CU00406831

The
Two Week
Traveller

Matthew Lightfoot

ISBN: 9781088945421
Amazon Print edition

Copyright 2019 Matthew Lightfoot

All Rights reserved. No part of this book may be
reproduced in any form without the prior
permission of the author, except for brief
quotations used for promotion or in reviews.

Do Anything You Wanna Do -Words & Music by
Graeme Douglas & Eddie Hollis © Copyright 1977
Rock Music Company Limited/Universal/Island
Music Limited. BMG Rights Management (UK)
Limited, a BMG Company/Universal/Island Music
Limited. All Rights Reserved. International
Copyright Secured. Used by permission of Hal
Leonard Europe Limited.

Whilst all the stories in this book are as factually
accurate as the author's memory allows, names of
people, places and businesses have been changed
in some cases.

Any requests, comments or queries can be emailed
to TwoWeekTraveller@Outlook.com.

This book is for anyone who would rather be eaten by a lion than run over by a bus.

.

CONTENTS

'Gonna break out of this city, leave the people here behind.

Searching for adventure, is the type of life to find.

Tired of doing day jobs, with no thanks for what I do,

I'm sure I must be someone, now I'm gonna find out who.'

Do Anything you Wanna do,

Eddie and the Hot Rods.

1 INTRODUCTION

A collective groan from our fellow passengers roused us from our perspiration-soaked slumber. It was mid-afternoon on a dusty road in the West African republic of Togo. We were travelling in a taxi-brousse, a twenty year old Renault 21 estate, designed for a French family of four, now carrying myself, my partner Kirsty, and six sweating Togolese locals plus a two-week old baby. Our driver slowed, almost involuntarily, as we all squinted into the shimmering heat of the road, and confirmed...yes, it's a police roadblock.

When travelling in Africa, you can always gauge the likely roadblock experience by the reaction of the locals. Looks of reassurance between driver and passengers and some collective pocket scrambling for loose change, indicate a likely smooth passage - no exiting of vehicles, some smiles, elaborate handshakes and perhaps a swift and furtive exchange of 'cadeaux' or 'dash.' The pole suspended across the road is removed, and you're on your way.

However, nervous murmurings, a slowing of the vehicle and frantic concealment of valuables means trouble. And this looked like big trouble.

A ragtag bunch of youths in ill-fitting khaki combat trousers and European football shirts were manning the makeshift barrier beneath an unrelenting sun. Two older men in grubby blue camouflage, lounged in camping chairs in the meagre shade of a yohimbe tree. Lethargic and somnolent, they showed little interest in our arrival, until alerted by the excited chatter of their young acolytes to the presence of two nervous, white faces, peering from the sweat-soaked interior of the Renault.

The hushed mutterings of our fellow passengers became a

collective sharp intake of breath as the men rose to inspect their potential victims at closer quarters. One was a short, squat man of around thirty. He was an unremarkable foil to the terrifying appearance of his younger colleague. Rising from his deckchair and stretching, it quickly became apparent that this man was a giant. Eyes widened in the taxi-brousse, as we took stock of his six foot, eight inch frame. He sniffed the air like a predator detecting prey, as his shaved head glistened in the sun's glare. His dark face looked like polished leather, scowling behind wrap-around shades as he approached us.

"Arretez," he growled, and our driver turned off the engine. As he reached through the driver's window to remove the key, we noticed he was wearing a pair of blue woollen gloves. The fingers had been removed, market trader style, in an obvious concession to the thirty five degree heat. He peered suspiciously into the vehicle and I felt the woman next to us tense. Her baby squeaked, as if sensing his mother's fear.

The two youths who were squeezed in beside the driver whispered and craned their necks toward the rear-view mirror as the Renault's boot was opened. The passengers knew the drill; stay in the vehicle, don't speak, don't look at the officers, pray they don't pick your bag to search.

In the rear of the vehicle, our rucksacks were conspicuous amongst the cloth bundles and canvas shopping bags. It was no surprise when they were dragged out and dumped on the dusty roadside. Our fellow passengers glanced at us nervously, giving us looks which said, 'rather you than me, mon ami!'

A gloved hand beckoned and I was summoned from the vehicle. I have a well-practiced routine for dealing with the police at roadside checkpoints, which usually serves me well. My first strategy is to become the friendliest man in the world.

"Hello, I'm Matthew!" I beam, as I confidently extend my hand in greeting. I then exchange a firm handshake, cemented with a winning smile, and maybe a friendly shoulder pat. Ice broken we engage in friendly, but polite conversation. I may drop in a quick lie of how I'm good friends with the British Consul, and the Governor of the local region, for good measure. Thoughts of highway robbery long diminished, we part company, the officer well satisfied with my promise to mention his exemplary conduct in high places.

Only this time, it didn't work like that. The man in the gloves looked at my proffered hand as if I was offering him a dead fish. He then pointed to our bags and barked an order in French.

"Open!" said one of the youths. Damn. An English speaker. That killed my next strategy of failing to understand anything being said to me, until they give up in frustration and let me pass.

I located the keys to the padlocks on our bags, and with sweating fingers, removed the locks. Eager hands deftly unzipped the bags and began what is best described as a frenzied rummage. Clothes were strewn by the roadside, as the main booty of electronics and toiletries was located and produced for closer inspection by Sergeant Gloves. Kirsty grimaced from the back of the Renault as one of the youths gingerly flicked at her dust covered bra with his flip-flop.

It's only when it's being examined by puzzled Africans that you begin to appreciate the volume of electrical equipment we tend to carry abroad. Phone chargers, camera battery chargers, electric shavers, E-reader cables, spare camera batteries, USB Cables...all emerged from an Asda carrier bag in a tangle of tech spaghetti. Placed on the floor, it was surveyed by the circle of officers and bystanders. Sergeant Gloves curled his lip in disgust at the lack of easy pickings.

"Passport. ID!" he barked, and his young interpreter helpfully repeated the message. I handed over my passport, and the interpreter passed it to Gloves with a flourish. A bead of sweat made slow progress down his forehead, and along the bridge of his nose, before dripping onto my passport as he flicked through the pages, occasionally turning it to peruse a particularly interesting visa stamp.

Eventually, the passport was returned, as the giant mumbled to his interpreter. The youth turned to me, whilst averting his gaze.

"My Captain says you have no permit for this region. Foreigners need permit. You must buy permits."

So here was the sting. The region in question was close to the Benin border, but I knew no permit was required. They knew no permit was required. They knew I knew no permit was required. But here was the excuse to extract the 'cadeau.'

"How much?"

Gloves mumbled as the youth looked to him for a price.

"15,000 CFA. Each."

About twenty pounds each. Could be worse but for Togo, that was a lot of money. Time for strategy three.

"I've never heard of this permit." I informed the interpreter, whose eyes twitched nervously, with Gloves looming over his shoulder.

"I think I need to check with the British Ambassador in Lomé, he's a good friend of mine.'

The interpreter scowled and slowly recounted my words to his boss. Gloves looked annoyed, and I wondered if he'd seen through my bluff. I was wearing a sweat-stained T-shirt, dirt ingrained shorts and a pair of sandals held together with black tape. I hadn't shaved for four days. I didn't look like the sort of character who would nibble on a Ferrero Rocher at the ambassador's residence.

Sergeant Gloves obviously felt that a more direct approach was required and stepped forward toward me, lowering his face towards mine. I tried not to recoil at his fetid onion and tobacco breath as he quietly spoke to the interpreter, whilst staring at me.

"No permit. No pass," was the message passed back.

I looked into my captor's shades, seeing only my own pleading eyes looking back. Sweat poured down my back. Seven pairs of eyes looked on from the taxi-brousse.

Then my phone rang. As now happens in an increasing number of locations around the globe, everyone instinctively reached for their pockets. My first reaction was to leave my iPhone where it was, safely tucked away in my shorts. But then I had an idea, and confidently produced the phone.

I recognised the number. It was Richard, a needy Sales manager from our company's North West office.

"Hello!" I answered cheerily, winking at 'Gloves' and his gang and nodding at the phone, the universal gesture for 'Just give me a minute while I take this chaps.'

"Oh, Hi Matt, it's Richard. Have you got a minute to discuss the Quarter One sales targets for the Customer Retention team?"

And with that sentence, I was transported to another world. Away from a dusty, fly-blown road in West Africa, to an air-conditioned office in damp, early winter Cheshire. From a likely highway robbery by uniformed bandits, to a morning of spreadsheets and commission plans, worrying that they'll have run out of ciabatta in the canteen.

"Hi Richard, great to hear from you." That stopped him in his tracks as it was never great to hear from him, and he knew it. I turned away from the semi-circle of would-be thieves, who were keenly monitoring the conversation.

"I'm in Africa. Being robbed. Play along with what I say." I hissed, then turned around, smiling.

"Sorry. Didn't catch that?" Richard was unsurprisingly confused, but I didn't let that stop me.

"Great to speak to you ambassador. I'm on my way now. Minor hold up at a roadblock." I then mouthed 'A-M-B-A-S-S-A-D-O-R,' towards the interpreter.

"Yes, the officers are just checking our paperwork. I'm sure everything is in order," I boomed, as the interpreter looked panic-stricken. The word 'ambassador' had clearly been understood, as the group shifted uneasily, looking at 'Gloves' for direction. He stood impassively, and I wondered if he was just going to shoot me on the spot to cover up the potential diplomatic incident.

"Can you hear me? I'm a little confused about the targets," Richard had his own problems to contend with.

"Yes ambassador, I'm looking forward to the banquet too. Should be there in a couple of hours." I could almost taste those Ferrero Rocher, as I watched the enthusiasm for the extortion venture drain from 'Gloves' face and he directed his gang to re-pack our bags.

"Can we have a call to go through the numbers Matt?" Richard was a world away, still grappling with his administrative issues.

"See you soon Ambassador!"

Less than a week later, I was back in that air-conditioned office in a gloomy business park in Cheshire. Another two-week long trip to a far-flung corner of the globe was over, and I was once again immersed in a world of spreadsheets and commission plans. I'd followed my usual post-trip ritual of a non-productive first day, recounting the adventures of my latest journey to interested colleagues. I'd then slowly slid back into my persona for 90% of the year- that of a middle manager for a large Telecoms company... and of course, I'd started to plan my next trip.

Whilst many people live by the maxim 'work to live, don't live to work,' my mantra was definitely 'work to travel.' Every single day of my annual leave allowance was used to travel abroad. I'd scrimp and save every holiday half day, timing flights and schedules to maximise use of my precious leave allowance.

I had a voracious appetite for travel writing, devouring the exploits of modern-day adventurers like Jonny Bealby, Richard Grant and Kevin Rushby, as well as the old masters such as Paul Theroux and Eric Newby, with a sense of envy. Invariably the work of a full-time travel writer describes a lengthy journey, taken over a period of months or years. For me, that type of odyssey was an impossibility. I needed to work to earn money to travel as I wanted, so was caught in a vicious circle, which typically limited each of my trips to two weeks. However, one element in my favour was a generous holiday entitlement of six weeks a year. Also, shorter trips meant an increased budget per day, which often enabled me to use rental cars, rather than public transport, to really get off the beaten track in the countries I visited. And the increase over the last twenty years in websites catering to the independent traveller, meant that careful planning often allowed me to visit more than one country in one holiday. I rarely tot up the number of countries I've visited, but at the time of writing this, I believe it's in excess of 140.

Colleagues regarded my travel obsession with bemusement. The usual response to my latest holiday location was 'Never heard of it, where's that?' or, more often, 'You're a total weirdo.' However, upon my return, I would usually be greeted at my desk by a steady stream of curious co-workers, saying 'Go on then...what happened?' Because something usually did. I seem to be one of those people that 'things' happen to. At conferences, employees from the company's other geographical locations would be introduced to 'Matthew, the bloke who goes to weird places.' On nights out, I'd generally be coaxed into recounting a travel tale, to a mixture of amusement, disbelief or drunken disinterest.

As in most modern organisations, we were asked to document our work processes and job descriptions, 'just in case you're run over by a bus.' Though in my case, this usual jokey yet gloomy cliché was most often appended with something along the lines of 'or eaten by a lion.'

'You should write a book.' That's a comment I've heard many times on work nights out. I always dismissed the idea. Anyone who travels independently to remote parts of the world will have adventures, and most will have ones which are scarier, funnier, weirder and more unbelievable than any of mine. I know, I've read a lot of good travel books.

However, I've never read a travel book which covers multiple trips. In dozens of countries. All visited in periods of less than two weeks. This is that book.

My hope in writing this story is that it shows anyone can embrace the adventurous spirit of those great travel writers, and explore the globe whilst also holding down a full-time job with a few weeks holiday allowance a year.

I hope my stories, gathered over thirty years of travel, will inspire a new generation of Two-Week Travellers.

2 BORN TO WANDER...AND WORK

My Grandfather, Jack Morris, died in 1960, seven years before I was born. A seaman, artist and raconteur, tattooed from head to toe, he filled the lives of my mother, Edna, and her siblings with tall-tales of a lifetime of travel and adventure on the high seas. In the pre-television days of my mother's childhood, story telling was an essential life skill, and she and her sisters memorised their father's recollections to be shared with the next generation. I was therefore raised on tales told of my grandfather and his shipmates racing camels round the great pyramids of Giza. I shook my little head in amazement as I heard how he rode on a bus through the trunk of a giant tree in a place called California. I sat, wide eyed, as my mum held one of my prized conkers, and told me how her dad had seen men's heads shrunken to a similar size, far away in South America. And best of all, I lapped up the story of my Grandad's monkey, Charlie, who set about the destruction of the family's terraced house, before succumbing to pneumonia and being laid to rest in the back yard, the last ape in North Leeds.

My mother's enthusiasm for the places she described, but had never seen, was infectious and I decided that one day, I'd follow in my late Grandad's footsteps. I'd see all those faraway places, and have those same adventures. Sadly for my mother, born into a working-class, northern family and leaving school at fourteen to work in a succession of factory jobs, travelling the globe was never likely. Although she and my father, John, did later become travel trailblazers in their own way.

My Dad was born in a tiny clifftop hamlet between the seaside towns of Scarborough and Whitby in North Yorkshire. There was no street lighting to illuminate the rough country lanes and no running water in the family cottage. The toilet was situated in a shed at the bottom of the garden, where a biting wind swept up from the North Sea, even during the short summer months. My father was the only son in a family of seven, so most of the least desirable chores fell to him, and in that isolated place, there were plenty of undesirable chores. To make some pocket money, young Johnny's only source of income was some illicit low level poaching - snaring of rabbits, which he would sell to the butchers in Scarborough after a ten mile walk to the town. If he was lucky, his ill-gotten gains would at least allow him to catch the bus home.

My dad's education up to the age of fifteen had been at the local village school, where the oldest pupils were taught in the same room and by the same teacher, as their five-year-old siblings. He soon realised that his opportunities for financial prosperity would be greatly advanced in one of the large towns to the North or South. Having never travelled further than Scarborough, at the age of sixteen, my father tossed a coin to decide where he would go to seek work. Tails it would be Middlesbrough to the north. Heads, would be Leeds to the south. Looking down, my Dad saw the profile of King George lying in the mud, and realised his future would be in the industrial powerhouse of West Yorkshire.

With a population of around half a million at the time, arriving in Leeds immediately after the Second World War must have been a terrifying prospect for a country boy, coming with nothing but the clothes on his back, and knowing no one. The city had a reputation for vice and crime, leading to the American armed forces banning its personnel from enjoying the seedy delights of the town centre after dark. My father ended up sharing a room in cheap lodgings with a Glaswegian labourer called Jock Harkins. Correction, he ended up sharing a bed with Jock. And Jock liked a drink. And after a drink he was a heavy sleeper. The shared toilet was down the hall...you can guess the rest. Fair to say, my father's introduction to big city life wasn't glamorous.

He got a job with a window cleaning firm, and was taken under the wing of another Scot, Harry Bendon, a well known pub singer, drinker and carouser. Harry showed my dad the window cleaning ropes by day, and the many pubs of Leeds by night. It was on one of those nights out that my dad spotted a Leeds lass swooning at Harry's slick taproom cabaret and, emboldened by his minor celebrity connections, the shy country lad made his move. My parents married in 1953.

Having learnt his trade from Harry, my Dad decided to go it alone. He saved up and bought his own hand cart and a set of ladders, and began building up a round of his own, cleaning the windows of the shops and offices of Leeds city centre. Hard work brought its rewards, first in the form of an ancient Austin van to transport his ladders, then in the early 1960's, my parents were able to buy a house and move out of their rented flat.

My thirty-something parents, with young daughter Sharon, were now part of an upwardly mobile, aspirational working class – the post-war 'never had it so good' generation. And after getting local curtains twitching by daring to paint their new, pebble-dashed semi in brilliant white, my parents' next move certainly ruffled some feathers in their street - they became the first residents of Green Road to take a holiday abroad.

With wages rising, and most companies now offering paid holidays to employees, the working class of the late 60's, had an exciting new opportunity to utilise their disposable income - the chance to travel abroad, something their own parents generally only experienced while in uniform and under enemy fire. The tumultuous years following the Second World War had paved the way for entrepreneurs to exploit a ready supply of ex-military aircraft and a general lack of industry regulation, to set themselves up as travel companies.

In Spain, General Franco's military regime saw mass tourism as a means of fast track growth for the country's economy, and poured resources into a greatly expanded Ministry of Tourism.

High rise hotels were constructed, often with reckless haste, in coastal fishing villages such as Benidorm on the Costa Blanca. Travel companies such as Clarkson's and Thomson's battled to undercut each other in a price war which meant that £20 for a two-week, family package holiday in Spain wasn't unusual. No surprise then that between 1961 and 1971, the number of Britons travelling abroad on holiday doubled to seven million. My family were amongst that number.

In November 1969, my parents, my sister Sharon, and a two-year-old me, set off from Leeds for Ringway Airport, near Manchester, for a two-week holiday in Alcudia, on the northern coast of Majorca. My father wore his only suit for the journey, my mother her best skirt and jacket. Not letting the side down, I was resplendent in a brown Prince of Wales check suit, topped off with a pin-on bow-tie. Doubtless a family appearing at the check-in desks at Manchester airport today in such attire, would be viewed as extreme eccentrics, or members of a bizarre cult, but my parents' dress code gives a hint of the glamour that was associated with a foreign holiday back then.

A small fishing village just ten years before, like many Majorcan settlements, Alcudia was undergoing rapid change, with new hotels and apartments springing up to cater to the huge increase in foreign visitors. I don't recall the name of our hotel, but dog-eared family snaps depict the usual white washed, multi-storey complex with an oblong pool and scrubby, palm-shaded grounds.

My recollections of the Alcudia holiday merge into a collage of memories from that and subsequent childhood trips to Majorca - the smell of pine trees, bad drains and sun cream; skidding a toy car on the cold tiles of a hotel room floor; the aroma of the food, so spicy and enticingly different to seventies English cuisine; a nest of feral cats living in a wall; my Dad slicing his foot open on a beach pedalo; Viva Espana, wooden castanets and souvenir bulls heads made of straw.

Later memories include learning the Spanish word for horse, after sliding head first into an improbably huge dump of roadside manure, and being cleaned up by a kindly shop keeper. 'Caballo.Caballo,' I repeated as my mother stood in the doorway, retching. I met kids from Munich and Manchester, and we ran wild in the grounds of our hotel, watching in thrilled horror from the bushes as the chef slit a pig's throat for a wedding barbecue.

To say that Spain had an impact on my parents is an understatement. They returned from that first holiday as commited Hispanophiles. My mother ordered a 'learn-at-home' Spanish course, and threw herself enthusiastically into a daily regime of lessons delivered via exercise books and 45rpm 'singles' which she played on our wooden radiogram.

After a lifetime of sodden seaside experiences in underwhelming, post-war English 'resorts,' staying in rule-laden B&B's and eating the same bland food every evening, Spain must have seemed like paradise, and no doubt my parents' enthusiasm manifested itself in every conversation they had upon their return, accompanied no doubt by square, orange-tinged snapshots taken on my Dad's prized Kodak.

Little wonder that the neighbours thought my parents had got ideas above their station. 'Airs and graces' and 'ten-bob millionaires' will have been phrases used locally. My mother entered the local newsagent to hear old Mrs Fenwick summing up the situation perfectly, "A bloody window cleaner going on a plane to Spain. I've seen it all now. Just who do they think they are?"

My parents didn't care. My dad worked a seven day week for fifty weeks a year. His two week holiday was his reward, and something to dream about through the cold, dark days of a Yorkshire winter. The package tour revolution of the 1960's had given them a glimpse of a different world and they had no intention of returning to the windbreaks and Mackintoshes of an English holiday.

They continued to visit Spain every year until my father died in 1992. Even after that, my mother plucked up the courage to go back on her own, those old Spanish lessons coming in handy at times, until her death in 2005. Strangely, for a couple who were early adopters of travel abroad, and who were curious of the world in general, they never showed any inclination to visit anywhere but Spain. My mother visited Florida with my sister in the nineties and enjoyed it, but it wasn't Spain. Spain was abroad, and to my parents, abroad was Spain. They had no desire to wander further afield. Me though, I was different.

I was a fat baby. Like the Michelin man in the tyre adverts, was how my mother described me. My hair was generously described as auburn, truthfully as ginger. I was also a bad baby, who cried incessantly at all times of the day and night. Fat, ginger and badly behaved, I didn't have a lot going for me as an infant.

Then, a single acquisition by my long suffering parents changed my demeanour in an instant. They bought a contraption called a baby-walker. Basically, a seat with four extending legs, each with a small wheel, designed to support a non-walking child and encourage it to use its legs to propel itself. For the first time, I was freed from the confines of cot or pushchair and was able to move when I wanted and where I wanted, to explore the outer limits of our house and garden. The transformation in my character was pronounced and immediate. The mewling, cantankerous cot-bound fatty, became a happy, laughing toddler scooting around at high speed in his Mothercare chariot. My parents realised I wasn't actually a bad baby, I was a bored one. Once I was able to move freely, I was happy. Something that remains true to this day.

Our family home was in a street of pre-war semi's. My school was a few hundred yards along our quiet road, and beyond that was a public park with woodland which extended for several miles. Although the area was classed as inner-city, heading in the right direction could mean walking in uninterrupted woodland for hours. My friends attended the same school as me, and all lived within a five minute walk of my home. Those circumstances meant that I was allowed out unaccompanied by adults, from what would nowadays be considered an alarmingly young age. At age four, my friends and I would make our way to school together. Homework was non existent for young children in the early 1970's, and after-school activities had yet to be invented. Therefore, 3.30pm meant playtime until our designated 'tea time.' It seems hard to believe now, but a normal school day at age five or six would probably entail waving goodbye to my mother at around 8.45 in the morning, and not returning home until 5pm.

The park and woods were our playground. Or any street with a vertical surface, at which we would boot the cheap plastic football which was our constant companion. With no adult protection, our sense of self -preservation had to be honed quickly – a life skill developed at a young age which has since served me well in locations around the world.

We could recognise local bullies from a long distance. We knew all the local dogs (dogs were free-range back then), specifically which were likely to take a malevolent interest in our vulnerable football. We quickly, and painfully gauged the weight limits of tree-branch rope-swings, and learnt which parts of the stream would submerge your wellington boots, or your head! Older kids taught us how to light fires in the woods and whittle spears and arrows from sticks using our pen-knives.

There was a hospital for the mentally impaired close by, and residents were generally free to wander in the community. We knew which were friendly and which were unpredictable. Who would chase you if you teased them, and who would cry. We all knew about Trevor, universally recognised as 'Hair Puller.' Trevor

15

was a middle aged man with a penchant for tugging the unruly mops of fair-haired boys, made all the more intriguing to us by his numerous missing fingers. I recall the terror of becoming his victim, aged around seven, while sitting on a friend's garden wall, with his father working in the garden only feet away. Though I knew what was about to happen, I was frozen by either fear or fascination, and can still picture Trevor's face as he approached, tilting his head to one side like a puzzled dog, eyes flickering, excited at the sight of my ginger mane. Then with a lunge from a three fingered hand, he had me. Gripping my scalp tightly, he shook my head three times, whilst emitting a curious hum of pleasure. I shrank to the floor, next to my friend's wall, Trevor smiled at me, and ambled away. My friend's dad continued working on his herbaceous border, oblivious to the assault which had taken place just feet away.

Nowadays, such an attack would provoke a social media outcry and vigilante manhunt. The poor child involved would need months of counselling to rid them of post-traumatic stress. I shuffled home, my hair more tousled than normal.

"Hair Puller got me." I informed my mother who was preparing tea.

"Are you alright?" A quick glance around the kitchen door frame, and she was back to peeling carrots.

"Yeah, it didn't hurt. I saw his hand. He's only got three fingers."

"Has he? How did he manage to pull your hair then? Go wash your hands, tea's nearly ready."

And with that, my 'hair puller' experience was over. I don't even think it got mentioned to my Dad. Trevor continued his reign of terror for most of my childhood, until, perhaps emboldened by a lack of reaction achieved by yanking hair, he overstepped the mark. Stories circulated that in addition to tugging Richard Johnson's curly locks, he'd also pulled the lad's trousers down outside Mr Quinns's newsagents. The authorities had to act, and Trevor was confined to the hospital grounds for the foreseeable future.

As the years advanced, so did my appetite for exploration. School holidays were an opportunity to roam further afield, and I would lead my band of friends on regular expeditions, using various means of transport. Discounted day-pass bus tickets allowed us to roam to the far boundaries of the city of Leeds. An unmanned local railway station at Headingley provided access to the North Yorkshire towns of Harrogate, Knaresbrough and York, without the inconvenience of paying for a ticket.

We walked, and cycled for miles, and, if on foot, generally hitch-hiked home, finding that bemused drivers would usually stop for a bunch of bedraggled ten year olds thumbing a lift, miles from civilisation.

For longer excursions we used our bikes, which were second, third or fourth hand and in most cases of the non-geared variety. Mine was a blue, hand-me-down Raleigh RSW 14. With it's small wheels and no 'cross-bar,' it was widely derided as being a 'girl's bike,' but I loved it. It was built for comfort rather than speed - I recall on one occasion straying into unfamiliar territory and being pursued by a group of older boys. My feet were a blur on the pedals as I sped forth, head down, in an effort to escape. Unfortunately, when I looked up, a couple of our pursuers had actually overtaken me on foot, and were able to halt my progress with a flurry of punches and kicks, which deposited the ginger kid and his girl's bike in the gutter.

On another cycling excursion, we'd travelled the ten miles to Leeds/Bradford airport at Yeadon, and were exploring the check-in area on our little bikes. Not surprisingly we attracted the attention of a security officer (he could actually have been THE security officer in those pre-terrorism days), who was soon pursuing us through the terminal. As we sped along with the breathless, elderly chap in pursuit, we almost collided with legendary rugby commentator Eddie Waring, who seemed highly amused at the spectacle. A couple of months later, we were again undertaking a cycle exploration of one of Yorkshire's transport hubs, this time it was Leeds City train station. As we pedalled along, swerving around commuters exiting WH Smith's, we heard a distinctive voice.

"Woah boys, slow down!" It was Eddie again, and he remembered us from the airport. This time we stopped to chat, and he told us that upon arrival in London, he'd told his disbelieving BBC colleagues that he'd nearly been run over in Leeds airport by a gang of ten-year-olds on bikes, while checking in for his flight!

I loved planning expeditions, and found I had a talent for identifying places to go, planning routes, organising schedules and marshalling a group of youngsters to get there and back in more-or-less one piece. My crowning glory though, was shared with Prince Charles and Lady Diana Spencer.

Wednesday 29 July 1981 was Royal Wedding day, which was decreed a public holiday in the UK. In order to deter hundreds of thousands of people from converging on London, transport companies and operators of other attractions around the country offered discounted rates to tempt the public away from the Royal nuptials. One such offer was made by British Rail. They announced that on Royal Wedding day, a fare of £1 would allow unlimited train travel on the East Coast line from Berwick in the North to Ipswich in the South. Obviously, London and surrounding stations were excluded from the offer.

As soon as my mother read out the details of the promotion from the local paper, I moved into planning mode. Her assumption when I headed to the enquiries desk at Leeds station the following day, was that a trip to the Yorkshire coast was on the cards. Only seventy miles by direct train to Scarborough was an obvious route to consider. Far too obvious for me. I was soon holed up in my bedroom with a pile of train timetables and maps of the UK rail network. My intention was to make full use of the British Rail offer and travel as far as was possible for my pound!

Early on the morning of Royal Wedding day 1981, myself and five friends set off on our journey from Leeds station. Our ages ranged from fourteen to eleven. We had no packed lunches, day-packs or anoraks, and certainly no mobile phones. Our mothers had no idea where we were going or when we'd be back. We took the high-speed Intercity 125 to Peterborough, then a train to Cambridge, where we picked up a connection to Norwich. Finally, from Norwich we boarded a train to the seaside resort of Great Yarmouth. We arrived in Yarmouth in the early afternoon, walked from the station to the beach; dared each other to jump off the pier onto the soft sand; bought some chips, which we ate on the beach, then rang our mothers from a payphone. Joan Potter had never left Yorkshire in her life, and had no idea where Great Yarmouth was, when eleven-year-old David called her. My mother knew it was over 250 miles from Leeds and refused to believe I was there. We then headed back to the station to begin our journey home.

I recall few details from the day, just the sense of excitement, companionship and shared adventure, to be finding our way, without adult assistance or guidance, to the other side of England. I also have a vivid memory of a middle aged man with a stalactite of mucous hanging from his spectacles, pursuing Robin Jones down the train. Robin's mop of blond hair had made identification easy when his high-speed gob found its unintended target, though perhaps the victim deserved it for ignoring the notices which said 'Keep heads in the carriage at all times.'

When we arrived home, my mother was perplexed.

"You went all that way, just to come back again. Why? You

could have had a nice day in Scarborough."

I probably didn't think to say it to my Mum at the time, but I'm sure that was the first time I realised something that I still find today when travelling - that the journey can be more important, and enjoyable than the actual destination.

As I approached my mid-teens, I was coasting at school, generally doing just enough to get by. Not being the cleverest in the class, or the naughtiest, seemed the best route to a quiet life. Out of school, my travel experiences were limited to the bleak post-industrial wastelands of the North of England, as I followed my football team, Leeds United around the decaying football stadiums of the old second division. Travelling on rotting rolling stock from the 1970's, deemed suitable only for 'football special' trains, we'd skulk out of damp, dark, small-town Victorian stations, to be shadowed by vindictive local police officers, and be chased by, or chase, youths who looked just like us, but spoke with the accents of Barnsley, Bolton or Burnley. Not the most inspirational travel experiences but they enhanced my geographical awareness of my own country. Also, witnessing more than one full-scale riot helped develop a sixth sense which is essential for travellers - the ability to sense when the mood of a crowd is changing; that subtle shift from latent discontent to explosive violence.

At sixteen, I took my 'O' level exams, and passed five, which was pretty good for the comparatively low standards of my school. Importantly, I passed English and Maths which qualified me for an office job. There was no thought of further education. From my point of view, my close friends were all leaving school, and starting to earn money for clothes, and nights out in the few pubs in Leeds where sixteen-year-olds with tight jeans and long fringes could buy beer. I knew that further education would preclude me from all that.

Nowadays, most responsible parents would put their foot

down and insist that their child stay on to study for 'A' levels, then possibly a university degree. Back then, I had no such parental pressure. My father felt that unless you planned to enter a profession where you actually needed a degree, such as a medicine or law, there was little sense in wasting five years studying, when you could be out grafting and earning.

Window cleaning was precarious. He had no written contracts, and if his work was sub-standard, or a rival undercut him on price, he would lose his livelihood overnight. Therefore, to my Dad, a job with security - a contract, paid holidays and sick pay, was the ultimate goal. If you could achieve those things whilst wearing a suit, and sitting in a clean, warm office, instead of climbing ladders carrying buckets of icy water in mid-winter, then that was worth more than any degree.

So, in June 1983, three weeks after leaving school and three months after my sixteenth birthday, I started work on a Youth Training scheme at the Leeds Permanent Building Society. I was paid £25 a week, and to my Dad's delight, I got to wear a suit. I also had my first experience of that nemesis of the two-week traveller – the dreaded Holiday Chart.

In the days before computerised offices, holidays were recorded on a large laminated board suspended above the boss's desk. This custom designed 'Holiday Planner' came with coloured strips of sticky plastic which could be attached to the calendar, to denote which employee was on holiday in which week. Diligent managers assigned different coloured strips per department, or even individual coloured strips per employee. Less efficient bosses (usually men) just scrawled names on the board in marker pen or biro.

I can't remember what colour strip I was allocated that summer. Not that it mattered. When I joined the office, the board was already a profusion of colour, with multiple coloured strips adorning the months of July and August. May, June and

September were less colourful, but most weeks already met the maximum criteria written in black marker at the top of the calendar – 'Maximum three off at once!'

I think I managed to secure a week off at the start of October, by which time I'd already left the Building Society. I'd landed a permanent job with British Telecom, with a starting wage of £55 a week, which was very good money for one of 'Thatcher's children.'

I also delighted my Dad by again getting to wear a suit. Unfortunately, I was also re-acquainted with an old foe, noting on my first morning the familiar coloured-strip striped calendar above the boss's desk. Availability limited to a week in May or at the end of September meant another year without a holiday, and this one really hurt, as my friends jetted off for two July weeks of high culture in Calella on Spain's Costa Del Maresme.

I vowed at that point to never again fall victim to the curse of the Holiday Planner. From now on, I'd be calling on the trip-planning skills of my childhood, to ensure I was quick off the mark, and my coloured strip would be the first on the board next year!

3 GO WEST!

After suffering the disappointment of missing out on a holiday during my first two years of work, I vowed that my coloured plastic strip would adorn the prized late July section of the 1985 holiday planner, and cajoled my friends into making the trip to Neilson's travel agents in Leeds, while everyone else in my office was still gearing up for the 1984 Christmas party season.

We were hoping for a quiet, traditional village on the coast of Spain, where we could immerse ourselves in the culture and cuisine of the region, whilst speaking the native tongue and exploring sites of archaeological interest. Only joking...we went to Benidorm!

The trip followed the same agenda as subsequent late eighties holidays to Magaluf and Ibiza. An all male group of teenagers, crammed into basic, high-rise accommodation close to the sea, leading a largely nocturnal existence, mixing only with similar youngsters from other British towns. We ate a dumbed-down, caloried-up version of the same food we ate at home, and drank ourselves into oblivion every night. We loved it.

Our daily schedule seldom varied, and explained why, upon returning to work sporting the same pallid complexions we'd had two weeks earlier, the first comment was usually 'Did it rain?'

We'd get up in the late afternoon, having adopted our own extreme version of the local siesta, to sit on the balcony and piece together the blurry events of the night before, and account for any members of the party still 'missing in action.' Once all were assembled, we'd set off for a very late breakfast, usually taken in one of the many British owned bars, showing violent action movies such as 'The Warriors,' or some gory horror flick like 'The Texas Chainsaw Massacre.' At around 7 pm we'd return to the hotel to 'get ready.' (Young men in the late eighties tended to cultivate elaborate hair styles, which required some serious groundwork before a night on the town). Ghetto blasters would be positioned on the balcony, considerately sharing our 'sounds' with other holidaymakers, and that patron saint of Spanish holidays, San Miguel, would be liberated from the room's ancient fridge to ease us into the evening. At around 10pm we'd head out, generally only walking a few feet before being coaxed into some neon-lit establishment by a bronzed cockney 'PR' rep with a permed mullet hair-do, assuring us of lethal Happy Hour measures of chemical grade spirits, and a surplus of inebriated members of the opposite sex.

If you can remember Spanish holidays in the eighties you weren't there, is an expression no one says, but probably should. In the days before digital cameras and phones, it was often the case that you'd only recall a place or event, when you revisited it on that exciting day you got your holiday photos back from Supa Snaps. Or maybe you wouldn't recall it at all, as an overexposed flash photo was passed round the pub to a circle of furrowed brows and muttered comments of 'Where the hell was that? '

Our night usually ended with a take-away meal at around 8am, when we'd try and work out who we'd lost, where and how. Also, whether anyone had got lucky and was enjoying a romantic sunrise on the beach, instead of staggering back to the hotel with the rest of us. Like a coven of vampires in tight football shorts, we'd aim to be in bed before the sun appeared over the high rise hotel blocks, and the families started making their way through the vomit-caked streets to the beach. Then we'd do the whole thing again. And again, for fourteen nights.

I usually returned to work after those holidays with sallow, spotty skin, and eyes like an insomniac raccoon, plus a few cuts and bruises, and on one unfortunate occasion, with only one eyebrow. My older colleagues would probe me for tales, and think I was ducking the question when I said I couldn't remember. In most cases, I actually couldn't.

By 1989, I'd been working at BT for six years and at the age of twenty two, had been promoted to a supervisory position. Not actually a manager, more like a glorified school prefect who enjoyed certain privileges over the rank and file of office juniors. My new found maturity was also demonstrated by the fact that I'd been going out with Karen for over a year. No more Benidorm trips with the boys for me. After a couple of holidays in the Greek Islands, I set my sights further afield, and a first trip outside Europe, to the land of the free and the home of the brave, the USA.

In 1984, a young multi-millionaire called Richard Branson had launched his new airline, Virgin Atlantic, supposedly after suffering the inconvenience of a delayed flight from Puerto Rico to the Virgin Islands. His aim was a high quality, low cost airline to shake up a status quo where British Airways was the only choice for UK transatlantic travellers, following the demise of Laker Airways in 1982. In 1985 Branson launched Virgin Holidays, an offshoot of his airline, offering seats on Virgin flights from Gatwick to New York, and Miami and Orlando in Florida. The choice of the two destinations in Florida allowed Virgin to pioneer a new holiday format which was to take the travel world by storm in the late eighties and early nineties – The Fly Drive.

A new type of package tour, the Fly Drive was a hybrid of a traditional package holiday and a do-it-yourself roadtrip. Virgin either offered the total freedom of a flight and car package, where the holidaymaker decided on their own route, and booked their own hotels, or a more structured itinerary, where hotels were booked for you. A popular option was the two-centre holiday, where hotel accommodation was included in the package in two separate locations, and you made your own way between them, and also had a car to explore while you were in each.

The two-centre option certainly delivered value for money. For £400 each, Karen and I flew to Miami, where we collected a Chevrolet saloon car – by far the best car I had driven at that point in my life. We had seven days accommodation in a Howard Johnson hotel in the Florida Keys, then made the five hour drive north to Orlando where we had another week on International Drive.

To say the USA made a big impression on us was an understatement. Put simply, it was 'abroad' like we'd never seen before. The standard of the hotels was so much better than those we'd experienced on European holidays, as was the food. An exchange rate of $1.80 to the pound, also made everything affordable for two young people on limited incomes. The fact that Karen was not yet twenty one, so couldn't buy alcohol, made a night out quite complicated, often requiring me to visit the bar twice, using my ID to buy Budweiser or Michelob from different bartenders.

We visited all the theme parks - though 'all' in 1989 was limited to Disney World, EPCOT, and Universal Studios. A highlight for me though, was simply driving in America, once I'd mastered an automatic. Exiting the car rental compound in Miami, I was trying to drive as if in a manual transmission vehicle, with one foot on the gas, the other on the brake. A hugely obese employee jumped in front of the car as I approached the gate.

"Wooaah guy, noooo! One foot only. You gonna have yourself an accident driving like that."

Wise words, as was his parting shot of 'Don't go near Liberty City.' The well known ghetto area in North Miami filled us with dread as we negotiated the City freeways, terrified that an incorrectly taken exit ramp would dispatch us straight into a street scene from the popular TV Show of the time, Miami Vice.

Once out of Miami though, we could relax and enjoy the journey. Travelling down the Florida Keys to Key West, crossing the famous Seven-Mile bridge in a huge electrical storm was an exhilarating experience. Karen didn't agree, suffering an attack of sudden nausea, prompted by the extreme electricity in the atmosphere, she made the crossing with her head out of the window, being hosed down by torrential rain as she vomited on the freeway.

On our last night in Orlando, we went out in the downtown area, which back then was a tourist-free zone. We met some

American kids, who tipped us off to the best places to buy beer with only one over-21 ID. At the end of a raucous night, we got a ride home with Kenny, a curly haired 21-year-old college boy in a borrowed convertible Chrysler LeBaron, the car described as being 'as big as a whale' in the B52's classic 'Love Shack.' I sat alongside Kenny as we cruised along Interstate 4, with the cassette player belting out some Country tunes. Karen sprawled across the huge backseat, the warm Florida breeze playing havoc with her curly perm. America was what travel was all about, and this was just one State. There were forty nine more to explore, and we promised ourselves we'd return.

For the next few years, our disposable income, and holiday allowance, was spent on trips to various American States. After our introductory two-centre holiday, we fully embraced the Fly-Drive ethos, and each year bought the cheapest flight we could find to a large city, then booked the lowest cost, i.e. smallest, rental car we could find.

It was a well known fact in the early days of Fly-Drive that American car rental companies never had any small cars. The rental company check-in clerk would try their hardest to upsell you to a family saloon. (I recall on one occasion the unsuccessful sales pitch including the cheery line 'If a truck hits that little car sir, you're just gonna be de-stroyed!'). We always stood our ground, saying a small car was fine. The clerk would go through the unnecessary charade of tapping on his keyboard, before announcing through gritted teeth, 'It's your lucky day sir! We actually have no super compact vehicles today, so you're getting a free upgrade. You tight English bastard.' Although of course he only thought the last bit.

This all worked very well until the early nineties, when the rental companies realised that English Fly-drivers simply booked the smallest car available, safe in the knowledge that they'd always be allocated a nice family saloon anyway. So they called our bluff, and bought fleets of the tiniest vehicles they could find, perhaps to punish us for all those free upgrades.

That was the reason I was pulled over by an incredulous Georgia Highway Patrol officer as I clocked 80mph in my bright red, five-foot-long, GEO Metro Sub-Compact, on a long cross country haul between Louisiana and South Carolina. Cars of that size were a novelty on US Roads anyway, and one travelling at that speed certainly raised a few eyebrows. Luckily, the officer had read somewhere that, 'in Europe, you guys have no speed limits on the freeway,' therefore sticking to a 55mph limit was obviously impossible for us, and he let me off with a warning!

We travelled across most of the States of the Union during those years of two week road-trips. Along California's fabled Pacific Coast Highway from LA to Carmel, where a mischievous poltergeist kept us awake for a whole night. Then on to San Francisco, where we'd failed to reserve a room and, finding a city bursting at the seams with travellers, ended up in a cheap flop house complete with murder scene carpet and windows thickly pebble-dashed with pigeon excrement. We drove to Las Vegas, through Death Valley in July, the blast of searing heat like opening an oven door when you wound down the car window. From New York, we headed north to coastal New England, a kaleidoscope of early fall colour. Then from Boston across the border and a rapid language shift as we reached Francophone Canada. We stood in the Texan desert at midnight, watching the mysterious Marfa ghost lights dance across the horizon, and were then startled by the headlight beam and horn blast of a train, dangerously close on an unseen track. We crossed the Mexican border from San Diego, and ran the gauntlet of struck-off US dentists in Tijuana, who told us we had terribly crooked teeth they'd just love to fix. Our two week holiday limit often meant a punishingly long drive for myself as the sole driver. Montreal to Toronto was meant to take around six hours, but freeway accidents doubled that, and we crawled into Canada's largest city late at night, exhausted and desperately seeking the neon of a hotel sign in that pre-internet booking era.

In early nineties Britain, an American holiday generally meant Florida, and our choice of location often baffled colleagues.

"Which theme parks are in Alabama then?" would be a typical

question I'd be asked.

Theme parks and popular tourist attractions weren't really what drove our holiday agenda though. After a few days in the city we'd flown into, we'd get in our car and drive. We'd most likely have a general destination in mind with a few distractions en-route, gleaned from the latest Rough Guide. However, for me, the beauty of the roadtrip was not really knowing where we'd end up, or what we'd find there.

Simon and Garfunkel once told us that we'd all come to look for America, and maybe that summed up our logic. It was the often downright strangeness of smalltown America we enjoyed, contrasted with the familiarity of language, and scenery easily recognised from TV and movies.

My Yorkshire accent was generally interpreted as being Australian, not fitting the American stereotype of Englishmen speaking either like Prince Charles, or Dick Van Dyke in Mary Poppins. Ordering food in a restaurant would usually be met with a quizzical frown from the waitress.

"Hey, are y'all from out of town? Don't tell me...Australia?"

"Wow! England! Princess Diana! I always get confused...is England in London or is London in England?" That was a question we were asked more than once, especially in the Southern States.

An occupational hazard in the South was a 'dry' town, especially on a Sunday. There's no worse feeling for a Brit on holiday than checking into a motel after a long drive, and heading out for a cold beer to find bars locked, and chains and padlocks on gas station beer fridges. If we suspected a town to be one of these unfortunate outposts of sobriety, we'd cruise down the main street, warily scanning shops and restaurants for signs of alcohol consumption. Only when we saw full glasses being raised, would we commit to staying the night.

It was on one of these alcohol reconnaissance missions, in a small town in Mississippi, that we spotted a bar bedecked in

Christmas decorations, with flashing lights and a fir tree haphazardly perched on the roof. A flashing sign announcing 'Christmas in July' caught our attention, probably because it was now September. We'd been driving for a few hours so decided to investigate. In the gloomy interior, the Christmas theme continued, with more tinsel and lights, and a liberal dusting of polystyrene 'snow' strewn across the floor and most other horizontal surfaces.

On the juke box, Garth Brooks sang about 'friends in low places' and an elderly man with a prosthetic leg resting on a stool sat in a corner, grinning at an empty dancefloor. Behind the bar, a prematurely middle aged, early thirties woman in a vest top, put down her magazine, stubbed out her cigarette and smiled a gap toothed greeting.

Karen and I ordered a beer each and after working out that 'Y'all are from out of town!,' Julie was eager to chat. We were the first foreigners she'd encountered in three years working at the bar, though she had been to New Orleans once, where she'd met a young Spaniard. She gave Karen a coy smile as she said this. She had a young daughter but no partner, and lived across the street from her widower father.

"Nothing much happens here," she shrugged, glancing across to the one legged man who had closed his eyes, and was now snoring along to another of Brooks' country classics.

We asked about Christmas in July and she explained that the bar's owner had the idea after seeing something similar in a film, and they'd just never got round to taking it all down. I was contemplating asking how many July's the decorations had been in place, when we all turned at the noise of a screech of brakes. A large blue pick-up truck, flying the ubiquitous confederate flag, had pulled into the car park and was now straddling two empty bays. A barechested, mullet-haired youth in very short shorts, sprang from the flatbed of the truck, and two men in their thirties lurched from the cab. All were holding bottles of beer.

We watched as they staggered and swaggered across the car park and Julie grimaced and sucked her teeth as they barged open the door.

"Julie! Julie! Julieeeee!" slurred the youth, as he reeled over towards the juke box and began punching the keys. The two older men pulled up stools next to us at the bar, and slammed their bottles down.

"Fill em up baby," snarled the largest man, his face pitted with acne scars.

Julie already had three bottles out of the fridge and placed them on the bar without speaking. It was clear our conversation was over. I could sense the smaller man staring in our direction. Karen shifted uneasily, feeling self conscious in her shorts and brightly patterned sun top.

"Who are your friends Julie?" he sneered, still sizing us up.

"On Vacation. From England."

The pock marked man looked over towards us and mumbled something I couldn't make out, then both men laughed. Brooks had been replaced on the juke box by Charlie Daniels and the younger man was cavorting around the dancefloor, kicking up a polystyrene snowstorm to Daniels' lethal fiddle.

"Come and dance with me Julieeee," he growled as he thrust at an imaginary sex partner, fists clenched around invisible female hips.

His two friends turned to watch and Julie flushed, glancing at us, embarrassed. Karen and I exchanged glances which said 'drink up and get out,' and I took a swig from my bottle.

The second man had now got off his stool and was leaning over the bar.

"You know what I think Julie...?" She ignored him.

"I said, you know what I think Julie?" His voice was louder now, with more than a hint of menace. She shook her head.

"I think me and my little brother and Richie here..." He paused and brought the bottle to his lips, then wiped his shirt sleeve across his mouth.

"I think we're all gonna have sex-ual intercourse with you in this here bar-room today." He pronounced sexual as two separate words. The youth on the dance floor whooped and punched the air. Scarface removed his cap and grinned lasciviously at Karen and I. Julie rolled her eyes, and lit a cigarette as the man stared across the bar at her, slowly nodding his head.

The film 'The Accused,' with Jodie Foster had been a big box office hit around five years earlier, and featured a shocking bar room rape scene. To Karen and I, it felt like we'd suddenly been transported to the sinister Deep South of movies like 'Deliverance' and 'Mississippi Burning,' but Julie seemed unaffected. She continued to flick through her magazine, ignoring the lewd comments being slurred at her from the other side of the bar.

Eventually, the rednecks got bored with Julie's lack of response, and headed over to the pool table. Karen and I had finished our drinks but didn't want to leave Julie with three potential rapists and a somnolent amputee.

"Don't worry about me. They're just playing. I've known these boys all my life. I can handle 'em." She smiled an unconvincing smile and urged us on our way.

Outside, Karen wondered whether we should call the police as a precaution. I shook my head, knowing exactly what would happen from childhood years of watching the Dukes of Hazzard. We'd call the police and the local sheriff would arrive - a fat man chewing tobacco and sporting a white Stetson and shades. We'd enter the bar behind him, to see our worst fears realised, with Julie pinned to the dancefloor amidst a polystyrene snowdrift.

"Hey!" The sheriff would shout and the attackers would pause.

"Hi Uncle Cleatus," the would-be rapists would respond, laughing.

"Nothing to see here." The sheriff would turn to us, removing his shades. He'd sniff the air. "Have you been drinking Sir? We don't tolerate that in these parts on a Sunday."

We drove on in silence. We'd come to look for America, but sometimes found something we'd rather have left undiscovered.

Despite driving many thousands of miles across America, I'd been fortunate to avoid any serious car-related incidents, bar the occasional run-in with the mirror-shades wearing officers of the Highway Patrol. Unfortunately, that all changed in Texas.

We were staying in the Chisos Mountains, in the remote west of the state, close to Big Bend National Park, which is named after a pronounced kink in the nearby Rio Grande. This is one of the most isolated areas in the United States, a harsh desert landscape on the Mexican border, rising steeply into the lofty fir-capped peaks of the Chisos range. Here, blistering hot days were followed by icy nights, with coal black skies lit by a million stars.

We were driving to the village of Lajitas on the Mexican border, hoping to meet the Mayor, Clay Henry, a fabled beer drinking goat. A thirty degree sun beat down on the asphalt as we travelled through a scrubby, dun-coloured terrain, brightened by an occasional colourful splash of cacti and yucca. Rounding a bend into a downward slope, I caught sight of movement to my right, as a number of small rocks bounced down an incline onto the road. I had a split second to decide what to do, and calculated that I could probably outrun the landslide with a burst of speed. I increased pressure on the gas, and as we accelerated, heard a succession of thumps from beneath the vehicle, followed by an ominous bang. Karen and I cringed involuntarily in unison, and I brought the car to a halt. We got out to see a river of yellowy brown liquid slowly coursing from beneath the vehicle into the gutter. It was clear we wouldn't be meeting any beer drinking goats today.

I looked around. Rough, sandy slopes to our right and some

craggy peaks about a mile distant to the left. The road ran in a perfect straight line for a couple of miles, before snaking off to the left around some low hills on the horizon. No signs of life and the road was empty, with not even a cliched rolling tumbleweed to keep us company. We'd been driving for nearly an hour and had only seen two cars. We'd passed a small settlement at Terlingua crossroads about six miles back, and I knew Lajitas was around the same distance ahead. A few hundred yards down the road, I spotted something looking out of place in the desert landscape. It seemed man-made. A sign! I walked towards the structure, squinting into the punishing Texan sun. It was a brown, wooden sign with yellow writing. Gas station ahead? Hotel? I wondered.

"Beware." I read aloud, then wished I hadn't. "This is Bear and Mountain Lion Country."

Karen was already heading for the safety of the car when I looked round. I had a limited knowledge of mechanics, but realised the tumbling rocks had probably destroyed the oil sump. I wasn't sure whether I'd cause further damage by turning the engine and air-con on, so we sat sweating, in silence, staring down the road, willing a car to appear.

After about half an hour, I was out of the car, hands shielding my eyes, as I peered into the sun's glare. A small dust cloud on the horizon and a glint of chrome - a vehicle! A battered maroon pick-up truck, driven by a Grizzly Adams lookalike, took around ten minutes to reach us.

"Y'all got a problem? ...Say, are you from Australia?" Grizzly was the local mailman. He covered the whole area, driving around two hundred miles a day, yet delivering to less than twenty properties.

"You folks ain't going nowhere in this car," he mused, stroking his dust flecked beard. "I can take you to Terlingua Junction, I think old Gerry has a tow-truck there."

Karen got into the cab with Grizzly, and I sat in the back of the truck, feeling the midday sun stinging my neck as we bumped along past a sign for 'Terlingua Ghost Town,' pointing up a rubble strewn dirt road on the left. We eventually arrived at a flat roofed, concrete structure with a handpainted sign, 'Terlingua Autos.'

"Ask for Gerry," shouted Grizzly as he pulled away with a wave.

An oil stained, white mongrel appeared barking from behind a shipping container as I approached a door protected by an iron cage. 'This shop is protected by a sawed-off shotgun, three nights per week. You guess which nights!' read a sign above a confederate flag car-sticker decorating the door. Before I'd managed to knock, the door opened with a creak.

Gerry was a tall, skinny, bespectacled, fifty-something, in a John Deere baseball cap which was two sizes too big for his head. He looked at Karen and I with a confused expression, scanning his forecourt in vain for the vehicle which had transported us to his remote neck of the woods. I explained our plight, and that the mailman had said he had a tow truck.

"Tow truck's not here right now." Gerry spoke in a slow drawl, referring to the missing truck in the manner of a parent discussing an elusive teenage son. "Guess ya'll better come on in."

We followed as he loped slowly into his workshop, followed by the mongrel who he greeted with a half hearted kick.

"Thing is, if it's a rental car, they won't let me fix it anyhow. Had a couple from Canada here two years back, same thing happened. They sent a tow truck from Midland to fetch it." Gerry chuckled and shook his head in disbelief at the stupidity of those big city fools, 250 miles to the North.

"You folks want a drink? Think you're gonna be here a while. I guess you need a cepo'tea?" He flashed a gap-toothed grin in admiration of his own English accent, which he explained he'd inherited, along with a box of tea bags, from a transient hired hand from the county of 'Cornwell in England,' a few years earlier.

Gerry brought us drinks in mugs which seemed to have been

used to clean paint brushes, and passed me a 1970's vintage phone on which to call the car rental company.

After selecting 'Two, for an accident or breakdown,' I was connected to Duane, sat in his air-conditioned call centre a few hundred miles, but seemingly a world of sophistication, away.

I described the accident and he sounded suitably sympathetic in a dramatically camp manner.

"A rock slide. Oh my gaaawd!"

It was when I came to provide an address that we hit a snag.

"Road from Terlingua Cross Roads....How are we spelling Terlingua? What town is that in sir? You don't know the street name? There is no street name? Ok what else is on the street? Are there any hotels or restaurants you can see? "

Gerry saw that I was struggling and gestured for me to pass him the phone. I sat back with my cepo'tea and listened to a half conversation, as he tried to convey the situation to a young man who was struggling to understand that places like Terlingua still existed in his country.

"Terlingua is the place. No it's not a town...it's a cross roads. But there is a ghost town. Yeah ghost, as in...ghost. Yup. Woooowoooo." Gerry's ghost sounded more like an owl trapped in a chimney, and he screwed up his eyes to better understand Duane's questions, and shook his head sadly.

"No, there is no Chevrolet dealership here. There might be one in Alpine, not sure, ain't been there for years. How far? About two hours. Yes sir. Two hours by car." Gerry was smiling now, amused at Duane's incredulity that anywhere could exist so far from an approved Chevy dealership.

"No sir. There ain't none of that here. There's nothing here! Whole lot of nothing!" Gerry passed the phone back to me, chuckling again.

Duane had now located approximately where we were, and confirmed that his company's nearest outlet was indeed in the town of Midland. As in the case of the stranded Canadians of two years past, a recovery truck and replacement vehicle would need to be despatched. The estimated journey time of 'about seven hours' brought home how far from civilisation we actually were. It also meant we'd need to try and hitch a lift back to our hotel which was around twenty miles away. Karen wasn't hopeful, but I recalled my childhood hitch-hiking days, and confidently predicted that 'you always get a lift on a quiet road.'

An hour later, I was still stood by the roadside, the radiance of my puce face tempered slightly by a film of dust. Karen slumped in the shade on Gerry's porch. Our host occasionally leaned out of his workshop with the cheery offer of 'another cepo'tea Matthew?'

I was starting to contemplate another six hours sat by the roadside waiting for the tow truck, when, through the blurred shimmer of the horizon, I spotted a car approaching. A battered, beige Peugeot stationwagon with black tape holding its driver's side headlamp in place, slowed as I frantically waved my arm.

I crossed the road, and a lank haired woman in her early thirties brought the car to a halt. She wore a tattered corduroy jacket and balanced a pair of shades above her forehead. A sullen expressioned teenage girl sat beside her in the passenger seat and two grimy faced boys peered from the backseat.

I explained our predicament and the woman shook her head.

"We're not going that far...sorry." It was a 'sorry' which suggested she actually meant it, and she drummed the steering wheel as she considered other options.

"We could drop you at the ghost town though. People there sometimes go to the lodge. If you don't mind a detour first?"

We weren't in a position to be choosy, so bade farewell to Gerry and jumped into the back seat. The two tousle haired boys, aged around four and six, stared up at us silently, each sported a matching luminous candle of snot suspended beneath a crusty nostril. Our driver introduced herself as Elaine, her daughter was Cody. The boys were Tyler and Jacob.

"Hope you don't mind fleas." Elaine shouted cheerily as we pulled away. "The dogs sleep back there. Those blankets are full of them." As usually happens in such a situation, Karen and I began to itch uncontrollably, shifting on the soiled blankets beneath us. To take my mind off fleas, I set about amusing the sad faced boys using my favoured party piece of 'Mr. Knee-Nipper.' Fashioning my right hand into the shape of a beak, in the style of Rod Hull's vicious emu puppet, I swooped around the boys' bewildered faces before plunging my hand towards their defenceless knee-caps. Locating the soft flesh just behind the knee, a gentle squeeze delivers a curious mixture of pleasure and pain and normally elicits a squeal of delight from the young victim. Only on this occasion, young Jacob merely winced and gave me a confused look which seemed to ask 'Why did you do that to me?' Luckily his mother hadn't noticed and we drove on in silence, with Jacob looking close to tears.

Elaine was friendly enough but there was an atmosphere in the car, and I wondered whether mother and daughter had been arguing. Elaine flicked on the radio to relieve the awkward silence. After driving for around twenty minutes, the road entered a ravine with rough sandstone cliffs on either side of the asphalt. The children shifted in their seats, the young boys craning their necks to see through the windshield, as they sensed the car slowing. Soon our speed had reduced to a crawl, and Karen I followed the youngsters' lead in scanning the road ahead, puzzled to be stopping with no obvious destination in sight.

"Here." Elaine brought the car to a halt and set the hazard lights blinking.

"Ready?" She placed a hand on Cody's knee and the girl nodded. Mother and daughter exited the car and Elaine opened the rear door to let the boys out.

"We'll just be a few minutes." Elaine smiled at Karen and I, as Cody opened the station wagon's trunk.

Distant thunder rumbled, signalling a likely afternoon storm, as Karen and I sat wondering what had drawn the family to this lonely stretch of road. The sombre procession of children bearing flowers from the trunk of the car gave us a clue. Elaine led them past us to a jutting promontory of rock on a bend in the road ahead, clearly marked with a tell-tale bruise of blue paint. A shattered triangle of licence plate lay in the gutter. The family stood in a semi-circle, Elaine and Cody holding hands. Eventually, Cody knelt and placed her bouquet on the roadside and remained on her knees, head bowed. Elaine turned and looked at Karen and I, a slight uplift of her eyebrows encouraging us, and we hesitantly got out of the car and joined the group.

"My man wrecked his truck here. The kids wanted to see where their daddy died." Elaine explained, her voice quiet but composed.

"We're so sorry.When was that?"

"Friday." Three days ago. I gulped, unsure how to respond.

"Lay your flowers boys." Elaine nudged Tyler and he knelt next to his sister, carefully placing his flowers beside hers. Jacob offered his bouquet to his mother, and she took his hand and guided it towards the gravel, resting the small bunch of posies alongside those of his siblings.

"Say a prayer now." The children all lowered their heads, though Jacob was distracted by a glinting fragment of smashed mirror and scrabbled in the dirt to retrieve it.

Karen and I stood in silence alongside Elaine, feeling ashamed that our minor holiday inconvenience had intruded on this family's terrible moment of grief. Another distant roll of thunder, this time longer than the first, caused Elaine to shudder.

"Come on kids, let's go."

Cody stood and I caught her tear stained eye. The sullen teenager was suddenly transformed back to being a vulnerable child.

"Time to take our new friends to the ghost town."

Terlingua developed as a mining camp in the late 1800's, following the discovery of cinnabar, a mineral used in the production of mercury, or 'quicksilver' as it was widely known. Wealthy Chicago shoe manufacturer Howard E.Perry staked a claim on the land in 1887, and formed the Chisos mining company, which by 1905 was estimated to be producing 20% of the world's quicksilver. The First World War saw an upsurge in mercury prices, and the small settlement was booming, with a general store serving 1500 workers, living in adobe shacks or tent frame houses. There was an ice-making plant, a jail, a two-story hotel with running water, and even a theatre. Sporadic mail deliveries arrived, and there was even a primitive telephone connection to Perry's hilltop mansion which boasted a wine cellar, Moorish arches and a ninety foot long porch.

However, conditions were harsh. Fumes from the mercury furnaces affected the gums and loosened the teeth of the miners. Many were left unable to eat solid food. The desert climate meant broiling hot days and freezing cold nights, and there was the ever present threat of rattlesnakes lurking amidst the rocky terrain. By the mid 1930's cinnabar reserves around Terlingua were diminishing, and it was no longer cost effective to re-invest in the mine company's aging machinery. The company ceased operating, and by 1940, only twenty residents were left at Terlingua, the rest having moved to richer seams elsewhere, leaving their homes to be reclaimed by the desert.

And that was roughly still the number of inhabitants when Elaine dropped us at the end of the dirt track leading to the village.

"I'd take you all the way but the road is rough and the muffler is held on with rope," she laughed, and we said our goodbyes. We even got a hint of a smile from Cody and a wave from Tyler. Jacob watched me warily from the back seat as the car pulled away.

We trudged up the rough trail, feeling hot and thirsty. Distant thunder rumbled across the Chisos range, and occasional clusters of grey cloud brought some temporary respite from the unforgiving sun. We passed a 1940's pick-up truck riddled with bullet holes, then began to notice wooden crosses scattered amongst the cacti alongside the track. Closer inspection revealed the graves of Terlingua's former inhabitants, killed in mining accidents or by the flu epidemic which struck the village in 1918. Few of the graves bore a name. Most were marked by a simple cross, projecting from the scrubby earth at a haphazard angle. Some of the graves had collapsed, revealing the splintered, decaying wood of a coffin, and it wasn't hard to imagine the contents being pilfered by desert critters or human scavengers.

We weren't sure what we'd find as we reached the top of the hill and spotted scattered shacks which had been reclaimed from the desert, and subjected to varying levels of refurbishment. What we definitely hadn't expected was a well stocked bar and an ice cold beer! The Starlight Theater must have appeared incongruous in its surroundings when it was first built to provide entertainment for the miners and their families, now it looked like a mirage.

We staggered up the stepped porch and I pushed open the door. It was dark and cool inside, with a long bar on the right, running almost the full length of the old auditorium. Three bearded men at the bar looked up as I entered, and I immediately recognised the mailman. He nodded a greeting and I heard the words 'Australians' and 'rock slide,' but no other words were spoken and his fellow drinkers barely glanced in our direction.

"What's it to be?" Asked the barmaid and I was half expecting to wake up, still on Gerry's porch and find this was all a cruel dream.

"Beer." I replied, salivating.

Two bottles of Lone Star were placed on the bar, beads of condensation trickling from the neck down the brown glass, as the tops were removed all too slowly. There are some drinks that you'll always remember, where, what and when, and that bottle of beer will stay with me forever. The barmaid seemed to recoil in shock as I grabbed the bottle, wrapped my lips round the neck and tipped my head back, glugging down the icy, malty liquid as fast as the bottle could dispense it. With two thirds of the bottle gone, a shot of 'brain freeze' pain across my forehead caused me to take a breath.

"Good huh?" The mailman looked on in admiration, as his drinking partners and the barmaid laughed.

We brought him up to date with our predicament and asked if he had any idea how we could cover the twenty miles back to our hotel. A muttered conference took place at the end of the bar, resulting in another ruminative stroke of his luxurious facial hair.

"You could try Celia. She goes to the lodge a couple of times a week to fetch water." After a couple more beers, he walked us to the door and pointed out her shack, a couple of hundred yards away, on the edge of the settlement.

"Mind she doesn't shoot you though," he called as we set off. I looked back expecting him to be laughing, but his face was deadly serious.

Celia's shack was a single story adobe structure, with a roof fashioned from ten corrugated metal sheets of varying age and states of disrepair. Numerous missing window panes were patched with cardboard, and a badly buckled wooden porch, running the full length of the building and facing towards the desert, was around a metre higher at one end than the other. A barrel had been positioned beneath the sloping lower roof eve, to capture precious rain water. A battered blue truck indicated that Celia was home.

Heeding the mailman's warning, we made as much noise as possible on approach, figuring that surprising Celia may result in an unwelcome encounter with a 'sawed off shotgun.' The only sounds in Terlingua were the distant rumble of thunder and the hiss of sand, blown by the warm desert breeze, so our shouted greetings of 'Hellllooooo' were soon acknowledged. A lined, nut-brown face, with white hair scraped back in a tight bun, gave us a hard stare from the corner of the porch. We explained our situation, as Celia tossed assorted bric-a-brac from two frayed armchairs on the porch to allow us to sit down.

"So watcha gonna do if I ain't going to the lodge?" She challenged with a mischievous glint in her eye. We shrugged and shook our heads. It was clear we had no other options. Terlingua's population would temporarily swell by about 10% without a lift.

"I was gonna go and fill my barrels tomorrow anyway, so no problem to go a day early." We breathed a sigh of relief. "You can help me load 'em up too."

As we lugged the large blue barrels onto the back of Celia's truck, she told us her story. A true child of the sixties, she'd left her conservative Mid-West hometown in 1965 with an older boyfriend, 'a bad boy,' and caught a bus to Los Angeles. They bought a flatbed truck, installed a double bed in the back, and with a tarpaulin roof and a couple of cats, they headed for the arid hills and valleys of the Mojave desert, East of LA.

"I fell in love with the desert then." Celia regarded the scrubby expanse in front of her home as she spoke, and we could tell she was thinking about times past.

"There were a lot of crazy people out there though, and my boyfriend got into mescaline. Heavy stuff. I left him and hitched to San Francisco. I was there from '66 to '71. Did all sorts of jobs. I learnt that if you have a tongue in your head and you're not too proud, you'll never starve."

She asked us what we did in England, and we were almost embarrassed to recount details of our mundane office jobs, though Celia seemed impressed that we'd landed in Terlingua on a mere two week trip.

"Most who come here stay for a while. Drifters. Dreamers.

Misfits. Like me!"

She smiled and continued with her story. She'd met an older man, Steve, and fallen in love. He'd had money but lost it all. He was offered a lucrative job - to go to Mexico to pick up a boat and sail it back to California, so Celia set off on the adventure with him. In the Mexican state of Baja California, they were arrested by undercover police, who had received a tip off that the boat wasn't all that they would be transporting back to the USA. Held on drugs charges in a filthy jail cell for six weeks, Celia wondered if she'd ever see her beloved desert again. Then one morning she was taken to an administration office and was met by a woman from the US Consul. She told Celia the charges were being dropped and she was being released. Steve was dead. Supposedly of a heart attack.

"Never found out the full story." She bit her lip as she looked at the desert. "Reckon he was murdered and they covered it up."

"Funny thing though. You'll think I'm crazy. I sleep out here on the porch. Sometimes at dawn, I wake up and there's this old cougar sat out there next to that big cactus, just watching me. First time he showed up, I freaked and ran for the rifle. I pointed it at him, but he just sat, watching. Then he got up and walked away. He's been coming a couple of times a month for the last twenty years. Seems he just sits watching me till I wake up, then he leaves.You know how long a cougar lives?"

We shook our heads.

"Well it ain't normally twenty years." She smiled mysteriously and stood up.

"Okay, lets go. Just need some beer for the journey."

We squeezed into the cab of the truck and set off towards the lodge, the onset of dusk and the storm darkening the sky ahead, with Celia drinking beer from the can, and tossing the empties through the window as we sped through the desert.

We may not have met the beer drinking goat, but if, as the song suggested, we'd come to look for America, it felt like maybe we'd come close to finding it that day, in the people we met, and the stories they told.

The year after our Texas adventure, I returned to America, this time on business. By now I was a Finance manager for a mobile phone company, working on a project to implement a new computer system. We were despatched to Denver, Colorado for a month in January 1997 to test the new system, at the headquarters of the American company who were developing the software. Our colleagues were suitably jealous, viewing the trip as a month long holiday. The reality was somewhat different with a twelve hour day, six day working week. We worked hard, and played hard, hammering our expense accounts at the end of every long day, averaging about five hours sleep a night.

My time in Colorado coincided with one of the coldest periods the State had ever experienced. Local news broadcasts urged people to cover all exposed skin, with frostbite likely to strike quickly as temperatures plummeted to minus 25°C. I set off to walk to my hotel from the office late on a Saturday afternoon and the streets were deserted. Stupidly, I'd forgotten to take a hat and had no hood on my coat. As I left the building, I felt the inside of my nostrils stiffen as the moisture immediately froze. The air was icy and dry, and each inhalation took my breath away. It was a twenty minute walk to the hotel and I quickened my pace, slipping and sliding on the icy pavement.

The news bulletin had delivered a lengthy lecture on early recognition of frostbite symptoms. Stage 1, was a burning or stinging sensation, so called frostnip, which I was now experiencing on my exposed ears. The next stage was a reddening and loss of sensation, followed by blistering, and blackening of the affected area, before death of the skin and subsequent loss of body parts. As I walked, the tingling on my ears subsided and I realised I was graduating to Stage 2. By now I was panicking, imagining staggering into the hotel reception, clutching my detached, blackened ears, to the horror of the dinner buffet queue and the amusement of my colleagues.

I tried pulling my coat over my head but this raised my upper arms to the level of my shoulders, resulting in me adopting the running gait of a zombie, which isn't best suited to an icy pavement. With the numbness in my ears increasing by the minute, I resorted to slapping them with my gloved hands as I careered along the darkening street. I was annoyed that I'd forgotten a hat and berated myself as I ran.

"Idiot. Bloody idiot." I bellowed, beating my ears frantically to stimulate blood flow as I stumbled along.

I alternated this approach with cupping my gloved ears to my head as I skidded along, shouting at myself and no doubt resembling the subject of Edvard Munch's 'Scream' painting, come-to-life.

The siren made me jump as the Denver Police Landcruiser pulled up behind me, illuminating me in the beam of a roof mounted spotlight.

"Stay where you are. Keep your hands by your side," crackled a disembodied voice.

After establishing that I wasn't an escaped lunatic, the officers were still bemused as to why anyone would choose to walk for twenty minutes at any time, let alone in Arctic weather conditions, as they delivered me to my hotel.

"I'm English. We like walking." I explained as I shuffled out of the vehicle towards the hotel reception, where my colleagues were eagerly waiting, to hear how I'd managed to get arrested on a half mile walk back from the office.

The punishing schedule in Denver had taken its toll, and when I returned home Karen said I looked like I'd aged ten years in a month. We'd bought a new house just days before my departure, and I was excited about the future. We both had new jobs which meant more money, and now owned a 'grown up' semi detached house in a suburban street. Most importantly, our increased spending power provided the opportunity to extend our travel horizons beyond Europe and America.

4 DISTANT HORIZONS

"UN Secretary General Kofi Annan is expected to meet Saddam Hussein in Baghdad for talks on Friday. Syria, Egypt and Jordan are urging Saddam to cooperate and the UN are hopeful of a positive resolution. However, they have evacuated staff from their Baghdad office in anticipation of possible US Air Strikes. In the event of air strikes, it's likely Iraq will retaliate with missile attacks on Israel. Gas masks have been issued in Tel Aviv. Thomson's and Thomas Cook are evacuating all their clients this afternoon. There are seats available on those flights for use by our clients, but you need to advise us in the next half hour if you want to leave. That's the end of the statement."

I scanned the faces of my fellow tourists, as the flustered tour company rep folded the sheet of typed A4 paper, and retreated to a half cleared breakfast table to field queries. Mouths open, eyes wide, heads shaking in shock and confusion. They'd only arrived in Eilat, Israel, the previous evening, and somehow the traditional welcome meeting had turned into a war zone briefing.

"Kofi Annan? Saddam Hussein? Baghdad? Where the bloody hell are we Geoff?" pleaded a teary-eyed woman with a strong Lancashire accent. "No wonder it was so cheap!"

And cheap it was. With tensions increasing in the Middle East as Iraq blocked access to UN weapons inspectors, deployed in the aftermath of the 1991 Gulf War, Israel wasn't an obvious choice for British package tourists. It was February 1998, and the sabre rattling between the United States and Iraq had been on the increase for months, culminating in the Clinton administration threatening missile strikes on the Iraqi Capital. Speculation was rife that Saddam would respond with counter strikes against Israel and Kuwait, and comments by Richard Butler, head of the UN weapons inspection team, that Iraq 'had enough chemical weapons to blow away Tel Aviv,' had led to panic in the region.

I'd spotted a cut-price deal with a specialist Middle East travel company, who had no choice but to carry on sending tourists to the area. For the big travel firms, Israel and Egypt were a tiny percentage of their overall business, so evacuating their clients was a minor inconvenience. For the companies who only dealt in the Middle East, pulling out would mean the collapse of their business. I'd gathered as many facts as I could (which wasn't easy in those early days of the internet) and decided that the risk was worth taking.

The area we would be visiting was two hundred miles away from Tel Aviv. More importantly, it was at the southern tip of Israel, on the country's slender nine-mile-wide coast, with the Egyptian town of Taba, and the Jordanian City of Aqaba less than five miles away. Even though Saddam was perceived to be a deranged tyrant, he was unlikely to launch an attack which impacted friendly Arab nations. The Israelis themselves seemed to agree, and the check-in area of our hotel was busy with families from the north, who'd decided on an impromptu evacuation holiday until the crisis blew over.

Needless to say, our fellow British holidaymakers didn't share my optimism, and most opted to take the flights home, one day after arriving. Karen and I found ourselves part of a tiny minority of foreign visitors, amidst an Israeli party fuelled by a siege mentality. Bars and restaurants deployed gallows humour to attract business – 'End of the World Party tonight,' 'Drinks 2-for-1 until the siren sounds,' were typical chalkboard ads, and the Israeli evacuees used the potential threat against their nation as a great excuse to let their hair down. The only hint that we weren't on a holiday island in the Balearics, was the occasional fighter jet screeching low overhead and the ever-present weaponry carried by young national service conscripts. This could be quite disconcerting, as a tipsy teenage girl in khaki fatigues danced on the table of a bar, assault rifle strapped to her back.

Luckily, Annan's diplomacy worked initially as he famously declared Saddam to be 'a man I can do business with,' and the threatened air strikes didn't materialise. US patience eventually ran out though, and by December of that year, American bombs once again fell on the Iraqi Capital. By then we'd already been on another trip, our first foray into Asia.

By the late 1990's, the new phenomenon called the internet, which would change travel planning forever, was still in its infancy, and was limited in its usefulness. Most people still booked holidays using Teletext, High Street travel agents or more specialist firms. One such London based company, offered unusual trips at an excellent price, and caught my attention when I spotted their advert in the back pages of a Sunday newspaper -

'A Journey across China on The Red Arrow Express.'

The trip included seven days in Beijing, a twenty four hour train journey to Hong Kong, then four nights in the island city which was in the process of being handed back to Chinese Governance. Hotels and flights were included for an unbelievable price of just over £500 each. More importantly for Karen and I, it fitted nicely into a fourteen day trip, and a September departure meant no mid-Summer wrangling around the dreaded holiday chart.

We met the rest of our twelve strong group at Heathrow, and realised we were around twenty years younger than the next most junior member of the party. The company's business plan quickly became apparent. Hook in a group of relatively wealthy, elderly travellers with an amazingly low price, then upsell them on daily trips, costing very little using local guides, but which could easily double the overall cost of the holiday.

I deployed a tactic I've used to good effect several times since, and totally shunned any of the organised trips. Our tour guide tried to sway us with tales of language difficulties, likelihood of getting lost, not understanding menus, straying into poor areas.... I smiled. Those were exactly the sort of things I wanted to experience.

China in 1998 was unrecognisable from the super-modern economic powerhouse I was to revisit twenty years later. Driving from the airport into central Beijing was like entering a toxic ash cloud, with a black fog of acrid exhaust fumes blurring the view ahead through the bus windscreen. 99% of the vehicles were battered yellow taxis. Known as miandis, or bread loaves, due to their boxy shape, these small mini-buses were everywhere, and seemed to be the sole form of transport for most of the population. The few cars which appeared to be private vehicles generally bore government number plates or a national flag, denoting the vehicle to be the transport of a diplomat.

Our hotel was a bland, business class affair, but was centrally located, so shaking off our jet-lag, we defied the tour guide and set off to explore. I picked up a card from reception with the name and address of the hotel in English, and its Chinese language equivalent beneath. Exploring Beijing was exhausting. The distances seemed huge, and we began to doubt the accuracy of the scale on our Rough Guide map. Also, with few 'free range' western tourists managing to escape from their tour groups, we became something of a sensation as we visited Tiananmen Square and the Forbidden City. Chinese visitors from the countryside were particularly excited to see us, and as crowds gathered, an ancient camera would be produced for a family snap with the exotic European visitors. Babies were held aloft, teens blushed and giggled, and bashful grandparents shoved to the front, as we grinned for the camera and revelled in our new-found celebrity status.

At the end of the day, I stuck out my arm on a busy avenue and a yellow taxi screeched to a halt in the third of four lanes. We dashed across to the car, and I brandished the card showing our hotel name. The driver looked slightly confused as I pointed out the Chinese lettering below the English name, but he gestured for us to jump in. We squeezed into the back of the tiny van and he tapped the Perspex screen in front of us, to ask for the hotel card. I realised we may have problems when I saw that he was looking at it upside down. I pointed at the Chinese letters and smiled hopefully. He grinned back sheepishly. We wondered whether he may be illiterate, or perhaps speak Cantonese, not Mandarin, but he drove on regardless. After about half an hour of driving, punctuated by the driver asking us in Mandarin for the name of the hotel, and us replying in English to look at the bloody card, we realised we were circling the same couple of blocks in the Wangfujing area, home of most of the big international hotels. Unfortunately, none were ours.

Eventually, I had an idea and signalled for the driver to stop outside the landmark Beijing Hotel on Dongvhang'an Street. I leapt out and dashed into reception, brandishing my hotel card. I established that the young receptionist spoke some English, and explained that we'd unfortunately got into a taxi with an illiterate driver who couldn't read Chinese. The girl looked at the Chinese 'address' on the card, and nodded, maintaining her serious demeanour.

"That says Welcome to Beijing, sir."

Our unsurprisingly confused driver seemed delighted when the receptionist came out and told him the name of our hotel. Not least because it was half an hour back in the direction we'd just come from.

We didn't mention the hotel card mix up to our tour guide on the rare occasions we saw him. The rest of the group regarded us with some amusement, and referred to us as 'the honeymooners.' Their assumption that we eschewed the organised tours to indulge in romantic in-room entertainment, couldn't have been further from the truth. We immersed ourselves in Beijing, enjoying the culture shock and strangeness of the City. Watching commuters perform tai-chi at daybreak, or pensioners' evening ballroom dancing sessions in a suburban square felt uniquely Chinese and totally foreign to us. However, on one occasion, a craving for western food saw us hunting for China's first Hard Rock Café, in the north of the city. Again, the Rough Guide map misled us, and we arrived after a gruelling two hour walk. Hungry for burgers, we were dismayed to see the dining tables being packed up at 8.30pm, as the restaurant became a Chinese disco. We soon had to forget our rumbling stomachs, as we became the dance partners of choice for a room full of Chinese New Romantics, and spent the night being repeatedly forced onto the dancefloor like two hungry, performing bears.

Twenty four hours on a train sounds no fun, but I loved the journey south to Hong Kong, and with no western cutlery on board, it was a perfect opportunity to hone our chopstick skills. There was little to do, except gaze out of the window, and as we rattled past a landscape of endless paddy fields, it occurred to me that every single field had at least one person working in it. That person would obviously know the person in the next field, who would know the person in the next field, and so on. Therefore, everyone living along that 1600 mile stretch of track, knew someone, who knew someone, who knew someone...I tried to work out, if the peasant in the first field in Beijing shouted a word to the peasant in the next field, who then did likewise, and so on, how long would it take that word to reach Hong Kong? Such is the nature of long-distance train travel - it gives you time to think abstract thoughts, that rarely occur to you when stationary!

Hong Kong was a shock for a different reason - food and drink were double the price we were used to in England and we found ourselves seeking out cheaper local options. On our last night, we met an English ex-pat who took us out for the night, courtesy of his expense account, and we learnt a valuable travel fact - that large numbers of visitors on expenses will soon distort a city's pricing structure, wherever in the world that is.

China had whetted my appetite for culture shock, and within a couple of months of returning from China, we'd signed up for another trip with the same travel company. This time it was a twelve day tour of Rajasthan in India, again for less than £500 each. On this occasion, we'd be travelling between the major sights of the region's 'Golden Triangle' by minibus, so were forced to spend more time with the tour group, although again, we opted out of any additional paid excursions, and 'escaped' whenever possible.

This trip allowed me to observe at first hand the reaction of street traders, hawkers and beggars to a tour group, as opposed to a couple of independent travellers. I noticed that our approaching bus would usually be spotted from a long distance. By the time we arrived at whichever tourist sight we were visiting, the vehicle would be consumed by a seething mass of women bearing colourful shawls, wicker baskets and fruit; small children brandishing bags of toxic-looking blue and red semi-iced water, and aged men wielding hissing cobras, occasionally with a twitching hessian sack, containing a wriggling mongoose slung over their shoulder.

We literally had to fight our way off the bus and through the heaving bodies. On one occasion in Jaipur, an overly persistent trinket salesman clung on so hard as I attempted to climb a staircase at the fort, that the neck of my t-shirt began to rip. To free myself, I was forced to shove him in his bony ribs, and send him hurtling backwards down the stairs, taking a shrieking clump of traders and their produce with him.

By contrast, I noticed that independent travellers were left comparatively unmolested. Hawkers were generally deterred quickly by a raised hand or a shake of the head (though confusingly, a head waggle means yes in India!) I wondered whether locals associated tour bus travel with wealth, or whether it was the age and style of dress of tour groups which suggested richer pickings. Either way, I noted that travelling independently definitely seemed to result in much less hassle, and resolved that my next visit to the country would be without the added hawker-bait of a tour group.

You never forget your first trip to India, and if it was culture shock we expected, the country certainly delivered. An explosion of noise, colour and smells at every turn. Extreme poverty, regular invasion of personal space, and the proximity of unfortunates with grotesque injuries and deformities made it an unsettling experience initially. I can still clearly recall exiting Delhi airport upon our arrival in the country. There was a chill in the air as dawn broke, and wood smoke tinged with aviation fuel stung our eyes as we filed out to meet our minibus. Behind a wire fence stood a silent mass of gaunt, grimy faces, wrapped in blankets, eyes wide, observing the new arrivals. Having boarded a plane from polished, sterile Heathrow, it was a shock to see these semi-homeless inhabitants of the airport perimeter within minutes of stepping onto Indian soil for the first time.

After a few days in Delhi, the city of Agra was next on the agenda, with everyone eager to visit the Taj Mahal and emulate Princess Diana's iconic bench pose of a few years earlier.

Unfortunately, Karen was stricken with a bad case of 'Delhi Belly,' and we were forced to go in search of a public convenience. There were long queues at the single toilet block assigned for public use, and Karen couldn't wait. Directed by a guard to an area of the site far from the opulence of Mumtaz Mahal's famous mausoleum, we found a concrete structure with a wooden door hanging from rusty hinges. Karen retched at the stench as she entered. There was no light and the floor was awash with a foul brown liquid which seemed to have overflowed from a broken squat trough which was just visible in the gloom. Unfortunately for Karen, she was doomed to spend some time in this hell hole. I stood outside shouting encouragement as she cried in terrible discomfort.

"There are crawling things on the floor. Oh God, there are things flying."

I supported Karen as best I could in her half hour of need. Eventually though, I spotted something which caught my attention.

"Are you Okay for five minutes? I just need to go and do something." She was in no position to object.

Karen later described suffering her bout of acute illness in that terrible lavatory, before emerging, blinking and tearful into the sunlight. I was nowhere to be seen. She slumped on a bench and closed her eyes, trying to forget the ordeal she'd suffered.

The calming sound of distant birdsong was suddenly shattered by excited shouts from a small road to the right. A tiny Indian man of around sixty, wearing a turban and grubby white dhoti robe was jogging backwards along the track as fast as his wiry legs would carry him. In his hands was a camera, which he was clicking at in a haphazard manner, whilst shouting in a squeaky voice.

"Yes sir, come, come, fast, fast, nice picture!"

Trundling along behind him was a wooden cart, with thick wheels of almost six feet in diameter, pulled by two huge, white brahman oxen. I was stood high at the front of the cart, reins in one hand, whip in the other, urging the great beasts onward, with a huge grin on my face.

"Karen, look, I'm driving it!" I yelled excitedly, pride at my new-found skill unfortunately outweighing any concern for my partner.

I'm not sure Karen ever forgave me for abandoning her, but looking back, those slightly blurry ox cart pictures are better than any taken that day on the 'Diana bench.'

As I often find with India, we were ready to come home by the end of the trip. (Though strangely, within a couple of months you generally develop an urge to return to the country again.) It was on the journey home that we experienced the worst problem that can afflict a two-week traveller. We were 'bumped' from our flight.

We were due to fly home on a Friday evening, but arrived at Delhi airport to scenes of chaos at check-in. That weekend marked the beginning of the five day period of Hajj, the holy pilgrimage to Mecca, which all Muslims are compelled to make once in their lifetime. Consequently, whole families had turned up to see relatives off on what for most, is a literal trip of a lifetime. The airport was full of rural families who had probably never been to Delhi before, let alone been inside an airport. Elderly barefoot men wrapped in frayed blankets wandered in amazement through duty free, as women with kohl-painted eyes cooked rice on gas stoves next to the Air India ticket counter.

Our tour guide, Javed, was engaged in a heated debate with the

Royal Jordanian Airlines ticket clerk. One of the drawbacks of our cheap fare was a flight via Amman. Unfortunately, this was also the likeliest route to fly into Saudi Arabia from India and Pakistan. It quickly became obvious from Javed's demeanour that our seats on the flight had been sold to someone else, most likely a group of rich Hajji's paying a grossly inflated price. The news that we couldn't fly home and would have to return to the hotel was greeted with shrugs by most of the group. i.e. the majority who were retired and were in no rush to get back. But for myself, Karen, and two middle aged teachers from Derby, who all needed to be back at work on Monday, this spelled potential disaster.

Back at the hotel, Javed was close to tears as he slumped over the reception desk, phone clasped between shoulder and ear.

"No flights with Royal Jordanian until next Wednesday. None with BA until Monday. Air India, Tuesday." His head waggled in agitation. With our holiday allowance exhausted, we shared his agitation, if not the head waggling.

Javed had put the word out amongst his network of 'fixers' that we needed twelve seats on any flight to England, any airline. As news could arrive 'at any time' we were forced to hang around the hotel for the whole of Saturday. This dampened any enthusiasm the retirees had for an extended stay. At around 6pm Javed burst into the bar, where the 'Delhi 12' had gathered. He was accompanied by a young man with a leather jacket and slicked black hair, bearing a passing resemblance to an Indian Alvin Stardust.

"This is Vihaan. He has a flight for us. You must give him your passports now."

"Give him my passport? Not bloody likely, I've never met the chap." Maurice was an ex Lord Mayor from Norfolk and was in no mood to hand over his UK citizenship.

"You must Mr. Maurice. He needs the passport to buy ticket. It's the only chance of escape we have." Javed added dramatically.

Questions were raised on which airline and what route, but Vihaan waved them away impatiently.

"Quickly, Quickly. Tickets will go."

Karen and I didn't care, as long as we were back for work on time, so handed over our passports, as did the rest of the group.

The following morning, at dawn, we were back at the airport which was still busy, but not as chaotic as on the Friday. Vihaan handed us our passports and tickets, which had a lot of Cyrillic writing on.

"DEL - TAS?" read Maurice. "We're not going via Tasmania are we Javed?"

Javed gulped. "Only flight available Mr. Maurice. Tashkent. Uzbekistan. Special plane."

How 'special' became apparent at check-in. There was no airline name visible, the only indication of our destination being some handwritten signs, again in Cyrillic script. The other passengers were all Uzbek traders, who had seemingly cleared out Delhi's textile and electrical markets, judging by the size of the bundles and crates they were checking in. Worryingly, the majority of the freight seemed to be by-passing the official weight checks, and bundles of rupees were exchanging hands and being furtively secreted in the pockets of customs officials. It seemed we were on a special flight chartered by the Tashkent Market Traders Association.

"These blokes look like cut-throats," commented Barry, a retired greengrocer from Essex. He was right, most of the men bore extravagant facial scars which made them look like a crew of pirates in baggy jeans and cheap leather jackets.

Upon boarding the plane, which again had no identifying logo, we were greeted by a flight crew who all sported a full mouth of gold teeth. Even the pilot looked like 'Jaws' from the James Bond films. He emerged briefly from the cockpit to cadge a cigarette from a stewardess, which he lit before returning to do his pre-flight checks, which mostly comprised of reading a glossy Russian magazine.

Our group was assigned seats in the 'First Class' section at the front of the plane, with slightly more leg room and comfier seats. Unfortunately, with the aisles further back full of crates and bags, some of the traders dragged the bulkier cargo to the front, and piled it precariously by the bulkhead in front of us. The plane took off with two women sporting head scarves and nine-carat grins, stood in front of us, whilst desperately clinging onto a large wooden crate to prevent it tumbling down the aisle. The stewardesses sat reading magazines and smoking.

It occurred to me that this was the sort of flight you hear about as a late item on a morning radio news bulletin. 'A plane has crashed en-route from Delhi to Uzbekistan with no survivors. There are believed to be twelve Britons on board.'

What on earth were twelve Britons doing on board a flight like that? You'd wonder for a brief moment, then carry on driving to work.

It was with some relief then, when we landed at Tashkent airport, which resembled a construction site, for a connecting Aeroflot flight to London.

"Tashkent is the second worst airport in the world, after Kabul," a Sikh businessman told me in the departure lounge. I wasn't arguing as I looked at the cracked floor tiles and paint peeling walls. I was just glad I'd be home in time for work in the morning.

5 GOING MY OWN WAY

The 1990's drew to a close with a trip to Fidel Castro's Cuba where we spent our first day and night confined to the hotel, as Hurricane Irene battered the South West of the island. Travelling through the region during the following week, it was hard to tell which homes had been damaged by the storm, and which were in a 'business as usual' state of dilapidation. I was aware of the country's fantastic free national health service, which exported doctors across the developing world, but was shocked to see Cubans queuing for rationed food staples in such a fertile land. Locals shrugged and smiled when I asked why they were unable to keep the produce they grew. The last bastion of Communism in the Caribbean was obviously not the utopia it seemed. There was however, a thriving black market in the vibrant bars and cafés, and I snapped up vintage Che Guevara bank notes and a newspaper-wrapped bundle of Havana cigars, straight from the backdoor of the factory, which my friends and I smoked to welcome the new millennium.

At the start of the new century, Karen and I broke our golden rule and tagged an extra week onto our annual leave, for a three-week trip to Australia. We criss-crossed the country by plane, supplemented by local rental cars, allowing us to visit a number of different regions. The scenery was fantastic and it was an unforgettable experience to snorkel in the waters of the Great Barrier reef, surrounded by multitudes of brightly coloured Korean tourists, their tour group denoted by the shade of their matching swim caps and lifejackets. After China, India and Cuba though, our brief taste of Australia maybe felt a little too familiar to me, with a lack of the culture shock I'd come to love.

At Ayers Rock without a hire car, we'd booked on a tour to see Uluru at Sunset and Sunrise. The coach driver was a boorish, time-obsessive, who bullied elderly passengers for being few minutes late back to the bus. After having our time at the aboriginal village cut short by his strict timetable, I took great delight in seeing his smug expression change to panic, when I told him we wouldn't be travelling back on his coach, and would find our own way the twenty-plus miles back to the hotel.

"You can't do that!" he spluttered through the open door, as passengers' heads popped up over their seatbacks to watch the heated exchange.

"Watch me." I shouted as I walked away, safe in the knowledge that you can always hitch a ride on a quiet road. We only waited twenty minutes, before being picked up by a couple from Bristol in a VW Camper, after spending an interesting morning learning the correct way to cook witchetty grubs in the ash of a fire.

Karen and I split up shortly after returning from Australia and she moved out of the house. As is often the case with couples who meet as teenagers, the transition we all experience as we reach our thirties, caused us to gradually drift apart. We parted on good terms and remain friends today. At work, I was now in a middle management position but had no desire for promotion. The next level of seniority brought with it the added complexities of often toxic corporate politics, which I had no appetite for. As long as I earned enough to pay for the things I wanted to do, and go to the places I wanted to see, I was happy.

I also had no interest in acquiring the latest 'stuff.' If I had a car, computer, and the latest must-have, a mobile phone, which worked, I saw no need to constantly upgrade to the latest model. I recall a conversation with a colleague around that time, in which she explained that her family had forfeited a holiday abroad for three years in order to save for 'a dream kitchen.' She also offered her opinion that travel was a waste of money, as 'at the end of the two weeks, you've spent loads, but have nothing to show for it.' I said nothing, but it made me reflect on my own priorities. I couldn't ever envisage a time where I dreamt about kitchens, but it was true that travel could be viewed purely as a cost with no real payback, beyond a chance to recharge your batteries for two weeks.

My view though was that the cost of travel should be seen as an investment. The sort of travel I envisaged paid back in terms of increased knowledge of the world and other cultures; learning to overcome challenges and setbacks; appreciating how much we have in comparison to others, rather than constantly always wanting more. The travel I craved, delivered experiences and memories that would last a lifetime. No matter what happened in terms of future personal wealth or physical health, you would always have those memories. I never wanted to feel at the end of a trip that I 'had nothing to show for it.'

However, before, realising those noble travel ambitions, I made the most of being single for the first time in fifteen years, by embarking on a road trip. I decided to revisit California for the first time in ten years to visit a mate, Iain, who was working in San Francisco. I also hoped to tie in a visit to a long-lost cousin who lived in LA.

The plan was to meet Iain in San Diego, where he was spending the weekend. After a couple of days boozing in Southern California, he would then fly back to San Francisco and I'd undertake a solo roadtrip along the Pacific Coast Highway. I'd then stay at his apartment when I reached 'Frisco.

Unfortunately, while I landed at LAX airport, my bag began a two day excursion around the airports of the USA. I therefore turned up for a big weekend in San Diego, clutching a carrier bag containing only a tube of toothpaste and a deodorant, that I'd bought en-route to the hotel. Luckily, Iain was able to lend me some clothes to wear. Unluckily, he was about three inches taller, and a stone heavier than me, so I hit the Gaslamp district on the first night looking like a schoolboy wearing his older brother's hand-me-downs.

I soon forgot what I was wearing after several beers, and to our delight we discovered that our Leeds accents were totally incomprehensible to the locals, enabling us to hold conversations in their presence without them having a clue what we were saying. Perhaps I overestimated how unintelligible we were though, as I have a blurred memory of a large redhead knocking me off a bar stool with a well delivered uppercut!

By Monday morning we were both in a sorry state. My rental car smelt like a frat-house carpet, as I dropped Iain off at the airport, was reacquainted with my bag and headed north on Interstate 5. It was a beautiful July morning, with a light breeze blowing off the ocean, as I flicked the radio tuner until I found a station playing 60's soul. I wound down the windows and sang along to Otis Redding, as I cruised at a steady sixty, fearful that a Highway Patrol breathalyser would reveal the extent of the weekend's excesses.

After an hour, my hangover started to really kick in with a rush of combined nausea and headache, and a feeling of impending intestinal doom. I decided to pull off the freeway at the next exit, and followed a sign to San Clemente. I followed the road along the seafront boulevard, and swerved into the car park of the first motel I spotted. I staggered into the gloomy reception and asked the elderly desk clerk for 'a room for one, any room.' Then, ignoring an overpowering smell of mothballs, I lugged my bag upstairs, opened the door and crashed unconscious onto the thin mattress of the single bed.

It was early afternoon when I awoke. I lay on the bed trying to remember where I was, and how I'd got there. My back was rigidly curved into the shape of the concave mattress, and my right eye was crusted, having been blasted by the air conditioning unit which vibrated under the window sill, with a steady thump-thump-thump rhythm. I reached for a stained and sticky remote control on the bedside table, and turned off the icy air, but the thump-thump-thump in my head didn't abate. I sat up and decided to make contact with my cousin Lenny in LA.

One of many interesting characters in my family, Lenny had left home at sixteen to find fame and fortune. Following his release from a Moroccan jail in the mid seventies (Another of those sailing boat collection capers which seemed so popular back then!) he landed in California, and taught himself how to build swimming pools. He'd since graduated to constructing recording studios, and was doing well via word-of-mouth contacts in the community of the latest genre, 'Gangsta-Rap.' Unfortunately, he hadn't embraced recent technology, and still had no mobile phone. Therefore, when I called, he explained that he'd be at work when I arrived and I'd need to call him on the site's landline. He had the number, but I had no pen to write it down.

'No problem,' I said. 'I'll pop down to reception to get one and call you back.'

The old man behind the desk eyed me suspiciously when I entered reception. He had a yellow, tobacco stained beard and straggles of white hair protruding from beneath a 'US Navy Veteran' baseball cap. His red checked lumberjack shirt was a perfect colour match for his eyes and bulbous nose end.

"Hi!" I smiled cheerily, ignoring the pain in my eyes caused by a flickering neon 'Welcome' sign behind the desk.

The old man didn't respond, as the sign behind him blinked erratically and ironically. He just stared, shaking his head slightly, as if I was speaking a foreign language.

"Do you have a pen I could borrow?"

The old man's eyes narrowed.

"You wanna what?" he shouted suddenly, causing me to jump. I took the unnecessary volume to mean he was deaf.

"A pen. Please." I increased my own volume in line with his and smiled again.

His eyes narrowed even more.

"A pen you say? You wanna pen?"

"That's right, if you have one I could borrow, please?"

"Whadduya wanna pen for?" His volume had increased further and he looked me up and down, with an expression of ill-disguised disgust.

"Erm....I just need to use one."

"You gonna use it in your room?" Brow furrowed, he stared hard into my eyes, again narrowing his own.

"Yes...if that's Okay?" I scanned the reception counter to see if there was a spare pen I could grab, but it seemed the old chap kept his biros safely locked away from thieving guests. Breathing heavily, he kept staring at me. I stared back, wondering how this seemingly mundane negotiation could go so wrong.

"What's going on Teddy?" The voice of an elderly woman came from the room behind the counter.

Teddy maintained his hard stare, as he replied without turning.

"It's the Australian guy. Wants to borrow a pen."

"What's he wanna borrow a pen for?"

"I'll be darned if I know." Teddy's lips curled in revulsion, as he turned away from me shaking his head, and headed into the back room. I could hear him muttering about 'taking a goddam pen to his room' whilst crashing around noisily, with his wife urging him to 'tell him he can't take it away from the motel.' This must be one hell of a special pen, I thought.

Eventually, Teddy shuffled back into reception, still shaking his head. In his hand was a large frying pan, which he placed on the counter in front of me. We both stared at it for a moment, then looked back at each other.

"What's that?" I asked, already half knowing the answer.

"It's a frying pen!" he bellowed. "You said you wanted to borrow a pen!"

I picked up the frying pan and walked out of reception. I couldn't summon the energy to discuss with Teddy the peculiar cadence of northern English regional dialect, and debate the vagaries of pronunciation, resultant of my flat vowels and his Californian drawl. I do though still wonder what Teddy and his wife thought I'd do with their frying pan in a room with no cooking facilities.

For the following week, I had an enjoyable drive up the California coast, with no set agenda and no firm plans, stopping in motels at small seaside towns, drinking, reading and thinking.

I arrived in San Francisco, and after devouring a literary diet of Charles Bukowski and James Ellroy for the previous week, enthusiastically submerged myself in the city's seedy underbelly. Iain's apartment was in the notorious Civic Centre area, and upon arrival he told me he'd never drunk in any of the bars within a mile radius of his home. "Why's that?" I asked and set out to explore.

For me, one of the pleasures of travelling in the U.S. is our shared language, which makes for easy communication with the random characters usually found sat at the bar of less salubrious establishments. Stan was one such character. A Vietnam veteran with a greasy, grey pony tail and Dennis Hopper 'Easy Rider' moustache, Stan was sat smoking in the window of a bar off Polk Street as I passed. Jim Morrison was on the Juke Box warning of killers on the road, and a patron was slumped in the doorway, asleep, a half eaten chicken leg resting precariously on his chin like a breadcrumbed cigar. My sort of place, I thought.

I'd been interested in Vietnam since reading Mark Baker's excellent 'Nam,' a collection of often harrowing anecdotes from the war, and soon fell into conversation with my new drinking buddy. Stan had been a helicopter rear-gunner from 1968 to 1971, and happily relayed disturbing tales of chopper drug runs to Laos, unauthorised machine gun strafing of villages 'we didn't like the look of,' and flying while 'as high as a kite and as drunk as a rat.'

"Most important kit on our Huey...?" Stan raised a quizzical eyebrow. "Not the guns. No sir. The Speakers! Always needed some sweet music while we flew!"

'Ride of the Valkyries?' I suggested, remembering the iconic 'Apocalypse Now' scene, with the squadron of Huey's skimming the waves as they clatter towards a VC village with murderous intent.

"Bullshit." countered Stan. "We didn't play no classical shit. Most of the guys were black. Motown and Soul was all we played."

I'd noticed a juke box on the wall, and with the beers flowing as freely as Stan's memories, I decided a trip down memory lane was in order. Plenty to choose from - there were about twenty volumes of the ubiquitous Motown Chartbusters CD's on offer. I selected a few appropriate tunes on my way to the bar for another round of beers, and when I got back to our table, Stan was back in 'Nam, singing along to Martha and the Vandellas, reliving the time of his life. Arms extended in front of him, fists clenched, holding an imaginary M60 machine gun, Stan was once again strafing Mekong Delta villages with a hail of tracer fire.

'Du-Du-Du-Du-Du!!!' the staccato report of Stan's make-believe firearm reverberated through the bar, forming a strange accompaniment to Martha Reeves singing about dancing in the street. For the first time, I saw the hint of a smile on Stan's face as he slugged a mouthful of beer from the bottle and recalled days of Motown, marijuana and aerial mass murder.

"We were Gods Matthew, fucking Gods." Stan's eyes closed as he savoured the moment, sucking on his roll-up, head nodding to the music, and once again feeling the damp heat of South East Asia on his face as he soared over the paddies.

Further along the same street, on an early Sunday afternoon, I was passing one of the area's many 'adult stores.'
"Pssst!" A tattooed teenaged girl stood in the doorway. "You speak English?"

I confirmed that I did, albeit with an Australian accent

apparently.

"Can you do my friend a favour?" She beckoned me into the shop.

Two middle aged, Japanese men in suits, were staring at an Amer-Asian girl in her mid twenties who was sat in a Perspex box, reading a book. The tattooed girl explained their predicament.

"Guys pay for a private show with Lori. She can close the curtain then. These two don't speak English and we can't make them understand. They've been stood staring at her for half an hour but we're not allowed to close the curtain." She nodded at a security camera, blinking red above the Perspex box.

"What do you need me to do?" I asked, always eager to help a girl in a perspex box.

"I'll give you ten dollars from the till. You give it to Lori, and she can close the curtain. Hopefully they'll then get the idea and pay, or leave."

It's not every Sunday afternoon you get an offer like that, so I accepted and was furtively slipped ten bucks, which I passed through a slot into the box and Lori drew the curtain.

Lori was half Chinese, and was studying to be a nurse. She worked in the box on weekends, saying it was easy money, though she had a dread of a family member or neighbour entering the store and discovering her secret career. She was interested in Europe, and was particularly surprised that in England we generally view 'Asian' as originating from the Indian Sub-Continent, rather than the Orient. We chatted for five minutes, and it felt like speed dating.

Then with a glance at the camera above the box, Lori suddenly asked "Hey, want to see my piercings?" and it no longer felt like speed dating. She dropped her towelling dressing gown, and hitched her leg up onto the plastic chair she'd been sat on.

"I have two in my outer labia," Lori announced proudly, as she pointed out two small rings.

"This one is called a Princess Albertina," she was delving deeper into her genitalia now and I was feeling slightly queasy, having skipped breakfast. "This is my fourchette, right in my vulva. That one hurt most."

"I can imagine," I gulped. Lori continued to make small-talk, telling me about her sister's recent wisdom tooth extraction, as she conducted a bizarre guided tour of her lower anatomy. Eventually, my time was up and I emerged, palefaced, from behind the curtain to be greeted by the two Japanese salary men, who nodded respectfully and grinned at me. Lori shook her head and picked up her paperback as they resumed their previous position in front of the box.

"It's going to be a long day." She smiled as I waved goodbye.

The bars around Civic Centre were a renowned den of thieves, where virtually anything could be purchased. On an evening, all manner of take-away food would be hawked around nightspots, having being 'liberated' from delivery driver's mopeds. On my last day in town, sitting in a dingy local bar, I became aware of a small, stocky black man lurking behind me.

"You play golf man?" he whispered, shuffling from foot to foot and glancing over his shoulder. "My brother's got a fine set of clubs for sale, out the back door."

He started at a hundred bucks, but I got him down to twenty, on condition that they also hail a taxi for me. Outside, I took delivery of a full set of clubs, bag, and balls.

Exiting the cab, I slung the clubs over my shoulder and strode into Iain's apartment building.

"Good game sir?" shouted the concierge.

"Not bad Pablo, 86!" I responded as I summoned the lift. Iain was surprised when I presented him with his leaving gift, not least because he didn't play golf, and also as I'd said I was only popping out an hour earlier for a newspaper!

My new-found single status coincided with an unusually successful period in the history of my football club, Leeds United. The team found themselves challenging for honours at the top of the Premier League, which also resulted in participation in European competitions. I was able to follow the team on a number of Continental excursions, though cultural immersion was generally limited to the bars of whichever city we were visiting.

A trip to Central Ukraine, and the city of Dnipropetrovsk, around 250 miles south west of Kiev promised to be more interesting than earlier excursions to Spain, France and Holland. Leeds had been drawn in the UEFA Cup against Metalurg Zaporizhya, whose own stadium failed to meet UEFA standards, so the game was moved to the nearest appropriate stadium, sixty miles away in the industrial city of Dnipro. Leeds usually travel with a large number of supporters wherever they play, but the logistical challenges in getting to this game, involving a flight to Kiev, followed by a ten hour train journey, limited the number of travelling fans to a couple of hundred.

Our group of four arrived in the city at dawn on an overnight train, and were quickly taking advantage of the strong local beer, priced at the local Hryvnia currency equivalent of about 20 pence a pint. Needless to say, the 1-1 draw passed in a blur. My main memory was of the Dnipro police force having seemingly raided the local dogs' home, in order to set up an impromptu canine unit. Hundreds of dogs of all shapes and sizes were chained to flustered looking officers stationed around the pitch. Most were straining at their leashes, barking manically and attempting to attack the next dog along the line, and any chants from the terraces were drowned out by a cacophony of yapping and howling.

The end of the game saw us stagger a short distance from the stadium to a smoky bar, packed with Ukrainian fans, where we were soon the centre of friendly attention. Bottles of the local 85%

proof vodka were ordered, and we were soon caught up in a seemingly never-ending round of incomprehensible toasts, slamming down glass after glass of the industrial strength spirit. My three friends and I exchanged worried glances as we were sucked into an alcohol driven, downward spiral of hospitality.

"This is going to end badly." My friend Lee shuddered as he downed another glass, to a resounding cheer of 'Bud'mo!' from our new friends.

Twelve hours later, it was morning and I was sat in the office of Dnipro's chief of police, seemingly in the midst of a serious diplomatic incident.

I'm unable to accurately recall what had happened the night before, but we managed to deduce that the over-exuberance of our new Ukrainian friends, had resulted in an altercation with the bar's doormen. At some point I was the victim of an attempted rugby-style spear tackle by one of the aforementioned bouncers. Luckily, on each occasion he tried to propel me headfirst into the concrete, I'd somehow managed to get my hands to the floor first, to cushion the impact. Eventually he'd flipped me backwards into some shrubbery, where I'd remained until the police arrived. Our passports had been taken and examined in the police van, where the human rights of our new drinking buddies were being loudly violated. Unfortunately, our passports were thrust back into Lee's hands in the dimly lit street, and the four passports taken had become only three returned. Naturally, mine was the one missing.

Perhaps naively, we'd wondered if this had been a simple accident, and that the officer had handed my passport in at the police station when he realised his error. We'd therefore turned up at Dnipro Police HQ, nursing life-threatening hangovers, only to see our 'enquiry' quickly turn into a serious 'allegation,' causing a three hour ascent through various layers of Soviet style bureaucracy. This culminated in me sitting in front of the top man, who was accompanied by a young English speaking interpreter, in his over-heated office.

The chief tapped his pen on the form in front of me. Three slow taps for dramatic effect. He barked an order which I didn't understand and fixed me with a piggy-eyed stare.

"He says you must sign the form," said the interpreter, a nervous, faintly moustachioed young man, who had been summoned at short notice from the English department of Dnipropetrovsk University.

"No way." I replied, and folded my arms. The chief's piggy eyes narrowed beneath his furrowed, sweaty brow.

The interpreter shifted uneasily in his seat. "Please," he whispered. I was getting nervous now.

"The form is written in Cyrillic," I pointed out the obvious, in case he hadn't noticed. "I don't speak Ukrainian. I could be signing anything."

The interpreter looked puzzled. He obviously hadn't been watching 'Banged up Abroad' as much as me.

"I could be confessing to anything. I could clear up their murder rate for the last ten years. I could admit to being the Dnipro Ripper!"

"I'll tell you what it says," my interpreter offered with a hopeful smile.

"But you could be one of them!" I hissed into his crestfallen face.

"It just says you lost your passport in the street," he read from the form. I looked doubtful.

"And that the police have been of great assistance and have tried to help you find it." The young man cringed slightly at this embellishment, and then flinched as the chief growled at us, while lighting a cigarette. I sensed I'd been given an ultimatum and the interpreter confirmed this.

"He says you must sign the form to clear up this misunderstanding, or he can't allow you to leave." His bright blue eyes implored me to sign, as the chief exhaled and blew smoke across the desk and into our faces.

My choices seemed clear. Either I must trust the interpreter, and the Chief of Police, sign the form and pray that I'm not single-handedly clearing up that year's unsolved crime stats. Or I rise majestically to my feet, bring my fist crashing down on the desk and tell the chief that I am an Englishman, and won't be bullied, then screw his document into a ball, flick it at him and stride confidently from the room.

Noting the holstered revolver hanging from a hat stand near the window, I decided that the second option may not be the best idea. I therefore slowly drew the piece of paper towards me, and, as the chief of police and interpreter nodded their approval, I signed my name and added the date. I then wrote in block capitals 'I DO NOT UNDERSTAND ANY OF THE ABOVE AND AM GUILTY OF NO CRIME.'

The chief peered at the form, his nose wrinkling with disapproval at the unexpected block capital addition. He nodded towards it, and raised his bushy eyebrows while looking expectantly at the interpreter.

I felt the interpreter shift in his seat. Looking at the form he uttered a single word and smiled hopefully. The chief's eyes narrowed. He picked up the form and stood to attention. I stood too, fearful that his next move would be to produce a pair of handcuffs from his drawer. He took a final pull on his cigarette, extinguished it in a brass ash tray, and extended his pudgy hand in a slow and dramatic manner. I heard the interpreter's sigh of relief as we shook hands, and the chief nodded towards the door to tell me I was now free to leave.

"What did you tell him I'd written?" I asked as we descended the stairs to leave the building. "I told him it was your address." He smiled, glad to have extricated himself, and me, from a sticky situation.

Unfortunately, that wasn't to be the end of my brush with Ukrainian bureaucracy. I now had no passport, and more importantly, no exit visa. Tim, the British consul officer in Kiev, was a stereotypical diplomat – well spoken, smartly dressed and very laid back, as he casually dropped into our conversation that it typically took five working days to secure an exit visa. Today was Saturday, so he was hopeful we could obtain one by the following Friday, allowing me to fly home in a week's time. The slight flaw in this plan was that I was due back at work on Monday morning. At that time I worked for a strait-laced accountant with no interest in football or tales of state-sponsored passport theft, or for that matter granting me an extra week's holiday at short notice.

"I can't stay here for another week." I slumped in my seat.

Tim obviously felt sorry for me and tried to cheer me up.

"Your flight leaves at 11am on Sunday. You may as well go to the airport anyway." This sounded hopeful. "You'll know by 10.30 that they aren't going to let you leave. I'll come and pick you up. We're going to a barbecue at the Polish embassy, you can tag along with us."

I slumped further in my seat.

"Their sausages are really quite something," he mused, licking his lips in anticipation.

We then set about arranging me a temporary passport, for which I needed photos. We screeched through Kiev's busy streets in Tim's huge 4x4, which he parked haphazardly on the pavement outside a photographic studio, hazard lights blinking. "Diplomatic immunity," Tim winked as we jumped out and entered the shop.

In the pre-selfie era, it seemed that Ukrainian teens would visit a photographic studio to obtain a portfolio of head-shots to send to potential suitors. There were a variety of backdrops to choose from - an Autumn forest, rolling waves and a stunning beach, or perhaps a U.S. style theme park. There was also a rail of outfits, mostly military or historical, in case the young person felt their leather-look bomber jacket or track suit top wasn't quite interesting enough for their portrait.

I was shunted to the front of a line of acne-adorned young men and girls with elaborate hair and too much make up, and was positioned in front of an appropriately stormy, dark grey sky backdrop. There was a light drizzle outside and my hair was damp, which the elderly photographer took as an opportunity to carry out some re-styling. He whipped out a comb and attempted unsuccessfully to carve a parting into my Grade-5-clipper hair. He also took exception to my posture, and roughly manhandled my jaw into an upward tilt, which he obviously felt gave me a noble bearing. The resultant image was widely described as looking like a particularly camp Russian sailor, and as I was forced to buy a sheet of 24 copies, then unwisely used it for my new passport, it was a photo I came to know all too well.

Arriving at Kiev airport on Sunday morning, my attempt at breezing through passport control without an exit visa was always doomed to failure. I was hauled from the line, and my friends pooled their remaining Hryvnia notes and passed them to me in a gesture of solidarity and 'rather you than me' survivor guilt. I was taken to a stale smelling room, where a succession of officials came to peer at me through a small glass window in the door. I could tell I was moving up the chain of command, as each new official got ten years older, had a wider band of service ribbons and a taller peaked hat than his predecessor. It was 10.30 and I was starting to think about a barbecued kielbasa sausage lunch, followed by unemployment, when two men entered the room and gestured me to follow them.

We moved quickly through a succession of corridors to emerge on the apron of the airport, where a military jeep was waiting. I was bundled aboard and we sped to an aircraft which appeared to be awaiting my arrival, with engines running and stairway already coupled to a tractor for removal. There were about thirty Leeds fans on the flight and I received a round of applause as I boarded, less than five minutes before take-off. News of my nearly-extended stay in Ukraine reached the local newspaper in Leeds, who claimed that I kissed the tarmac on arrival at Heathrow. A slight exaggeration, but it was fair to say that I was unusually pleased to be walking into the office that Monday morning.

6 CHANGING TIMES

The beginning of the new millennium saw a revolution in the travel industry, which would have seemed unlikely a decade earlier, and positively incomprehensible to my parents when they took their first package holiday abroad in the late 1960's.

Mass internet use began to gather pace in the mid 1990's, and the guidebook of choice for most budget travellers, Lonely Planet, was one of the first large companies to see the potential of this new channel of communication, setting up its website in 1995. Lonely Planet's Thorn Tree forum, named after a fabled backpackers cafe at the Stanley Hotel in Nairobi, quickly became the 'go-to' information exchange for independent travellers, just as the café noticeboard had, on a much smaller scale, twenty years earlier.

Other technology giants had their eye on the nascent internet travel market too. In 1996 Microsoft launched its booking site Expedia, which was followed a year later by LastMinute.com, enabling travellers to search for, and book, discounted flights and hotels. Budget airlines Ryanair and Easy Jet, quickly followed by names such as Buzz and Go! launched in 1997, aimed at a young, internet-savvy market, with attention grabbing fares which, like those early 1960s package tours, often seemed just too good to be true.

The key difference between these companies and what had come before, was the focus on booking via the internet, rather than ringing a call centre, or visiting a High Street shop. Online booking was the buzzword, and soon everyone was doing it. The launch of personal email providers Hotmail and Yahoo at around the same time, meant that travellers were able to bypass travel agents and make arrangements from the comfort of their own homes. (Though 'dial-up' internet access could be a frustrating affair when trying to book airline seats in those early days.) Also, even the smallest hotels, in the most remote corners of the world, were able to set up an email account to communicate with potential guests. Some even set up their own simple websites.

Travellers could now research destinations and make their own flight and hotel bookings. Then, in 2000, a start-up business launched in a room above a pizza take-away in Massachusetts, added another piece to the self-booking jigsaw. TripAdvisor was the first site to solicit reviews of cities, attractions, hotels and restaurants from travellers, rather than so called experts. Suddenly, the promotional 'blurb' in package company brochures was rendered irrelevant. As the number of online reviews grew, it became possible to get up-to-date information from unbiased sources on just about anywhere in the world.

On September 11 2001, the terrorist attack on New York using hijacked passenger aircraft delivered a seismic shock to the travel industry. Stringent new security measures, nervousness over potential future attacks, and a reluctance by many people to travel abroad, saw airlines and travel companies left with a huge volume of unsold seats and hotel rooms. Faced with financial disaster, companies were forced to accelerate their use of internet-based marketing and customer communications. They found it worked well, was cost effective, and customers liked it. By the end of 2002, it seemed everyone was booking their holidays 'online'.

For me, the new millennium brought further opportunities for solo exploration of parts of the world which interested me, but may not have been top of Karen's list of 'must sees.' I'd read Nelson Mandela's autobiography, Long Walk to Freedom, and South Africa's turbulent 1980's history had been the news backdrop of my teenage years, so in November 2001, I took a flight to Cape Town and booked into a small hotel on Kloof Street in the city centre.

Back then, before the 2010 World Cup prompted the authorities to 'reclaim' the streets, many of South Africa's city centres were virtual no-go areas at night and on a weekend, and even in daylight working hours you needed to keep your wits about you. It was that raw urban edginess, contrasted with the stunning natural beauty of Cape Town's beaches and mountains, that made the city one of my favourite places in the world, and somewhere I've returned to a number of times since.

I spent four days in Cape Town itself, exploring the usual tourist haunts. I was lucky that Table Mountain's spectacular rolling 'table cloth' of cloud stayed away while I was at the thousand metre summit, so was able to enjoy the spectacular views across Table Bay to Robben Island. I caught the ferry to Mandela's old enforced home, enjoyed an interesting talk from an ex-inmate, and saw the cell where 'Madiba' spent twenty seven years in captivity. I visited the District Six museum to hear the story of residents forcibly moved from their homes, for an upmarket housing development which never even happened.

On my first night in town, I was drinking in a pub near the recently re-gentrified waterfront area, and got talking to a weather-beaten old Afrikaaner at the bar. A thinning crew-cut sat atop a badly sun-blasted scalp, but he still boasted an impressively bushy white moustache. Upon hearing it was my first night in Africa, he taught me a lesson which I've called upon many times since in locations around the world.

"What you have to remember," he explained with a finger jabbing toward my chest, "Is that in Africa, the law of the jungle prevails. It's survival of the fittest." He took a swig from his beer, then wiped the frothy residue from his moustache as he warmed to his subject.

"It's hunter and hunted. And you are the hunted!" He flashed a malevolent smile, looking to the barman for approval.

"Think about lions and antelopes." He prodded the finger again. He seemed to be waiting for a response, so I nodded.

"The lion is lazy. He doesn't like hard work, so will observe the antelope herd from a distance. Will he target the big, strong antelope running at the front? No! He will identify the oldest, the weakest, the sickest antelope. The one at the back, struggling to keep up. Then he will ATTACK!" He fashioned his wrinkled, nut-brown hand into the shape of a lion's jaws, and clamped it around the throat of an imaginary gazelle.

"The human predators in Africa are like lions. Lazy. They will watch the herd to identify who is the weakest... That is who they will single out for attack." His voice lowered, and the bar tender nodded his agreement.

"So!" He turned to me, voice raised again. "The lesson is, in Africa, to avoid becoming prey, you need to be the biggest, strongest, nastiest, fucking antelope in the herd!" His fingers became two stubby, tobacco-stained antlers extending from his crimson forehead to emphasise the point.

"You know how to do that?" I shook my head.

"No! Of course you don't. Because you don't have predators in England like we have in Africa. So, I'll tell you!"

He stood up, placing his empty glass on the bar. Sticking out his chin, he expanded his chest above an impressive beer gut. Shoulders back, he clenched his fists, arms rigid by his sides. His eyes fixed on mine, and his lip curled back to expose an impressive set of dentures. Then he strode towards me, stopping with his nose six inches from mine, brow furrowed, eyes burning into mine with a look of pure hatred. He then inhaled sharply and loudly through his nostrils, hawked a globule of phlegm from his throat and mimicked spitting it dramatically onto the bar floor. The bartender craned his neck over the bar to ensure he had only mimicked it.

"You've got to look like you're going to rip the head off the next bastard who looks your way." He settled back onto his stool.

"Finishing with a good old mouthful of spoeg helps to emphasise the point that you take shit from no one. Understand?"

The following day was a Saturday, and against advice I'd received at my guest house, I lingered outside a bar on Long Street beyond the unofficial weekend lunchtime curfew that was in force in the City Centre. I watched as shops and other businesses put up their shutters and closed, and within the space of an hour, the previously busy road became almost empty of pedestrians. I set off walking towards the waterfront and ahead of me, noticed two obvious tourists, an overweight middle-aged couple in bright t-shirts and shorts, lumbering down the street.

I wasn't the only one to spot them. The urban lions of Long Street had scented prey. Two youths in baggy shorts, one wearing a baseball cap, the other in a bright green puffa anorak, jogged across the road to size up their potential victims from closer quarters. I contemplated changing direction, but the side-streets were even quieter than the main road, which at least had a smattering of passing traffic. I carried on walking as the boundaries of aggressive begging and light-touch mugging were blurred, with the tourists forced to hand over a 'donation' to the youths as I passed on the other side of the road.

Having just feasted on the fat wallet of a tourist, I hoped the skulking teenage predators may be satisfied, but I sensed them turn their attention to me, as I involuntarily quickened my pace. Just in time, I remembered my training of the previous evening. Slowing down, I pulled back my shoulders and lifted my head. I took a deep breath and clenched my fists, my expression turning to what I hoped was one of imminent violence. I set off walking like I had a large roll of carpet under each arm. Almost forgetting my pièce de résistance, I turned towards the youths who suddenly seemed hesitant, and inhaled dramatically through my nostrils. I then loudly hawked up the resulting concentration of mucous, and viciously expelled it towards the pavement.

"I am the biggest, nastiest antelope in Cape Town." I snarled to myself as I strode onwards. After a few minutes I looked back, and the would-be muggers were gone. My first, but not last, use of the big antelope strategy had gone well. I'd escaped unscathed, apart from a thick slug-trail of phlegm down the leg of my shorts.

Driving into the centre of Cape Town from the airport, the first thing a visitor notices is the sprawl of wooden and tin shacks along the N2 Motorway. This is the Cape Flats townships, home to many of those displaced from District Six and other urban areas, by the apartheid regime's Group Areas Act of 1950. Seen by most white Cape Town residents as an area to avoid at all costs, it housed around 80% of Cape Town's population, so I felt it was an area that warranted a visit. Mini-bus tours of the main townships of Gugulethu, Langa and Khayelitsha were conducted by local residents, so I booked onto one, and set off with a guide and group of three Belgians. We visited township homes, artisanal workshops and a school, and even stopped for lunch at a new venture, a guest house which allowed visitors to spend a night in the township.

The tour rounded off with a visit to a local bar or 'shebeen,' where a group of around ten youths were drinking beer from bottles and playing pool. The Belgians seemed a little nervous at their boisterous presence, and sat in the corner with bottles of water, but I bought the lads a drink and joined them at the pool table. At that time, the South African national football captain, Lucas Radebe, played for Leeds, and before leaving home I'd bought some publicity photos of Lucas and got him to sign them. I'd already given a couple away to kids I'd met around town, and now pulled the three remaining photos from my bag. After a couple of seconds pause, while they digested who it was in the photo, and that the great man had actually signed them, the room erupted into a riotous debate over who was the biggest fan of football/Lucas/His old team Kaiser Chiefs/Leeds United, and should therefore be given a photo.

Word quickly spread to the street outside that a good friend of Lucas Radebe was in the bar and within minutes, scores of excited youths were pouring through the door. Many were tattooed and bore some spectacular scars, which indicated they were probably a member of one of the many local street gangs. Our guide had already told us that most gang members would be carrying firearms, and as the arguments raged on who should get the photos, I saw the Belgians nervously retreating to the minibus. Bottles of beer were thrust at me as I was jostled amidst a clamour of shouting, arguing young men, all eager to meet Lucas's best mate. I eventually announced that the three remaining photos would be awarded on the basis of a quiz about Lucas and Leeds United.

I stood on a chair, bottle of beer in hand, and shouted out the questions to a yelling mass of around fifty township youths, while the Belgians peered incredulously into the bar from the safety of their bus seats, at the most unusual, and raucous, pub quiz they'd ever seen, and I'd ever hosted!

I rented a car for my final week in South Africa, and drove around the coastline of False Bay, then onto the wine region around Stellenbosch, a town which seemed to have been the inspiration for a Beautiful South song lyric, as it seemed that everyone really was blond and beautiful. The scenery rivalled anything I'd seen anywhere in the world, and some of the beachfront properties were stunning. They were also quite affordable compared to the UK's inflated house prices, due to a strong Sterling to Rand exchange rate, plus the ever-present elephant-in-the-room which was South Africa's violent crime problem.

I drove to the southernmost point of Africa near the Cape of Good Hope, and rounding a bend on a mountainous road, I came upon a snake of cars lining up behind a VW Golf, which was stopped, blocking the lane, hazard lights blinking. A large male baboon was sat on the vehicle's roof, masturbating nonchalantly. The occupants of the car seemed to have no idea what was happening above them. I slowed as I passed, and the baboon cocked his head to one side, as if to flirtatiously catch my eye, as he flailed at his exposed pink lipstick. The couple in the car looked at me, as if asking what they should do. I shrugged, smiled, and drove on, wondering whether the onanistic ape had taken a shine to me, or was perhaps making a comment on my driving skills.

My trip to South Africa was the first I'd booked without the assistance of any agent or travel company. Internet-sourced flights, rental car and hotels, and an agenda gleaned from the Lonely Planet guide and Thorn Tree message board, delivered a cost-effective trip that was surprisingly easy to arrange. It seemed that the world had suddenly become a much smaller place. I think that was the first time I realised I could literally go anywhere in the world in my two-week holiday window, and do just what I wanted when I got there.

And on my next trip, what I wanted was to shoot at a wooden camel with an AK47 assault rifle.

I'd read countless books on Vietnam, covering both the American war of the 1960's and 70's and also the end of the French Colonial period in the 1950's, and had developed a keen interest in South East Asia, so I booked a flight to Saigon and decided to make up an itinerary as I went along. Saigon was as colourful and chaotic as I'd expected, and it wasn't hard to imagine battle-worn G.I's with thousand-yard stares, enjoying a spot of R&R in the many bars and clubs around Pham Ngu Lao. The city's motorbike taxis were the chosen mode of transport for most travellers, and provided an exhilarating, late-night rollercoaster pillion ride home, with your designated rider swerving at breakneck speed through packed lanes of honking motorbikes, rickshaws and pedal cycles.

After a couple of days wandering the city streets and markets and learning how to cross the multi lane roads (in the gradual lane-to-lane hopping style of the eighties video game, Frogger), I decided to take a bus thirty miles north of Saigon to the town of Ben Duoc in the Cu Chi district, to see the famous Vietcong tunnels. This seventy five mile long complex of narrow, waist-height subterranean corridors formed a network of supply and communication channels for the guerrilla fighters of the Vietcong. The tunnels became the main base of operations for the 'Tet' uprising of 1968 which saw 80,000 North Vietnamese and Vietcong troops launch attacks on more than a hundred towns and cities in South Vietnam.

Conditions in the tunnels were terrible for the fighters. A lack of air and light, coupled with an abundance of poisonous snakes and insects, must have made for an unnerving existence, and US bombing meant troops often had to remain underground for weeks at a time.

Some of the tunnels had supposedly been enlarged to accommodate the super-sized frames of western tourists, but exploration was still not recommended for anyone of a claustrophobic nature. In most of the tunnels, I could move through the inky blackness of the labyrinth without crawling, but I was forced to stoop low and bend my legs into an uncomfortable shuffling crouch. This made for slow progress, and guided only by the flickering beam of a cheap battery torch, it wasn't hard to temporarily lose your way. At that point, with a mild wave of panic rising inside you, it was easy to catch a brief glimpse of the terror the occupants of the tunnels must have felt, as nearby U.S. bombing shook the foundations of the whole structure.

After exploring the tunnels, I headed to the infamous shooting range. A rite of passage for South East Asian travellers, it was an opportunity to get up close and personal with some serious military hardware. An urban myth of the time, which actually may not have been a myth, relayed tales of a similar operation, close to Phnom Penh airport in neighbouring Cambodia. The unique selling point of this particular shooting gallery, was that it allowed tourists to take pot shots at a variety of livestock using rocket propelled grenade launchers, amongst other hardcore weaponry. It supposedly cost fifty US Dollars for stoned travellers to dispatch a live cow with an anti-tank missile, as passenger jets soared in to land a few hundred yards away.

With an obvious respect for animal rights, or perhaps a shortage of cows, the Cu Chi tunnels shooting range had substituted the live animal targets for painted equivalents on twelve foot tall wooden billboards. You simply selected your weapon of choice, and picked up a handful of live rounds from a plastic bucket. An attendant in military uniform had a quick look at how many shells you planned to fire and gave you a price. I considered going for the nineties gangsta-chic look of an Uzi, but eventually opted for the classic, mujahaddin style, AK47 assault rifle. I paid my ten dollars and was shown to a stand around two hundred metres from my allocated target - a lopsided, hand-painted camel. Other potential 'trophies' ranged from a predictable lion and elephant, to the less obvious ostrich and giant eagle, to the downright surreal, despondent donkey and smiling pig in a bowler hat.

My camel was obviously an attempt to add some Middle Eastern style excitement to the proceedings, and I decided to take him down with a terrifying volley of fire to the hump. The young attendant loaded my magazine with the rounds of ammo I'd purchased, and said something which, at the time, I didn't understand. He obviously took my bemused expression as an affirmative, so clicked a couple of switches on the machine gun and handed it back to me. I soon realised that his question was whether I wanted the rifle on automatic fire mode. Unfortunately, I only realised this upon squeezing the trigger. I was wearing ear protectors but the upward jolt of the rifle away from my shoulder as I squeezed the trigger, dislodged them. The force of the weapon's recoil caused me to stagger backwards, while still spraying bullets into the air with a deafening report. With my large black ear defenders knocked askew on my head, I must have looked like Mickey Mouse on a suicide mission. I crashed into the attendant, who seemed unmoved by the incident, but quickly surveyed the sky above us, presumably to ensure I hadn't brought down any passing aircraft.

During a lull in the shooting, I walked down the field with a young German to inspect the targets. The animals painted on the billboards bore few signs of bullet wounds, leading us to suspect that the rifle sights were deliberately misaligned. We hastily made our way back to safety as we spotted a couple of Swedish girls wielding Uzi's, unsupervised, as the attendant tucked into to a bowl of noodles.

Back in Saigon, I was on the pillion of a motorbike taxi, waiting to pull out into the heavy traffic at the large roundabout at the end of Ham Nghi Street. I surveyed the 'Wacky Races' style scene, wondering how my driver would ever manage to breach the non-stop stream of motorbikes, rickety cycles ridden by old men in conical hats, and graceful schoolgirls in white Ao Dai's. As we waited, I felt something digging into my thigh through the pocket of my shorts. Puzzled, I reached in, and amongst the sweat-stained bundle of Dong bank notes, located a foreign object which I retrieved and held out for examination. I've no idea what the driver thought about his passenger brandishing a live Kalashnikov shell on a busy Saigon street. At that point a tiny gap appeared in the traffic stream and he accelerated forward, casting the occasional wary glance in my direction through his mirror as we sped to my hotel.

The next morning, I became the final victim of the Vietnam war. I awoke in my cramped single room, to the sound of the ceiling fan clattering and banging above me. I'd asked the old lady on reception if she could get someone to oil it, without response, and in a way, I liked the fact it allowed me to wake up each day feeling like Martin Sheen in the opening scene of Apocalypse Now. As soon as I tried to swing my legs over the side of the five-inch-thick mattress, I knew I was in trouble. I felt like I'd been run over. Then reversed over. As I stood up, my thigh muscles felt like they were about to burst out of my skin, and a shooting electric shock of pain in my calves caused me to fall back onto the bed. I realised that the enforced crouching gait during my tunnel exploration, had obviously utilised muscles I'd never previously had to employ, and I'd been scuttling about in the tunnels for about an hour. Unable to walk, I sank to the grubby linoleum floor and dragged myself into the bathroom. I managed to haul myself into the bath, where I alternated between hot and cold immersion, while trying to massage the excruciating muscular pain from my legs.

After half an hour, I was able to stand and walk, albeit like I had broom handles strapped to my legs. It was clear though that crossing Saigon's roads while walking like a clockwork soldier would likely result in a swift end to my personal game of Frogger. Luckily, the hotel had a clunky old lift, as there was no way I could have descended a flight of stairs. The old lady gave me a cheery wave as I staggered through reception, and out into a sunlit Saigon morning, to run the usual gauntlet of motorbike taxi drivers who were lounging on their machines outside the café next door.

The most forceful of their group stepped forward to greet me. A rake thin, bow-legged man in his late thirties, with a wispy hint of a moustache and shiny track suit bottoms which looked like pyjamas, he went by the unlikely name of Peter.

"You need motorbike sir? Where you want to go?" he asked half-heartedly. I'd been at the hotel for a couple of days and had always chosen to walk, so he probably had me marked down as a lost cause. Today though, I definitely needed a ride.

"I need a massage, Peter." As soon as I said 'massage,' his eyes lit up and a beaming smile appeared beneath his fluffy moustache.

"Ah, massage Sir. Sexy time. Fuckeefuckee. Very nice." He turned to the other drivers who all grinned their approval.

"I know place, sir. Sexy girl. Very nice, very clean, very cheap."

"No, Peter, I don't want sexy girl. I need a proper massage."

Peter remained enthusiastic.

"It's okay sir. I know place. Very nice. Boom-boom. Massage good. Lady-boy."

"No, No, Peter, definitely no lady-boys. I need someone who can do a proper massage. I can't walk." I limped forward to emphasise my disability.

The fact that I wanted an actual massage caused some furrowed brows and debate amongst the drivers. Eventually, someone came up with an address, and Peter was all smiles again.

"Come sir, proper massage. No sexy time. But maybe also, if you want later..."

With the help of the other drivers, I was loaded onto the back of Peter's Honda Dream, and we set off into the traffic, with my legs stuck rigidly out in front of me, unable to bend to reach the footrests.

We eventually arrived in a street in which every shop seemed to be a hair stylist, ranging from modern ladies' hairdressers to roadside barbers offering simple clipper-cuts, and shaves for the few men who could muster up any facial hair. Peter pointed me through a door, and I dragged myself up a narrow staircase to emerge in a long room with around a dozen mattresses on the floor. Half were occupied by semi-naked, middle-aged Vietnamese men, whose limbs and sweating torsos were each being yanked and stretched by a white-clad teenage girl.

A plump elderly woman approached and spoke in Vietnamese. I pointed to my legs and grimaced, to little effect. The woman shook her head and called a couple of the younger girls over, but it was clear they spoke no English either. They looked at me suspiciously, and I guessed they thought I was there for 'sexy time,' especially as the older woman was looking me up and down and seemed to be sizing me up as a potential client.

I decided to try and demonstrate the cause of my problem and began to mimic my gait in the tunnels, crouching as best I could and groaning loudly, as I staggered around the room. The masseuses stepped back in alarm, perhaps fearing that I was experiencing sudden and debilitating diarrhoea. A couple of the floorbound men shifted uneasily on their mattresses as they watched my performance.

Whether the masseuses interpreted my mime correctly is debatable, but it had the desired effect. I was soon laying on my stomach on the floor, as a nubile girl of around twelve, deftly trod on my legs, her toes probing the painful tissue and gradually kneading away the pain. After half an hour of being walked upon, I rose like Lazarus from my mattress, and after paying a small fee, skipped back down the staircase. Peter was waiting in the road outside.

"You have nice time sir? Lady was good, yes?" He grinned mischievously.

"She had magic toes, Peter." I winked as I hopped energetically onto the bike, once again confident that I could survive another day of playing Saigon Frogger.

I wanted to explore more of Vietnam, and had booked a flight to Hanoi in the North of the country. First though, I decided to head south by ferry to the seaside town of Vung Tau, later to become tabloid-infamous as the beast's lair of shamed seventies rocker Gary Glitter. The town and surrounding beaches were pleasant enough, but things were quiet midweek, so on my last day in town I rented a scooter and headed north up the coast. I set off early and made good progress on winding roads which snaked along the shoreline, with lush jungle to my left and the crashing waves of the South China sea to my right. There was little traffic and it was a pleasure to ride the quiet lanes, away from the constant horns and sweaty clamour of downtown Saigon. Occasionally I passed through a village where I would attract a tail of sprinting, squealing children playing 'catch the farang,' an ever-popular game in areas where foreign faces are a rarity.

After lunch of spicy pho broth at a roadside shack, the road took me into the Binh Chau-Phuoc Buu Nature Reserve, an area of forested hills and swamps fronted by rocky beach inlets. I was feeling drowsy after a morning of riding in the hot sun, and was contemplating a nap in the shade. Pulling into a sandy carpark on a small clifftop, I was spotted by a group of young men who shouted a greeting and waved me over. A barbecue was being fired up and a huge bag of tiger prawns, newly acquired from a beach fisherman, were being liberally dusted with chilli powder and lime, in preparation for the grill. The lads also had two large cool-boxes filled with the local Saigon Green beer and imported bottles of Tiger. From the grins on their faces and slightly dazed expressions, it seemed their picnic had been going on for a while.

There were eight present, but only two of us spoke English. Minh, or Mike, as he preferred to be called, was twenty-two and was visiting his Vietnamese relatives, having grown up in Chicago, and would be my interpreter for the rest of the day. Mike's parents had fled the chaos and hardship of post-war Vietnam in 1978, becoming part of the estimated one million strong exodus of refugees who became known as 'boat people.' From a camp in the Philippines they were eventually resettled in the USA in 1980, and their son was born soon after. Mike's father was able to train as an electrician and now owned his own company, going out of his way to help other new arrivals to America to get a foothold in the employment market.

It was clear that Mike was viewed as something of a celebrity prodigal son amongst his cousins and their friends in his parent's old village. His hundred-dollar trainers and designer label Polo shirt were in stark contrast to the ragged shorts and mis-sized t-shirts they wore, though a couple of the lads sported shop-clean Chicago Bears baseball caps – obvious recent gifts from their wealthy overseas relative.

I was the first 'farang' they'd ever met, and as the beer flowed and the prawns sizzled on the grill, I was peppered with questions about life in England, via Mike's interpreting. Not for the first time in Vietnam, my hairy legs were the centre of the group's attention. With my fair hairs highlighted against tanned skin, my legs resembled those of a balding polar bear in comparison to their relatively smooth limbs. Unfortunately, a couple of the bolder lads took the opportunity to test the staying power of my follicles and administered a few sharp tugs to my painful surprise. My hairiness seemed to impress my new friends, my muscles less so. I was about a foot taller than the rest of the group, and they seemed to assume my biceps would be similarly proportioned. The first tentative squeezes of my upper arms therefore resulted in disappointed bemusement and slightly embarrassed debate amongst the gang. Obviously tapping on a computer keyboard all day didn't deliver the same upper-body work-out that a day in the paddy-fields did.

The long afternoon of drinking culminated in a drunken game of beach football as the sun began to dip beyond the headland to our right. I was conscious that I had a scooter journey of around twenty miles back to Vung Tau, followed by a ferry the next morning and a flight to Hanoi in the afternoon. However, my attempts to say farewell to my new mates were greeted with mock horror.

"No, no, you can't go yet. They want you to come back to the village. You're the guest of honour tonight!" Mike explained as his cousins and friends nodded their grinning agreement.

Fifteen minutes later our cavalcade of five scooters puttered off the small main road, past some iron roofed shacks and along a bumpy dirt track. I was glad none of the lads had opted for a pillion ride on my bike, as the backend fish-tailed wildly in the dirt, my balance not helped by the several litres of beer I'd consumed throughout the afternoon. We eventually arrived at a small settlement of houses in a cloud of dust, accompanied by sounding of horns and scattering of toddlers and livestock.

All the men of the village, plus Mike's Dad and brother, turned out to greet us, as the womenfolk smiled demurely from a distance, and we all piled into the largest house. This shack was of breeze-block construction with a corrugated tin roof and unglazed windows, which allowed around thirty village kids to crane their heads above the window-sills to observe the strange foreign visitor. We all sat in a circle on the tiled floor and plates of rice and seafood were produced. And more beer. This time small bottles of Heineken, and lots of them.

A variety of intriguing condiments on small plates appeared. One was a saucer full of small, thin, red chilli peppers. I noticed a few glances being exchanged across our seated circle and Mike attracted my attention with a nudge. He was holding one of the chillies between thumb and forefinger.

"Dare you?" he challenged, as the rest of the group fell silent. I wasn't averse to a spicy curry at home, so accepted the challenge, providing Mike went first. He tugged the stem from the chilli, dropped it into his mouth, chewed and swallowed. Then I did likewise.

Within around five seconds, it was obvious I was the victim of a wicked deception. Mike had used sleight of hand or a placebo chilli, and his laughter told me that the type of offensive pod which was now destroying the lining of my mouth, had been nowhere near his.

The laughter which initially engulfed the group subsided quickly when it became clear that I was in serious trouble. In an effort to cleanse my tongue of the malevolent presence which was stripping away its surface, I'd swallowed the pepper. The searing pain now spread to my throat. My whole mouth was beyond fire, the entire lining felt molten. My tongue seemed to have swelled to three times its usual size and my throat was constricting. Tears flowed from my eyes and I tried to say 'You little bastard' to Mike, but my voice box had been incinerated, so I was reduced to a husky plea for help as burning mucous poured from my nostrils.

The group realised their prank had backfired and panic ensued. Amidst excited shouts, I was laid on my back on the cold tiled floor, and help was summoned in the form of an ancient crone who scurried silently from a back room, brandishing an earthenware jar. My mouth was prised open and Mike's father firmly held my nostrils closed. I wondered if the old woman was a shaman who was about to perform an emergency tracheostomy, and tried to wriggle free, but unseen arms held me in position.

The circle of frowning men cleared to allow the ancient witch-doctor to perform her magic ritual, and I cringed as she approached brandishing a shining silver implement, which she immersed in the jar. Seconds later, I felt a dry, rough textured substance fill my mouth, poured from the old woman's tablespoon. Again and again she dipped it into the mysterious jar, then thrust the sweet magical dust between my blistering lips until my mouth was bulging. Bulging with sugar.

The relief was instantaneous, and she encouraged me to swallow, thus allowing her to spoon more of the contents of her sugar pot between my teeth until I was lying, mouth agape, totally filled with the miraculously soothing granules. All I needed was a cherry adorning the white pile spilling down my chin, to have made an attractive dessert at a cannibals' banquet.

Once it was clear that I was out of imminent danger, the party continued, with the men laughing and drinking around my prone, red faced, sucrose over-dosed body. Eventually, I was able to expel the sugar from my mouth via a combination of spitting and swallowing, and Mike thrust a Heineken in my direction in a gesture of contrition for his cruel prank.

At around 8pm, I scraped the excess sugar from around my mouth and bade my friends farewell. The whole village turned out to wave me off, but as I turned the key in the ignition of my scooter, I couldn't fail to notice the concerned expressions return to their faces. My headlamp wasn't working. Everyone in South East Asia is an enthusiastic, self-taught scooter mechanic, so there followed half an hour of bulb removal and replacement, wire tweaking and removal of various electrical components from behind the light mounting. After much scratching and shaking of heads and muttered debate, one of the men had a literal light-bulb moment, and announced his idea. The assembled circle nodded agreement and I was confident a solution had been found, as he skipped away to a nearby hut.

I'd assumed he would return with a vital electrical fitting, or maybe a local mechanic. Instead he jogged back clutching a small, plastic, battery-operated torch and a roll of sticky tape. And so it was that I rode out of the village, onto an unlit road on an inky black, moonless night, pursued by a howling pack of children, and after a day of heavy drinking, with my path illuminated by a small torch taped to my handlebars.

It was a twenty mile journey which took around an hour and a half, as I cautiously proceeded along the winding country roads, my visibility limited to around five feet ahead. Occasionally, to help ensure I stayed wide awake, a pack of feral dogs would spring from the undergrowth and snap at my wheels and ankles, as I accelerated to safety. For some variation, a stray water buffalo would decide to take an evening stroll along the road, and loom suddenly before me in the gloom, its startled eyes glowing red in the faint beam of my tiny torch. My hangover was already beginning to kick in when I finally arrived back in Vung Tau, knowing I had to be up again in a few hours to begin my journey north.

Twenty-four hours later, I was in Hanoi, having travelled over a thousand miles, and seemingly a couple of seasons from Saigon. In contrast to the steamy humidity of the South, Hanoi had the damp, chill air of Northern Europe in October. If the bright lights and western style billboards of Saigon had resembled Hong Kong or Bangkok, Hanoi had a definite feel of old China - more reserved and traditional. Even the headwear of the locals differed - In the south, the traditional Chinese conical hat offered protection from the fierce tropical sun. In the North, a khaki pith helmet adorned most men's heads.

The chaos on the roads was the same, if not worse than Saigon, although the southern multi-carriageway roads through town were less common than older, narrow and often tree-lined avenues. Hanoi seemed much cheaper than Saigon too. I found that I could have a good night on the town and still return to my guest house with change from five US Dollars.

I rented a bicycle for a dollar a day and explored the city. It felt more European than Saigon, with its French colonial boulevards, parks and lakes, and street stalls selling fresh coffee and baguettes. What certainly didn't feel European was the local market with stalls displaying whole roasted dogs, teeth bared in a rictus snarl, but tails extended in a disconcerting death wag. Their meat was sold in slices, like cuts of ham, by smiling teenage girls.

After a few days in Hanoi, I took a bus a hundred miles east to the coastal town of Ha Long. I checked into an overpriced single room with peeling paintwork and no heating, then spent a dispiriting, drizzly evening, eating noodles in an empty karaoke bar. It felt like I'd travelled halfway round the world for a night out in Cleethorpes. The reason for my visit wasn't to experience the bright lights of Ha Long though, it was to see the town's eponymous Bay.

Ha Long Bay was declared a World Heritage site in 1994 and

features in every 'must see' list of Vietnam. Covering almost a thousand square miles, the bay comprises of around fifteen hundred forest-capped limestone islands, rising precipitously from a brilliant, emerald green ocean. There are a wide range of options to experience the bay. It's possible to take a multi-night tour on a traditional Vietnamese junk boat with your own upmarket private cabin. Or you can hop on one of the daily tour boats from Bai Chay Wharf, for a day's sailing around the islands with optional kayaking and rowing boat excursions.

I opted for the latter, but as the karaoke machine kicked into life before we'd left Ha Long, I began to wish I hadn't. The boat was half full – an approximately even split of western travellers and Vietnamese locals. I fell into conversation with Jason and Hailey, a couple of heavily pierced and tattooed stoners from Toronto, who had just flown in from Cambodia. We stood at the stern of the boat, away from the high pitched karaoke, and drank-in the surreal scenery, with a drifting sea mist tickling the higher limestone peaks adding to the other-worldly feeling.

Our boat eventually moored in a bay surrounded by floating platforms containing what appeared to be wooden garden sheds. These were fishing villages with each platform of around twenty square feet in size, containing the living quarters of an entire family. The fisherfolk supplemented their income by providing piloted rowing boats to tour boat passengers, and soon Jason, Hailey and I were clambering on board a tiny wooden craft, manned by a ragged youth of around fourteen, and his spectacularly snot-nosed toddler brother.

As we rowed slowly through the murky haze, more islands materialised in the mist, and Jason produced a Cambodian souvenir in the form of a huge spliff which he struggled to light in the drizzle. For the next hour we drifted amongst towering vegetation-covered peaks and through limestone caves in a fug of marijuana smoke. Paddling slowly back towards the tour boat, with our pilot and his young sibling seeming suspiciously relaxed, a sudden break in the cloud ahead revealed a hazy sun, followed by a translucent rainbow arcing above a towering limestone pinnacle on our right.

"Wooaahh!! Trippeeeee!!" squealed Hailey, flinging her tattooed arms skywards, as Jason closed his eyes and nodded thoughtfully, while caressing a silver ring in his nostril. Seconds later we were being soaked by a heavy shower of warm, mist-like rain, the tiny floating droplets illuminated in the sun's rays, as our boat's karaoke machine suddenly sprang into life, and a squeaky oriental teenage voice shattered the dreamlike ambience.

Less than forty eight hours later, I sat gazing through the drizzle at another indistinct rainbow. This time there were no limestone peaks or emerald ocean. No rowing boat, Canadian hippies or karaoke. I was sat in traffic on Leeds Outer Ring Road, heading to the office and the dreaded first day back at work. The worst day of the year for a Two Week Traveller.

7 BETTER MAKE THAT ROOM A DOUBLE

I returned from Vietnam to begin planning my next holiday, whilst, as usual, recounting anecdotes from my trip to colleagues in the staff canteen or on work nights out.

I had started to notice that one colleague always seemed very interested in my stories, and in travel in general. I'd known Kirsty for around ten years. She worked in our company's Finance department and was a regular on our frequent work nights out, which generally entailed a pub crawl round Leeds followed by a late-night curry. Recently separated, her husband had viewed holidays as a time for relaxation rather than adventure, but Kirsty had that inquisitive nature and adventurous spirit, which separates travellers from tourists. Her new single status therefore promised the opportunity to broaden her horizons and explore some of the world's more interesting and challenging locations

A group of around ten of us were sat in an Indian restaurant in the centre of Leeds at midnight on a chilly November Thursday. I'd just booked a flight to Cambodia for the following February so was regaling the group with details of my plans. Having heard my Vietnam stories, Kirsty was starting to consider a South East Asian trip of her own. She quizzed me on flights, likely costs, where I was planning to go in Cambodia and how I'd get there. At that point, I didn't have much of a clue!

Our Aussie colleague, Tim, wasn't the most tactful person in the office, and after eight pints of Stella and with a mouthful of onion bhaji, he could be relied upon to get straight to the point.

"Jesus mate, it's obvious she wants to go to Cambodia, book her a farkin' ticket."

I'd enjoyed my solo travels and would have normally blustered my way through some elaborate excuse as to why a work colleague couldn't join me, but Kirsty and I had always got on well. She had a great sense of humour and a laid back, positive outlook, coupled with a curious nature similar to my own. Tim was right – we were a perfect match, though as he chomped his way through his Naan bread, it's unlikely the belligerent Aussie could have foreseen that Cambodia would be the first of well over a hundred countries which Kirsty and I would visit together!

The Cambodia trip started inauspiciously. We had a stop-over in Bangkok, and having visited the city before, and eager to impress my new travel partner, I suggested we visit 'a little bar I know on Sukhumvit Road.' It was a longer walk than I remembered, and I was soon regretting my bizarre decision to wear jeans and trainers for our first evening in the muggy heat of the Thai Capital. Eventually a blue neon glow came into view, in the approximate area I recalled there previously being a rustic local music bar. Where the old bar had open-plan frontage facing onto the busy road, the large windows were now tinted with dark glass, preventing us from seeing inside. A pounding bass thudded away in time with the flashing bright white lights around the door, and it was obvious the bar had seen a change of ownership since my last visit. This no longer looked like my type of place. However, Kirsty was a few years younger than me, so, eager to show I was still 'down with the kids,' I looked as enthusiastic as I could and pushed open the door.

It was pitch black inside, with pumping dance music and a flickering strobe light, which seemed to be triggered into blinding action by anyone opening the door. I could make out what seemed to be a bar area, lit by blue and green neon at the far end of the room, so set off in that direction. I took about five steps and was suddenly waist deep in water. I stumbled forward in shock, just managing to regain my balance before my head was submerged in the tepid, stagnant pool, with a chlorine concentration that took my breath away. I turned to see Kirsty, hands over her mouth, standing alongside a deck chair on a fake beach, her shocked face illuminated by a flashing pink light. There were mounds of gravelly sand with assorted plastic aquatic wildlife, and a fake palm tree festooned with fairy lights. It was clear I'd stumbled, literally, into the latest incarnation of the bar – The Bangkok beach!

Still waist deep, I turned towards the bar and for the first time spotted the staff. A line of six Thai teenagers, all wearing sailor outfits, were clutching trays and watching me wade through the indoor 'sea.' They all sported welcoming smiles, but I noticed a mixture of bemusement and slight concern on their faces as I flailed towards them and hauled myself from the pool, back onto the gravel covered shelf which constituted the beach.

Not losing 'face' is an important aspect of Asian culture, and I think I was subconsciously considering this point as I struggled to my feet and strode nonchalantly to the bar and ordered a drink. My jeans were soaked, and water squelched from my trainers as I walked. My t-shirt was wringing wet up to chest level, and I was soon shivering in the icy blasts of the air conditioning, but I insisted on pulling up a deck chair and sitting looking across the stagnant 'sea' whilst enjoying my drink. Eventually one of the young waitresses brought me a blanket - obviously concerned that a European visitor dying of hypothermia in a tropical themed bar wouldn't be great for business.

Once in Cambodia, as I'd expected, Kirsty took the South East Asian culture shock in her stride. We visited the harrowing Tuol Sleng genocide museum, site of a Khmer Rouge prison and torture centre, and the nearby Killing Fields museum at Choeung Ek. The latter is the site of one of many mass graves which have been identified throughout Cambodia, dating from the bloody revolution of 1975. The museum houses a Buddhist stupa containing five thousand human skulls found at the site, many clearly showing damage from blunt force blows which led to the victim's death. Wandering the lightly wooded former orchard with a guide, I noticed something lying in the scrubby grass and bent to retrieve it. Holding it up, I realised what it was.

"Tooth. There are many here," said the guide quietly.

I surveyed the ground around me and soon spotted another

tooth. Then another. And another. I crouched and ran my fingers through the grass, and realised that dozens of human teeth littered the area around me. Some smaller than others, clearly belonged to children.

"They smashed their heads on this tree," the guide explained, pointing to a nearby stump, still discoloured by the staining effect of human blood. A shocking place, its slightly amateurish presentation made it somehow even more harrowing.

Back in Phnom Penh, we scooted round town, three to a motorbike taxi, and enjoyed the city's often seedy nightlife. On one occasion however, we had to hastily retrieve a left-over pizza we'd donated to some five year old street urchins, forgetting that we'd gone for the 'happy' version, seasoned with a light marijuana topping, which was popular in traveller cafes! We took the boat to Siem Reap, riding on the roof rather than in the stifling cabin interior, and ignored the advice on the Thorn Tree forum on renting a scooter, which said it either wasn't allowed, or that you'd be attacked by local taxi operators for self-driving.

We had no problem renting the scooter and no issues with taxi drivers as we explored the ancient Khmer ruins around Angkor Wat. Driving ourselves allowed us to visit each of the temples when we wanted, and to avoid the tour buses which would disgorge scores of tourists, and could instantly transform a peaceful, forested ruin into a noisy theme park hell. We spoke to other travellers who had been told that it wasn't possible to rent a scooter and had been driven around the temples by impatient motorbike taxi drivers, who set their own agenda and didn't want to travel further afield, to the less visited sites. It was an important learning point – don't believe everything you're told, do your own research.

We decided to spend a few days at the coast at the end of our trip and looked at options to get to Sihanoukville, south west of Phnom Penh. The journey was only a hundred and fifty miles, but would take around five hours by bus, so I asked a taxi driver how much he'd charge. Had we been on a longer trip, the twenty five

US Dollar fare may have seemed excessive. On a two-week long trip though, where time was scarce, it made perfect sense to pay a little more to reach our destination more quickly.

This was to be my first experience of using long distance taxis in Asia and the drivers we used to get us to and from the coast, provided an unfortunate insight into how difficult it can be to find an efficient and safe driver in the developing world. Both were terrible, in contrasting and unexpected ways!

The Phnom Penh driver I got to take us to Sihanoukville was a well groomed, fashionably dressed man in his late twenties. His car was a shiny, red, five year old Toyota, with tinted windows and polished silver wheel trims, which was obviously his pride and joy. I harboured suspicions of 'boy racer' tendencies as we made slow progress through the streets of the capital, busy with motorcycles, tuk-tuks, pedal rickshaws and the occasional elephant. I expected that the quieter roads beyond the city may result in an opportunity for our driver to show us the full power of his 1300cc engine, and fastened my seatbelt in anticipation.

I needn't have bothered. I'm pretty sure our man never managed to get into top gear on the whole journey, preferring to coast along, with the engine screeching its disapproval at being driven at 30mph in third gear. The road was long and straight, with few vehicles except the occasional slow moving truck, which our driver seemed happy to chug behind for miles, while we choked on belching, toxic exhaust fumes. Two of the 'slower option' buses actually overtook us as we laboured along, our driver's hands gripping the wheel as if he was negotiating a terrifying mountain road. I actually became convinced that he wasn't aware that his vehicle had five gears, as third remained his default position with a rare, exhilarating foray into fourth, as we moved into heady speeds in excess of 35mph.

Timing wasn't our man's forte either. After we'd sat in a lorry's carbon monoxide slipstream for a few miles, it would suddenly occur to him that overtaking may be a good idea. Unfortunately, he'd execute the manoeuvre travelling uphill towards a blind summit, and wouldn't think to increase his speed in order to pass quickly. We'd therefore reach the top of the hill travelling alongside a slow moving truck, on the wrong side of the road, engine screaming in third gear, with Kirsty and I cowering in the back seat, hands covering our terror stricken faces. We eventually arrived in Sihanoukville six hours after leaving Phnom Penh, and our driver seemed keen to collect us in a few days. With a flight to catch, and still able to taste those truck exhaust fumes, we decided we'd be better returning with a local driver.

This time, I studied the taxis parked by Sihanoukville's market to find a likely candidate. I identified a small, elderly man in smart blue slacks and sandals, reading The Nation Post, whilst sat on a stool next to a blue Toyota. The car seemed in good condition, if older than the one we'd arrived in, and the man looked studious in his small wire-rimmed spectacles, like a respected headteacher approaching retirement or a friendly grandfather.

Unfortunately, if I'd assumed his mature, learned appearance was indicative of many years safe and efficient driving experience, I was to be sadly disappointed. Within a few minutes of leaving Sihanoukville on the road north, I was left wondering how our man had managed to reach such an advanced age. In hindsight, it was no surprise that he'd stopped at a roadside Buddhist shrine to leave an offering of bananas as we'd departed, to grant us good karma for the journey. He chattered away constantly in good English, his eyes rarely straying to the road from the rear-view mirror he used to observe his increasingly nervous passengers. If our previous driver had seemed reluctant to exceed 40mph, our new man didn't seem able to drive below that. With one arm on the wheel, the other out of the window, we flew round bends at seventy, tyres screeching and a dust cloud billowing behind us. Whereas on the outbound journey, we'd become accustomed to studying the curly swirls of Khmer lettering on the back of trucks, we now flew past them in a blur, accompanied by a horn blast which sent more than one oncoming cyclist tumbling into a roadside ditch.

I resisted the urge to be a backseat driver until our driver started scrabbling in his jacket, which was on the passenger seat, to retrieve a photo of his son's family, as we swerved round a slow-moving van on the wrong side of the road. At that point I tactfully informed him that we were in no hurry to get back, and that he could take his time. Please. Maybe he could even stop to show us his family snaps rather than doing it at 70mph. We still arrived back in Phnom Penh in roughly half the time it took us to get to the coast. At that point, I decided that next time we were facing a lengthy road journey, I'd attempt to rent a car and drive myself, wherever in the world we were.

By the time Kirsty and I departed on our next trip, we were a couple, rather than just travelling partners, though we didn't broadcast the fact at work, and Kirsty hadn't yet got around to introducing me to her family, who lived around seventy miles from Leeds. We set off for Morocco with her having told them she was going with a friend from work, which technically, I suppose, was true. We spent a few days in Casablanca, then, following through on my Cambodian self-drive promise, we rented a car and set off to explore the country.

It was the morning of May 16, 2003 as we headed south towards the coastal town of Essaouira. We arrived in the ancient walled city in the early afternoon, seemingly in a different century, as our car was surrounded by dozens of shrieking men on horseback wearing traditional baggy trousers and djellaba robes. We later discovered they were training for the Berber festival known as 'Game of Gunpowder', and that evening watched as the riders tore along the sandy expanse of the town's beach in formation, before firing their muskets skywards, a demonstration of their horsemanship and weaponry skills.

Kirsty and I both had company mobile phones at the time, but 'roaming' charges were expensive, and, not wanting to be bothered by work calls, we generally kept them switched off. Also, before 2007 and the launch of the first Apple iPhone with its 'pinch screen' feature, internet browsing on mobile phones was generally a poor experience. Public Wi-fi in hotels and restaurants was virtually non-existent, so at that time, a mobile phone was a lot less useful when travelling than it is today.

It was therefore sheer good fortune that Kirsty chose to switch on her phone on our second day in Essaouira. I saw the concern register on her face, as she began to scroll through a huge number of text messages from family and friends. The wording varied, but the general tone was the same. 'For God's sake, please let us know you're OK.'

On the day we'd left Casablanca, Al-Qaeda terrorists had launched a series of attacks on the city. Fourteen suicide bombers had attacked restaurants and hotels, killing thirty three people and injuring over a hundred. The fact that we had been eating and drinking in that same area just twenty four hours before the attack was a sobering thought. Though the attacks were big news in Morocco and around the world, we were totally oblivious to them, having no internet access and not seeing any TV news. UK TV bulletins had reported that Europeans were amongst the victims, and Kirsty's parents, unable to reach her, had contacted the UK Foreign Office. They confirmed she wasn't one of the named victims, nor was her travel partner.

After the relief of hearing she was safe, Kirsty's mother's first question was 'and who's this Matthew Lightfoot you're with?' (Although she actually called me Matthew Lightbody). Given the raised eyebrows that some of our subsequent trips have prompted in Kirsty's family, it was an unfortunate, yet probably appropriate way for them to find out about our relationship.

From Essaouira we travelled to Marrakech, which was in a state of high alert, with further attacks considered likely. The police and military were a visible presence as we sat outside a bar on Rue de la Liberté, in the new part of the City. The pavement tables were busy with a mixture of locals and European tourists, attracted to the area by the more liberal licencing laws which permitted alcohol sales, unlike in the conservative old town where intoxicants were banned. We sat and watched, as the police randomly stopped vehicles to carry out stringent searches using sniffer dogs, unloading the occupants of cars and vans, including families and the elderly whilst a wagging spaniel skipped and snuffled around their possessions on the roadside. Pedestrians were questioned by masked officers in body armour, their machine guns clearly visible as a deterrent to any would-be terrorist.

I felt reassured by the presence of the authorities, and was thankful that the Moroccan government had obviously decided on a show of strength to thwart further attacks. Then I glanced down the road to my left. Approaching at a quick pace were three young men of Southern Asian appearance, wearing flowing shalwar kameez robes and skull caps. Each had a wispy, long beard and was leaning forward beneath the weight of a large backpack. It's wrong to stereotype people by their appearance, but in a country still reeling from its worst ever terrorist attack, and in a city on edge and fearing further atrocities, the appearance of the young men caused a sudden murmur of apprehension outside the bar. All heads turned towards them as they approached, their steps seeming to quicken as they got closer. I heard the smash of glass, and turned to see a group of French tourists abandon their table at speed and scramble inside the bar. There followed the noise of a mass scraping of metal chairs on concrete, as others followed in a rapid evacuation from the bar's street-side tables. For some reason, Kirsty and I stayed put. I later likened the experience to my childhood brush with the infamous Hair-Puller. I knew I should move, but seemed frozen to the spot, watching the terrible scene unfold in slow motion. At any second, I expected a police officer or soldier to notice the potential attackers and unleash a deadly hail of gunfire which would obliterate the threat, and also anyone stupid enough to remain sitting outside the bar clutching a glass of beer.

By now the youths were almost level with us, but incredibly seemed to be invisible to the police, who carried on searching mothers with babies and old men leading overloaded donkeys, whilst totally ignoring the young men and their potentially lethal backpacks. Time seemed to stand still as they drew level with the bar and stopped. The few remaining customers sitting at the tables alongside us froze; those inside cowered behind the now closed doors, peering anxiously towards the street; a waiter held his tray across his chest, subconsciously shielding himself inadequately against the forthcoming blast.

One of the young men turned to allow his friend to forage in his rucksack and emerge holding a piece of paper. The collective sigh of relief was audible as the map was opened and studied, directions agreed, and the youths set off to find their hostel. The customers from inside the bar repopulated the outdoor tables and, like Kirsty and I, no doubt began debating the moral dilemma of pre-judging people based on their appearance, and perhaps also the efficiency of the Moroccan police force's anti-terrorism training.

The following evening, we explored the Djemaa-el-Fnaa square in the medina quarter of the old town. Translated as the 'Assembly of the Dead' in reference to its historic use for executions, wandering the square at dusk certainly felt like a trip back to medieval times. Smoke from countless barbecue grills drifted across the orange glow of gas lamps, as stall holders enticed locals and tourists to sample their tagine, couscous, snail soup, sheep's brains, stuffed spleen or skewered heart. It was the nightly halqa, or street theatre, which was the real attraction here though. Story-tellers held court; jugglers and fire eaters wandered through the crowds; acrobats bounced and span, monkeys in three piece suits danced; medicine men dispensed dubious snake-oil remedies, all to a soundtrack of cobra-charming flutes and the clank of golden cups wielded by water vendors wearing elaborate, tasseled hats.

The square is popular with tourists but the majority of visitors seemed to be locals going about their daily business – buying groceries or maybe an amulet to ward off arthritis or the evil eye; getting a henna hand tattoo re-inked or obtaining a reading from an ancient fortune teller seated beneath a golf umbrella; or perhaps having a troublesome tooth extracted by a hirsute man wielding a fearsome set of pliers.

The square felt totally foreign to us, and was a great culture shock experience, though Kirsty was treated to an extra shock which is apparently quite common in the Djemma-el-Fanaa. As we watched a six year old ride a unicycle along a cable suspended precariously about ten feet from the ground, I saw Kirsty suddenly leap forward, eyes wide with surprise. She'd experienced a furtive backside fondle from a thin, pointy faced Moroccan man in a leather jacket who was now rapidly making his escape through the crowd. I lost track of him momentarily, but then spotted him again, at the opposite side of the circle of people watching the acrobatic cycling child. He seemed to be manoeuvring into position to assail the buttocks of a young blonde girl who was watching the show with her boyfriend. I told Kirsty I'd be back in a minute, and stealthily made my way through the crowd, until I was able to sidle unseen alongside the crafty groper. As he focused his attention on moving closer to the blonde girl, I slowly reached around behind his back, and up under his leather jacket, to firmly clasp one of his skinny arse cheeks. He lurched forward then turned to face me, eyes wide with a mixture of shock and panic. His look turned to horror as I gave him a cheeky wink and my sexiest pout, and he set off at speed, pushing and stumbling through the crowd, his ardour well and truly dampened for the evening.

We returned from Morocco realising that fate had dealt us a lucky hand and that we'd missed being caught in a terrorist atrocity by a very narrow margin. It was our second close call in quick succession, as our Phnom Penh hotel had been burned to the ground by a rioting mob within a month of our return from Cambodia. We hoped it wouldn't be third time unlucky, as we considered where to head on our next trip, and how to travel once we got there.

8 DRIVING YOURSELF. CRAZY!

As usual, once back at work, I set about planning our next trip, to Sri Lanka, and quickly came up with a potential itinerary – We'd take a scenic train journey from Columbo to Kandy, legs dangling precariously from the open door of the carriage as we clattered through the jungle; stop for lunch at the elephant orphanage at Pinnewala; then on to the tea-growing hill towns of Kandy and Nuwara Eliya. From there we'd somehow find our way to Galle on the south coast, then catch the train along the line which hugs the Indian Ocean all the way back to the capital.

I reckoned that should take around ten days, leaving us with a few days to explore the ancient cities around Polonnaruwa, and maybe scale the spectacular natural rock fortress of Sigiriya. The problem was that these Buddhist archaeological sites were scattered over a fairly large area, a four hour drive north of Columbo. Recalling our Cambodia experience, self-drive seemed the best solution, but finding a rental car which came without a local driver was proving difficult. I therefore sought advice from the Thorn Tree message board on the Lonely Planet website. Specifically, I wanted to know if anyone had any contacts who could rent me a self-drive car in Sri Lanka, and whether anyone had driven in the country themselves. It seemed an innocent enough question to me, but to some of the forum's users, my suggestion seemed akin to suggesting a tour of the badlands of Afghanistan on a tandem.

People questioned my sanity, and said that I would endanger myself and Kirsty by attempting to drive myself in Sri Lanka, or anywhere in Southern Asia for that matter. Others questioned why I would want to drive, when I could hire a car plus a local driver for roughly the same price. The general response to my question was that no one on the forum had self-driven in Sri Lanka, no one would consider doing so, and no one understood why I was thinking of driving myself.

There were a number of reasons why I favour self-drive, beyond the often questionable ability of locally hired drivers, all of which I still firmly uphold fifteen years later, having driven in around a hundred countries, and on every Continent. (Except Antarctica!)

The first is the obvious consideration of our limited holiday time. On a two-week trip, we wanted to see as much of the country we were visiting as possible, so could ill afford the additional time spent arranging, waiting for, and travelling on public transport, if it could be avoided. Also, as a keen photographer, there's nothing so frustrating as whizzing past a great photo opportunity on public transport, knowing you'd never travel on that particular road again. A rental car allowed us to stop when, and as often, as we wanted.

Another factor was cost, and the availability of good deals which often meant that self-drive was surprisingly cheap, if you know where to look! I always tried to use local companies rather than the big international brands. Not only were they usually a lot cheaper, but their vehicles were rarely anything like new, which is an important point. When driving in the developing world, the very last thing you want to see as you exit the rental company office, is a shiny, brand new vehicle, upon which every new scratch, dent and stone chip will be immediately visible, and chargeable. Far better that the vehicle has seen some 'action.' As long as it functions mechanically, I allow myself a satisfied, and relieved, smirk upon being assigned a car with some serious bodywork damage. And over the years, those cars which could tell a few tales have led to some of our own.

In Zanzibar, we collected a battered 4x4 which looked very much like it had rolled down a cliffside a couple of times. It also had the dubious 'extra' of housing an ant's nest in the boot. In Tibilisi, Georgia I rented a car which seemed to have no mechanical defects, until I applied the brakes when travelling downhill, failed to stop and rolled straight through an ungated level crossing. Another close call!

Of all the cars I've rented though, none was as unlucky as the Toyota Prado 4x4 we rented in Malawi. On this occasion I became aware very quickly that the brakes didn't work. Within minutes of pulling out of the rental company compound, onto one of Lilongwe's busiest roads, in fact. I returned to the office and the friendly owner, Sunge, explained that unfortunately he had no other vehicles available to rent. Anyway, the brakes DID work. There was just a 'special way' to apply them. We jumped into the car for a demonstration, and Sunge pulled out onto the main road and accelerated towards a line of cars, stopped at a red light. As the speedo touched 35mph he applied the brake, and nothing happened. Quickly he stabbed at it again twice in quick succession and on the third depression we screeched to a halt.

"You see. It works okay." He beamed. I wasn't convinced.

"Hit it once, no stop. Hit it twice, slow down. Three times, stop! Easy." He handed the keys back to me and I was faced with a choice. Refuse to take the car and delay our departure by trying to locate another vehicle at short notice. Or perfect the 1-2-3 braking routine. I was sure I'd master it with some practice, so set off again, but decided it was probably best not to tell Kirsty about the 'special' braking system.

After a couple of close calls on the first day, my 'brake three times' instinct had kicked in, and I was driving relatively normally. Kirsty had frowned a couple of times at my unorthodox, last minute approach to stopping in the face of obvious obstacles, but hadn't noticed my three-tap pedal routine. That was until we visited the Zomba Plateau. This two thousand metre high granite slab of mountain had loomed large in my consciousness for the previous few days. I wondered how steep the road up to, and more importantly, back down from the summit would be, and whether there would be any guard rails.

The answer was very steep, and as I'd expected, there were no guard rails, not even on the sharpest bends, as the bumpy road wound its way down the mountain. We'd spent an enjoyable afternoon with Victor, a handyman at our guest house, and part-time guide, exploring the pine forests and lakes of the plateau. The highlight of our hike was approaching a cluster of huts in a sunlit glade, to hear the voices of angels coming from a tiny wooden chapel. We approached to see two teenage girls, sat in the shaded pews of the old building, singing a beautiful acapella hymn. No doubt European youngsters would have dissolved into a fit of embarrassed giggles at being observed by unexpected visitors, but the girls smiled shyly and carried on, as they spotted us peeping through an open window. Not wishing to intrude, we sat in the shade of the building and listened to the peaceful choral paean, accompanied by the noisy twitter of wild birds in the forest surrounding the village.

Half an hour after this idyllic chill-out session, I was soaked in panic-induced perspiration and white-knuckled, as I gripped the steering wheel to begin our descent down the mountain. Victor was sat beside me and at first seemed bemused by my cautious 5mph progress, and curious foot jabbing motion. He looked at me quizzically and I glanced in the rear-view mirror and caught Kirsty's eye on the back seat. She seemed to sense all was not well, so I decided to break the news.

"Okay. We have a slight problem. The bloody brakes don't work." I grimaced.

The mood in the car suddenly changed, as Kirsty and Victor's newly gained awareness of the situation enabled them to share my feelings of impending doom, on the white-knuckle ride down the mountain. Driving in first gear kept our speed reasonably controlled, and the brakes generally locked on pretty well on the third foot tap. It was, however, quite alarming when they would suddenly disengage totally, resulting in an immediate acceleration, which was particularly terrifying if it occurred on a steep bend. It took us around twenty five minutes to get to the bottom of the mountain, at the head of a procession of trucks and cars, honking their horns in annoyance at my slow progress, and providing an embarrassing fanfare as we rolled into town.

We dropped Victor off and stopped at a supermarket, with the atmosphere somewhat frosty, now that Kirsty was fully aware of the mechanical failings of our vehicle. Unfortunately, driver error was now going to contribute to the car's bad luck streak. I definitely checked the rear-view mirror just before I reversed out of the parking space, but for some reason failed to notice a small, white hatchback which had pulled in behind us and stopped. I crunched the gear lever into reverse, released the handbrake and accelerated. The bang was enormous as we smashed into the side of the car. I glanced in the mirror and saw the scared eyes of a small local man staring back, silently voicing the question Kirsty now asked incredulously, and loudly.

"Why did you do that!!?"

Momentarily I considered blaming the brakes, but realised that probably wouldn't help. I pulled the car forward and got out. To my horror, I noticed a little girl of around five, her hair in tight corn-braids, wide-eyed and traumatised on the back seat of the hatchback. A crowd was gathering, and I raised my hands to accept the blame, and began apologising to the girl's father, who had now exited his vehicle and was surveying the damage. I was aware of the potential for a lynch-mob mentality to develop in such situations in certain African countries, so at the very least I expected to have to part with a serious amount of cash in damages. If the child was injured, I could be in danger of physical assault, or worse.

There was a large dent in the passenger side door of the hatchback, and some scuffs of blue paint from my spare-wheel cover, which the driver was attempting to scrape off with his fingernail. I stood back, trying to gauge the mood of the gathering, excitable crowd and the driver. He was a small, smartly dressed man, and I felt sure I could handle him if things turned nasty, but not a crowd of angry locals. To say I was surprised by his reaction was an understatement, as he straightened up and turned to face me, with a gentle smile on his boyish face.

"It's okay, no problem." He raised his hands as if HE was

apologising to ME.

"I'm so sorry. It was my fault. Your car is damaged, and I must pay." I blustered, momentarily thrown off guard by his reaction.

"No, no. Its fine. My car is old. You don't need to pay me anything." He smiled again and my cynical mind began wondering if he was driving illegally.

"But your daughter is upset. Is she okay?"

He glanced to the back seat where the little girl looked anything but okay, and nodded.

"She is fine. It's all okay. No problem."

Again, the reaction was so unexpected, I began to suspect an elaborate scam. Would he drive away, then report me the police, in order to extract a bigger pay-off to drop the charges? I began jabbering about accident reports, insurance and compensation. The sort of bureaucratic detail we find so important in the developed world, but which are irrelevant in rural Africa. The man looked puzzled at my insistence that I should be giving him money. To him, it made no sense. The vehicle was old anyway. It had plenty of dents and scrapes. One more made no difference, as long as the car still worked. His daughter was shaken, but otherwise unhurt. The act of financial recompense, which our culture takes for granted in such a situation, or even views as an opportunity, was totally alien to him. He even declined my offer to buy his daughter an ice cream.

"Thank you but she is not hungry," he replied as the unfortunate child looked close to tears. Not only had a crazy European nearly killed her but her chance of an ice cream had also been cruelly snatched away.

We shook hands, and parted, but only after an old man had appeared with a bucket and chamois leather, and diligently removed the scuffs from our unlucky Toyota.

Unfortunately, those scuffs were the least of my worries the following morning. We spent the night at a hostel which doubled as a centre for local artists. During the hours of darkness, and obviously inspired by some of the works on display, our vehicle was visited in the car park by an aspiring young graffiti artist, specialising in a style which could probably best be described as Urban African Cave Art.

Loading up our bags in the morning, my attention was immediately drawn to two crude stick-men figures scratched into the paintwork on the driver's side door. Each was about six inches high and was a stark white, etched deep into the dust-covered blue paintwork. The scene depicted in the childish tableau was expertly summarised by the night watchman, Godfrey, when I summoned him from his hut.

"It is a man. And a lady." His reading glasses rested on the tip of his nose as he bent to survey the figures.His face fell in horror, as the full scale of the obscenity became apparent to him.

"Oh dear. The man's Pee-Pee...it is going into the lady."

This was unfortunately true. One of the stick figures seemed to have an additional limb, equal in length and thickness to the others, which was protruding at a ninety degree angle, towards the opposing stick figure, who boasted a swirl of unruly curly scratches atop its oblong head.

A God-fearing man, the image had clearly upset Godfrey.

"It is a very terrible thing. Very bad. The children..." His voice tailed off, as he silently contemplated their likely descent to the fiery depths of Hell, for the production of this car-borne abomination.

To say the scratched 'car art' caused quite a stir during our remaining time in Malawi is an understatement. When stopped at a gas station or supermarket, the scratched figures would soon be spotted. Petrol pump attendants or passers-by would surreptitiously walk past a few times, to confirm what they'd seen.

They'd then tip off others, and soon a giggling, pointing gaggle would form, standing a discreet distance from our car. Upon our return, most would turn away, embarrassed to be caught viewing our hard-porn paint job. Occasionally, a concerned local would remain, shaking their head and muttering "Very bad. A terrible thing. Those children..."

Luckily, Sunge didn't share their disgust when I returned the car. He screeched with delight and began taking photos to add to his Facebook page. I asked if he'd be able to paint over the graffiti.

"Are you joking?" he laughed. "I'm keeping them on there. I might even ring the Nyasa Times, to see if they'll run a story and I can get some free advertising." I doubted whether Hertz or Avis would have been so forgiving.

Sunge's laidback attitude was typical of many of the local car rental companies I've dealt with. In the Philippines, my car was delivered without any paperwork at all, which would leave me exposed to police questioning and possibly extortion, so I insisted that I was provided with some form of contract. The rental company employee disappeared into a petrol station and returned with a paper towel, bearing the words 'Man is okay to driving car' scrawled in red marker pen. Luckily, I never had cause to explore the level of my insurance cover!

Many local firms only have a couple of vehicles for rent, so have no need for a fixed office base. This is often the case on Caribbean Islands, so I wasn't surprised to be told to meet my car rental contact at a dockside bar, when we landed by ferry on the small island of Dominica. Kevin was a lugubrious rasta in his early twenties, his three-foot long dreads bulging inside a crocheted tam hat. The Suzuki Jimny he led me to, was pleasingly dilapidated, and I handed over my Eastern Caribbean dollars, Kevin tossed me the keys and we agreed to meet back at the bar in four days.

It was 2016, a year before Hurricane Maria wreaked terrible devastation on the small island, so its tourist infrastructure was fully functioning, though was still pleasantly low key, without any of the large all-inclusive resorts which blight so many islands in the region. We'd spent an enjoyable few days driving the single coastal road and hiking in Morne Trois Pitons National Park, and on our last night, my Bluetooth reggae track exchange with a local barman DJ, had resulted in him handing me control of the sound system. Not for the first, or last time in a rundown shebeen in a small Caribbean town, the locals were treated to one of my eclectic roots playlists, sourced over the years from the phones of aficionados in countless similar bars around the world.

The following morning found us relaxing at our guest house in the hills above the tiny capital, Roseau. We had a ferry to catch to the neighbouring island of Martinique at 2.30pm, and I'd arranged to meet Kevin at the bar an hour before that. It was now 11.30am and I was making full use of the guest house WiFi, lounging on our balcony, amidst the song of forest birds, whilst focusing on a different kind of twitter, to keep track of the Leeds United game taking place around four thousand miles away. I could hear Kirsty packing her bag in the room, and a rustling of paper preceding an anguished cry of 'Oh my God!'

She joined me on the balcony brandishing our ferry tickets, with an accusatory look on her face which told me I'd screwed up.

"The ferry is at 12.30, not 2.30." We both paused momentarily while the impact of this news sank in. The boat only ran twice a week. Our two-week trip was utilising ferries and local flights to travel between Antigua, Guadeloupe, Dominica and Martinique, before flying home from St Lucia. Missing the ferry would cause a major rethink of our plans, cancellation of non-refundable accommodation and costly purchase of replacement flights and ferries. We had an hour to get to the ferry, a half hour drive away, and we hadn't even packed our bags or showered. And we had a rental car to return.

All hell broke loose. We both hurtled into the room and began stuffing possessions into our rucksacks. We hadn't even paid for the accommodation, so were forced to thrust a bundle of dollars into the hands of a maid as we tore down the stairs, unshowered and half dressed. The little Suzuki was soon screeching down the mountain roads, scattering goats and chickens, as I frantically tried to call Kevin to rearrange our rendezvous. Not surprisingly he hadn't answered by the time we pulled into the ramshackle town, with its brightly painted clapboard houses and narrow streets filled with booming reggae. I despatched Kirsty at the ferry terminal where our boat was moored, black smoke belching from its funnel hinting at an imminent departure. She joined a jostling queue of locals, while I set off to try and return our car. My first stop was the bar where I'd met Kevin upon our arrival. The old lady behind the counter and her sole customer, an obese market trader with a shaved head, turned slowly and regarded me with vague disinterest as I burst through the door.

"Do you know Kevin?" I panted, sweat dripping down my face, as the ferry's horn blasted out a plaintive rebuke to late arriving stragglers.

The old woman had a spectacular squint and few teeth. She opened her mouth as if to reply, then closed it again without uttering a word.

"Kevin? Rasta? Sits outside." I was waving the car keys in front of the fat man, who looked puzzled and shook his head.

I heard the horn of a truck, and realised I'd double-parked and was blocking the road. I left the bar and began a frenzied circuit of the town centre, trying unsuccessfully to find a parking spot, with the occasional ominous blast from the ferry's horn spurring me on. Eventually, at the far side of the harbour, I spotted a street vendor moving a barrow of plantains from a pavement-side pitch, and as he vacated the space, I swerved the Suzuki into its place. I locked the door and set off running, with the shouted admonishments of market traders clearly indicating I was illegally parked. Kirsty had already been forced to embark and was leaning on the rail at the stern of the ferry watching my approach. Assuming I'd managed to locate Kevin, she was therefore somewhat surprised to see me carry on running past the boat.

A familiar scene unfolded as I burst into the dimly lit bar again, with the old lady and her portly customer turning slowly to greet me. This time however, there was no time for pleasantries.

"Keys! Give to Kevin. Rasta!" I yelled as I tossed the car keys towards the bar. Not surprisingly the old crone ducked, and the keys bounced into some unseen recess behind her. I didn't have time to explain further. I set off running towards the ferry, with smoke now billowing from its funnel, gangplanks in the process of being withdrawn, and mooring ropes untied. It was actually beginning to slowly pull away from the quayside, as a couple of stevedores became aware of me bellowing 'Hold the boat!' and momentarily stopped retracting a gangplank to allow me to scramble aboard.

About an hour into the surprisingly rough passage to Martinique, my phone rang, and I recognised Kevin's number. I was about to start explaining where his car and its keys were, but he stopped me. He already knew. The small-town jungle drums had alerted him to the sweating Englishman careering through the town and almost missing a ferry, and the car was safely back in his possession. Kevin was already back outside the bar waiting for his next client.

The Caribbean is a place where driving is usually a pleasure. Most roads are of reasonable quality, drivers generally have an acceptable level of road-sense and away from major towns, the roads are quiet and often spectacularly scenic. The same can't be said of all parts of the world. Some of the craziest driving I've encountered was in the Middle East. The three-lane highways in pre-war Aleppo in Syria were a challenge to pedestrians and drivers alike. At a red light, cars jockeyed for position, engines revving, drivers eyeballing each other in anticipation. As soon as the light turned green, every single driver applied their horn to full effect and accelerated, seeking a gap in an adjacent lane in which to swerve into, without any indication, before driving as close as possible to the bumper of the car in front. It was dog eat dog. Sink or swim. And I loved it! Defensive, nervous driving would simply invite motorised bullying, so the only way to proceed was to become as aggressive as the locals. It was the first time I'd had to employ the 'big antelope' tactic on four wheels.

Aleppo drivers also had an interesting approach to roundabouts, as I observed from our hotel room window, which afforded a view from above, of a large roundabout linking a number of dual carriageway roads. I watched, fascinated, as drivers approached on the right-hand side of the road to attempt to correctly negotiate the roundabout in an anti-clockwise direction. If, however, they noticed that traffic was backing up ahead of them, they would simply swerve across to the other side of the carriageway and navigate the circle in a clockwise course, against the flow of approaching traffic. It looked chaotic, but everyone seemed to understand that the first rule of Syrian driving was there were no rules, and the traffic generally kept moving!

The urban motorways of Beirut in Lebanon were more of a high-speed challenge than the traffic choked avenues of Aleppo. Here, the manoeuvres were as erratic and aggressive as in Syria, but were carried out at much faster speeds. Driving was a cross between Formula 1 and the cartoon Wacky Races, and again I found it an exhilarating experience, as I raced along at 70mph, weaving between lanes, hand firmly on the horn at all times. Good fun, but I'm not sure it would be healthy on a daily basis, especially after a hard day at the office.

Bad roads are an occupational hazard when self-driving in much of the developing world. I've generally found that local rental companies are the best source of information on the likely state of a route. Care should be taken however, to establish when the local 'expert' last travelled on a particular road. A single rainy season, or even a recent storm can have a seriously detrimental effect on a poorly maintained surface or an ancient bridge, meaning a road which was deemed in 'good condition' a few months ago, may now be totally impassable.

One of the best examples of this this was in the Southern African nation of Mozambique. After decades of conflict, including a long running independence struggle against Portugal, followed by a bloody civil war, the country was again deemed reasonably safe to visit. My manager at work at the time, a keen photographer, was, however, being overly optimistic when he excitedly told me he couldn't wait to see my wildlife photos. Most of Mozambique's elephant and rhino population had succumbed to the guns of the guerrilla fighters of RENAMO and FRELIMO, and Gorongosa National Park lost 90% of its mammals between 1977 and 1992.

We therefore weren't expecting a safari when we set off to drive north from the shabby capital, Maputo. We'd read about undiscovered, unspoilt Indian Ocean beaches, crumbling historical cities and laidback fishing villages, all located well off the well-trodden tourist trail. It was around three hundred miles to the town of Inhambane along the M1 motorway which we were assured was a 'very good road.' We'd therefore assumed a five to six hour trip. In reality, it turned into double that. I'd previously experienced some seriously large potholes on the motorways of Northern Brazil, but it soon became clear that this M1 had nothing in common with it's smooth, multi-laned UK namesake.

The pot-holes were frequent and varied in size and depth. Some were small, round, deep and deviously concealed by the dusty surface, to suddenly appear as you dared to accelerate above 30mph, causing a loud bang as your tyre plummeted into the void. Others were vast crater-like expanses, fifteen feet across and six inches deep, which I tried to slalom around, until there were so many that I admitted defeat and slowed to a crawl, in order to trundle in and out of the hole at walking pace.

Africa's roads are a colourful procession of village life, and Mozambique's main motorway was no different. Our enforced leisurely pace allowed us to interact with locals carrying huge bundles of charcoal fuel on their heads, whole families on trundling donkey and bullock carts, and old men on rickety cycles who sometimes came close to overtaking us. As always, we stopped to take photos of children playing in rivers or walking to school in frayed, but lovingly washed and ironed uniforms. The sight of their own grinning faces reproduced on the LCD screen always caused squeals of delight and disbelief. On a long stretch of hot, decaying asphalt, we passed a teenage girl with a small baby carried in a sling on her back. We stopped to offer her a lift and she gratefully accepted. It was only when she quietly explained that both she and her infant were suffering from potentially deadly malaria, and were walking fifteen miles to see the nearest doctor, that we appreciated the importance of this crumbling road to the locals.

Rounding a bend, we swerved to avoid tree branches placed in the road, a tell-tale sign of a breakdown or accident ahead. Unfortunately, it was the latter. A car had rounded a bend on the wrong side of the road and hit a pick-up truck, head-on. Two youths riding in the flat-bed of the truck had been thrown from the vehicle, and one was seriously injured. The other was concussed and seemed to have a broken arm. With emergency services several hours away, discussions were underway as to which of the assembled passing motorists had the fastest vehicle to transport the most seriously injured boy to hospital. We were the only vehicle heading north, so the youth with the broken arm was laid, moaning, on the back seat of our car, next to the malarial mother and child, and we were tasked with taking him back to Inhambane.

The gas lamps were already flickering on the dhows moored in the harbour when we pulled into town, to be met by the family of the now semi-conscious boy, in front of the cathedral. His mother's tears, and the general sombre demeanour of other relatives, led us to wonder about the fate of the other youth. The girl had fallen into a deep sleep on the back seat, and she rubbed her eyes as we gently roused her. She smiled and thanked us for the lift, pulled the sling tight on her back to secure her baby, and disappeared into the sidestreets. We were left to reflect on how a three hundred mile journey on a 'good road' often turns into an adventure in Africa, and how self-driving can easily draw you into the often perilous daily existence of the local people.

That perilous existence can sometimes cross the line into ruthless opportunism though, as we found on a journey through the highlands of Uganda. We'd picked up a car in the Rwandan capital Kigali and were driving to Kampala, via the Bwindi Impenetrable Forest, on the border with Democratic of Republic of Congo, where we'd secured permits to track mountain gorillas. The drive took us through improbably steep, mountainous rainforest, on dirt roads which had turned into thick rivers of mud after days of incessant rain.

Our 4x4 coped well with the challenging terrain but, rounding a bend on a mist shrouded hillside, we were faced with a raging torrent of muddy brown water, pouring like a deluge of gravy from the hillside and across the road. Forced to stop, I got out to gauge the depth and strength of the flow by wading across, only to have to dodge a fast-moving tree trunk which had been dislodged by the water's force. It was clear that attempting to cross would likely result in our vehicle following the log down the hillside, so we got back in the car and switched off the engine to wait for the rain, and hopefully the flood, to abate.

One of the marvels of driving in Africa is the prevalence of small children. Ever present on the roadside near towns and villages, in hand-me-down school uniform or rags; wheeling hand-crafted wooden toys or tugging a homemade balloon in the form of an inflated carrier bag on string; alone or in running, tumbling, skipping barefoot gangs, children are everywhere. In rural areas, you may drive for hours and only glimpse an occasional farmer working his land, but should you stop your car, you'll be surrounded in minutes by multitudes of curious kids, who seem to emerge from nowhere.

Within five minutes of turning off our engine, we caught a first fleeting glimpse of pink amongst the roadside foliage, which soon revealed itself to be a girl of about six, in a bright pinafore style school dress, liberally spattered in mud. She was soon joined by an older girl of around eleven. They observed us cautiously from the treeline, until they were joined by two more ten year old girls, all sporting the same mud coated, pink uniform, and as a foursome, felt confident enough to approach.

We wound down the window to be greeted with the now

familiar refrain of 'give me money.' In most cases nowadays, this more direct approach seems to have replaced the requests of a previous generation who asked for pens/paper/sweets/soap etc. It seems the kids have learnt that cold hard cash is king!

I responded as I usually do, with a simple 'why?' which seemed to temporarily flummox the girls, and they shifted their clay-coated bare feet uneasily, until the oldest girl got the conversation back on track.

"Give me money, mzungu." This time accompanied by a gap-toothed smile, and employing the term generally used to refer to white people by children in East Africa. A Mzungu is a ghost, and so the story goes, when local people first saw whites, they believed them to be pale skinned spectres, come to steal their souls.

More pink uniformed girls had now arrived, accompanied by a group of little boys, clad in khaki, and they all tried their luck unsuccessfully at the 'give me money' game, as the rain poured down, and they stood, drenched and shivering on the muddy roadside.

Within an hour, word had obviously travelled quickly through nearby villages, and we were entertaining a crowd of around sixty rain-sodden children. It had become clear that 'Give me money,' was doomed to failure, so we'd moved onto the other games I use to amuse kids, when interacting with them at one of the ubiquitous delays that African travel throws up. I started by taking their photo, then showing them the image on the LCD screen. We then moved onto learning English language animal names, assisted by my impersonation of each beast. This was followed by showing them English coins and explaining who the Queen is. Finally, I resorted to teaching them Leeds United football songs.

When proceedings had descended to this stage, with Kirsty shaking her head, I knew it was time to move on. The rain had slowed, and the flood waters were flowing less rapidly. Much of the road had been washed away though, leaving a narrow, muddy ledge above a steep slope, falling away into a blur of cloud shrouded hillside far below. I gingerly edged our car along the thin slither of remaining road, guided by dozens of mud-soaked young helpers, all yelling advice and issuing directions with an array of confusing hand signals. We reached the other side safely, and rewarded the kids for a job well done, not with the requested money, but with fruit, biscuits and some glossy colour pictures of mountain gorillas torn from our Lonely Planet.

If only the next obstacle had been so easy to negotiate. About five miles further along, the road ended abruptly and vanished into a vast mound of grass covered earth. The steep bank flanking the road seemed to have been peeled away by a giant hand and dumped across our path. It was a serious landslide, and the fact that no villagers were yet on the scene told us it had only just happened. We stopped the car and reflected on the narrow margin which had prevented us being hit by this muddy avalanche, which would have deposited our vehicle in the valley far below.

It didn't take long for news of the landslide to reach the nearest village, and soon we were joined by a crowd of rain-soaked locals sporting an incongruous mix of mis-sized wellington boots, colourful traditional shawls and blankets, and the usual smattering of western aid-donation clothing, bearing the mysterious logos of universities and corporate entities in far-away Europe and the USA. Known as 'Kafa ulaya,' the clothes of dead whites, in Nigeria, these branded items from the developed world are prized possessions throughout Africa, although the new owner of the garment clearly has no idea of the meaning of any logo or slogan they're displaying. (In a crowded local market in the Zambian Capital, Lusaka, I was once sold a bunch of bananas by a skeletal, yet cheerful septuagenarian lady, sporting a t-shirt informing us that she was 'Bouncy Beth.' I shuddered to think what she would have thought, had she actually attended 'Lisa's Hen-do, Blackpool 2013.')

The group of locals standing with us in the misty rain regarded me with bemusement, as I tried to muster them into action to help clear the road. Only literate Ugandans speak English, with most of the rural population speaking the local Luganda language, of which I obviously had no knowledge. Therefore, I resorted to miming a digging action, which only seemed to confuse them further. My attempts at a demonstration of the required job also failed miserably. I couldn't believe how much a manhandled sod of the soaking earth weighed and after hauling three armfuls off the road, I was knackered, and caked in mud.

As I caught my breath, a young man with a bright yellow sou'wester hat obscuring most of his face, tugged my arm. "Chief coming." He pointed towards a diminutive, bow legged figure picking his way down the muddy track towards us, sheltering beneath a large red and white umbrella, which he'd apparently acquired while playing 18 holes at a golf course in Bear Creek, Missouri.

A gentle smile played on the old man's face as he surveyed the landslide and the mud soaked mzungus standing before him. Clad entirely in dead men's clothes, he had the wizened countenance of an eighty year old, and the mischievous eyes of an eight year old. The potential for monetary gain was obvious. The road was impassable without some serious manual labour, and he controlled the only workforce for miles around. He was also probably well aware that we were heading to Bwindi National Park, with our expensive pre-purchased gorilla tracking permits. The odds were stacked in his favour and he knew it.

"Five hundred Shillings to move." He nodded towards the muck pile and I noticed a group of youths approaching along the track, brandishing an assortment of shovels and rakes. I did a quick calculation in my head and realised that five hundred shillings equated to about ten pence, which seemed highly unlikely. I retrieved my phone from a soggy pocket and accessed the calculator app. I tapped out 5,0,0, and passed it to the old man.

He screwed up his eyes and held the phone at arm's length. Then smiling again, he jabbed at the screen with a calloused finger and passed it back. Three additional noughts had been added to my 500.

"Five hundred thousand! That's a hundred pounds." I spluttered. We were carrying that amount of local currency, but in the absence of cash machines in the small towns we'd be travelling through, it would leave us seriously short of cash to pay for hotels and meals. Also, the average monthly wage for a family in a rural area was only about three hundred thousand shillings. In such situations, it's important to try and achieve a balance. Driving too hard a bargain could cause insult, or, even worse from our point of view, could result in the offer of help being withdrawn altogether. On the other hand, handing over an amount equivalent to nearly two months wages, would only reinforce the view that travellers are bottomless money pits to be exploited to the maximum. I shook my head and tapped on my phone, to delete one of the old man's zeros.

"Fifty thousand." The chief snorted and gave a hand signal to the tool carriers which said, 'Turn around lads, the job's off.'

I took back control of the phone, its screen now smeared with mud and droplets of rain and tapped the numbers 1,0,0,0,0,0. The tool carriers paused, the assembled villagers craned their necks to catch a glimpse of the latest offer, and the chief screwed up his eyes and peered at the screen. He sighed in mock frustration at the protracted negotiation and shook his head slowly. The screen was tapped once more, and the phone thrust back in a manner which said 'take it or leave it.' 250,000 shillings, the equivalent of fifty pounds. Kirsty and I were debating our next move in this mountainside fiscal chess match, when we heard a vehicle approaching along the road behind us, and a crowded mini-bus skidded to halt behind our 4x4. The banging Nigerian Hip-Hop pumping from the speakers seemed totally alien in the remote setting.

The driver and his mate disembarked with the cocky swagger typical of local bus drivers in Africa. The driver turned up the collar of his leather jacket and grimaced at the cold and damp, but didn't remove his mirrored shades. He nodded a greeting to Kirsty and I, and approached the chief, as his colleague dismissively kicked at the mudheap on the road.

This seemed like good news. I was sure a local driver could negotiate a fairer rate to clear the road, and we could split the cost. I couldn't hear the discussion between the bus driver and the chief, but it concluded with an order to the gathered locals to pick up their tools and begin to clear the landslide. The driver approached us, smiling, and I told him where we'd got to in our negotiations.

"250,000 shillings is too much. The old man was robbing you," he grinned, flashing a gold-capped front tooth. "I have arranged a fair price with him. We will pay him when the road is clear."

He omitted to mention what the price would be, and retreated to the minibus, closed the door and cranked up the sound system. Kirsty and I set about helping the villagers shovelling the huge mound of mud from the road, our task not helped by locals driving motorbikes and herds of cows and goats across the top of the obstacle as we worked. After an hour, the landslide had been reduced in height to about half a metre, and the bus driver's mate supervised the positioning of wooden planks to provide a makeshift road surface across the mud. A hand signal back to the mini-bus indicated satisfaction with the work, and the driver emerged.

"Give me one hundred thousand," he requested somewhat furtively, and I assumed he'd driven the price down to two hundred thousand, and that we were splitting the cost. Satisfied with the outcome, I handed over two damp, fifty thousand notes. I watched as he sauntered over to the chief and they turned away from the crowd of toiling villagers to finalise the transaction. The driver then bade us farewell, and I thanked him for renegotiating the price and sharing the cost of the work. With a flash of gold tooth and an elaborate handshake, he was back in the bus, marshalling his assistant and passengers to push the vehicle up the planks and over the landslide, with wheels spinning and the exhaust spewing out black smoke.

We followed, and with four-wheel-drive engaged, easily bounced across the mound of earth. I paused at the far side, and leant out of the window to thank the villagers. The old chief caught my eye, and gave me a respectful nod which I took to mean 'We'll call that a draw. We both got what we wanted.'

I waved and as he raised his hand in acknowledgement, I couldn't fail to notice that he was clutching one, single, orange fifty thousand shilling note. We drove on and I was left pondering exactly who had been robbed by who!

If the Ugandan villagers' opportunism had been the result of an act of God, the same couldn't be said for the mishap we suffered in Namibia. We were driving through North Western Damaraland, having visited the two-thousand-year-old bushman rock drawings at Twyfelfontein. We were now heading for the infamous Skeleton Coast, one of the most remote and inhospitable regions in Africa, if not the world.

I'd read a lot about this barren, fog shrouded coast of soaring dunes and gravel plains, bordering the icy waters of the South Atlantic. Hundreds of rusting shipwrecks are scattered along the 125 mile long coastline, testament to the treacherous currents and crashing waves which give the area its forbidding name. Early Portuguese sailors called it 'As Areias do Inferno,' The Sands of Hell, as even in the unlikely event of unfortunate seafarers escaping a stranded vessel to reach land, the chances of then surviving the hostile Namib desert were slim.

We were travelling on the remote C39 gravel road, through a Martian landscape of dusty plains and low, rust coloured hills, heading towards the infamous skull and crossbones festooned gates to the Skeleton Coast National Park. With a huge billowing cloud of dust trailing our VW Polo, we hadn't seen another car for almost an hour, when I noticed a hand painted sign by the roadside which read 'Tyre Repairs.' Around a hundred yards distant, set back from the road was a wooden shack with a corrugated iron roof, which I assumed to be the strangely located tyre shop. I'd found that maintaining a speed of around 35mph provided the optimum balance between speed and stability for the thin tyres of the Polo on the rough gravel track. We therefore drove to an accompanying soundtrack of loud bangs and bumps, as stones bounced off the car's undercarriage and we slewed in and out of ruts in the road surface. The noise of our approach had obviously alerted the two occupants of the hut and they ran out excitedly, waving their arms in greeting. We waved back, commenting on how isolated the shack was, for a passing vehicle to cause such excitement.

The cause of the exuberant greeting became apparent a couple of miles down the road. Travelling up a slight incline, I became aware that the back end of the car seemed to be fish-tailing a bit more violently than it had previously. I stopped to investigate and found a fist sized gash in the wall of the now deflated rear tyre. It seemed too much of a coincidence that we'd sustained a puncture a few hundred yards from a tyre repair shop. Unfortunately for the shop's proprietor, the rough road surface we'd been driving on, had conditioned us to alarming noises and erratic handling to such an extent that we hadn't even noticed we had a puncture!

I changed the tyre easily enough. Unfortunately, the spare was a tiny 'space saver,' with about the thickness and tread of a motorcycle tyre. We knew that whilst a four-wheel-drive vehicle isn't absolutely necessary to drive the Skeleton Coast, it is highly recommended. Unfortunately, the cost of a 4x4 had meant we'd decided that a smaller vehicle would have to suffice. This decision had seemed to be vindicated earlier in the trip, when the nifty acceleration of the VW hatchback had outpaced a belligerent adolescent elephant, who'd taken a dislike to us in Etosha National Park. Now, faced with a journey of over a hundred miles through one of earth's most inhospitable and isolated regions, with no spare tyre, it seemed less sensible.

A chill grey blanket of fog was rolling in from the sea as we paused for a photo by the famous skull-adorned entrance gates. I hadn't been over-optimistic enough to expect a gas station at the entrance to the coast road, but I had harboured a faint hope of a shop, or some other sign of life. Unfortunately, there was nothing. Just the two of us, in a tiny car, with a hopelessly inadequate tyre, and no spare. After contending with rough gravel roads, we were now facing a different challenge. The initial stretch of road is constructed from compacted sand and salt, and is therefore totally smooth. Too smooth, in fact. After being soaked by the rolling sea mist, it takes on the characteristics of black ice, making the tyres of even four-wheel-drive vehicles spin alarmingly, with no real grip of the road surface. We therefore proceeded tentatively, peering through the windscreen at a landscape of ill-defined horizons, where the shimmering salt of the road surface merged into a smudged grey sky, occasionally brightened by glimpses of inky blue ocean. Swirling sand drifted across our path, so visibility remained poor, even when the patchy mist cleared, and a faint sun illuminated the road ahead. Kirsty and I had read about the eerie, other-worldly feel of the Skeleton Coast, and now, driving this endless straight road in an ill-equipped vehicle, with no sign of life for miles around, we could fully appreciate the feeling of isolation such a lonely place inspires.

I'd sourced a map of ships wrecked on the coast, and on a couple of occasions we stopped the car, and braved a chill Atlantic wind to hike over the dunes to a deserted beach, where we watched the waves crash over the decaying corpse of an unfortunate vessel, and wondered at the fate of its one-time occupants.

Back on the road, our feeling of making slow progress was heightened by the landscape we were travelling through. Flat, featureless salt plains stretched to the horizon on our left, and to the right, scrubby dunes were punctuated by an occasional glimpse of wave lashed beach. It felt like the loneliest place in the world, and we drove in dread of another blow-out, which would have stranded us there. We'd seen few other vehicles and as late afternoon approached, a night spent stranded on the Skeleton Coast wasn't something we wanted to experience.

We were fast losing the afternoon light as we paused to savour the stench of the huge Cape Fur Seal colony at Cape Cross, before continuing forty miles south, to the only real settlement in the area. The desert village of Henties Bay is set atop towering dunes and blasted by drifting sand and winds whipping in from the South Atlantic. We checked into a motel and raced each other to the shower, eager to wash away the crust of salt we'd accumulated during our drive. Then, relieved to have reached relative civilisation where we could get our tyre repaired, we set off to celebrate, by experiencing the bright lights of the Skeleton Coast.

The first bar we entered was crowded with young locals enjoying the refined pursuit known as 'Tequila Suicide.' i.e. drinking a shot of tequila, snorting a line of salt, then squirting juice from a fresh lime into your own eyeball. We had a quick beer, then left. With a long drive ahead the following day, we didn't feel like being coaxed into participating in this particular local custom. The next bar was a bit more laid back, with soft lighting, piped mood music and a more mature clientele. We pulled up a couple of stools and sat at the bar, alongside a couple in their late fifties who were drinking cocktails.

Again, everyone seemed to be local, and our arrival caused a flurry of interest, not least from our neighbours at the bar, who introduced themselves as Helen and Don, South Africans living in a beachside trailer in the village. Helen had a vaguely reptilian appearance, with thin, weathered brown skin, stretched taut over a skeletal face, beneath dyed brown, bobbed hair. Bright red lipstick highlighted a set of dentures which had obviously been fitted when her head was a lot larger. Consequently, they made frequent attempts to escape from her mouth, only to be recaptured by a combination of an extended, serpentine tongue and flamboyantly puckered lips. Helen's fashion style seemed inspired by a 1950's Parisian brothel, with stick-like fishnet-stockinged legs emerging unappealingly from beneath a black PVC mini skirt. Don had the air of a provincial 1970's newsagent, with a cheap, short-sleeved shirt unbuttoned to chest level, and a pair of beige slacks straining to contain a sizeable beer gut. His thinning hair was teased into tufty spikes on top, and straggly rats-tails at the back, hinting at a one-time mullet. Don's most noticeable feature though, related to his overactive sweat glands. Dark patches patterned his shirt, a glistening sheen reflected the light off his forehead, and tiny perspiration beads rested precariously in the gap between his nose and thin, twitching lips.

Helen and Don were friendly and interested as we told them

about the day's roadtrip adventure. Helen lit a cigarette, and blew the smoke into my face as I spoke, and Don stared at Kirsty, nostrils flaring as he breathed heavily and noisily through his nose, his lips curled in a curious leer. When Helen leant forward to stare into my eyes, to tell me she could see into my soul, I became a little suspicious of the reason for their interest. That suspicion became more pronounced as her bony fingers began to caress my knee, and her lizard tongue lingered a little too long on her lips, after one particularly lengthy battle to regain control of her teeth. I turned to Kirsty with a facial expression that attempted to convey the immortal words of Alan Partridge. "Kirsty, these are sex people!"

Kirsty had already realised that, as Helen told me I had nice hair and began to ruffle it playfully. Meanwhile, Don's underarm sweat patches were expanding rapidly, and seemed destined to meet somewhere near the gold chain nestling in his cleavage. They invited us back to their trailer for some of Don's special cocktails, but we were already explaining that we had a very early start, so were planning an early night. Helen's eyes lit up, and we knew it was time to go. Self-driving is a great way to get off the beaten track and meet the locals. Unfortunately, they can sometimes be a little bit too friendly!

Meeting people in their own environment was, for us, another major draw of self-driving. In the days before sat-nav and worldwide digital map coverage provided by phone apps like Waze, getting lost was a fact of life, and a great way to interact with locals. Appearing suddenly in a location well away from any recognised tourist routes, clutching a map and displaying a suitably confused expression, usually resulted in being viewed like a visitor from another planet. I would smile and engage a likely looking local, pointing at my map and mispronouncing my intended destination. I would estimate that in 90% of cases, it would quickly become apparent that the person I'd selected had never previously used, or maybe even seen, a map. Often, they would peruse it studiously, tracing a route with their finger, and nodding sagely. Then I would notice they were holding it upside down!

With my chosen local 'guide' looking baffled, a crowd would quickly gather. My map would be passed between a variety of seemingly knowledgeable locals, who would loudly debate the best way to reach my desired location. With no shared language, directions were often eventually provided via complex diagrams drawn on my map, or some other scrap of paper provided by a helpful onlooker. Heated arguments would sometimes develop with raised voices and flailing hand signals. In most cases I would return to the car and Kirsty would say "do we know the way then?" I'd nod and drive off, waving to my crowd of new friends, then invariably have to stop again a mile down the road to ask someone else.

We got lost in a Brazilian Favela and the Costa Rican jungle, where we had to rely on an aged woman and a six year old child to guide us across a flooded river. We drove for miles along a mountain track in Bosnia, which ended abruptly at an isolated farm, where we were taken in, fed, watered and redirected by a bemused family of cowherds. We've taught countless impromptu English lessons in village schools (generally focussed on animal noises!) Asking directions also resulted in me helping to wash a cow in a river in Ukraine, and milk a herd of goats in Syria. Kirsty and I have also participated in an assortment of roadside agricultural activities; picking, planting, ploughing, hoeing and threshing, after stopping to ask field-hands the way on rural roads around the world.

On a gloomy June afternoon, we were attempting to negotiate the confusing sprawl of roads south of the Armenian capital, Yerevan, in a rented Lada 4x4, which resembled a small armoured car and handled like one too. After enjoying some amazing scenery on our trip through the Caucasus, we were now experiencing the grim architectural flipside of the former Soviet states. We were travelling through a 'Mad Max' style, post-apocalyptic, industrial landscape of soot-coated factories, and ugly concrete edifices adorned with the undecipherable swirls and squiggles of the Armenian alphabet. Road signs were equally bamboozling, and it was no surprise that we were hopelessly lost.

I pulled up next to a row of roadside butcher's stalls, where youths in blood spattered white overalls hacked the meat from carcasses suspended on hooks, watched by flocks of tethered, nervous sheep. The smell of lamb kebabs sizzling on a charcoal grill alongside each stall made my mouth water, and the presence of your evening meal, bleating and moaning next to the barbecue on which it would be roasted, gave a new meaning to 'farm fresh' produce.

I was greeted by a grinning crowd of young butchers, with the usual mixture of bemusement, hand-shakes and eagerness to help. There followed the familiar ritual of holding the map upside down and shouted arguments about where I was heading and the best route to take. We were soon pointed on our way, chewing on a welcome sample of tangy, juicy grilled lamb, infused with the scent of woodsmoke and diesel fumes.

After driving for a couple more miles along a dual carriageway clogged with trucks belching toxic black smoke, it was clear that we were still lost. I could see the apartment blocks and government buildings of Yerevan, framed beneath the snow-capped peaks of Mount Ararat away to my left, so decided that heading in that vague direction would be the best course to follow. Checking my mirror before changing lanes, I spotted an old black Mercedes with tinted windows and headlights on full beam, weaving in and out of the traffic a few hundred yards behind us. Clearly in a hurry, the driver was taking no prisoners, as he pulled onto the opposing carriageway and drove into the flow of traffic, headlights flashing and horn blasting. Kirsty noticed my furrowed expression and began to observe the car in the side mirror.

"Undercover police?" she wondered.

"Maybe. Or perhaps gangsters escaping the police."

The somewhat 'pimped' appearance of the car made this seem more likely, and we monitored its progress as it leap-frogged the traffic behind us, until we were the next vehicle in its path. I had no desire to become embroiled in a road rage incident with the obviously suicidal driver, who was now almost nudging our rear bumper, so I slowed down to allow him to pass. Unfortunately, he seemed to slow down too, so I pulled into the inside lane. Again, he tucked in right behind me, lights flashing and the rasp from his illegal exhaust clearly audible.

We'd been made aware of the potential danger of bandits and highway robbery in remote areas of Georgia and Armenia, but hadn't been expecting to be targeted this close to a capital city. I decided I wasn't going down without a fight. "Hang on," I said to Kirsty, and crunched the gear stick forward into third. A quick check over my shoulder to ensure the outside lane was clear, and I rammed my foot down on the accelerator. The Lada jerked forward, engine screaming and tyres spinning. I overtook a couple of trucks and a slow moving car, then ducked back into the inside lane in a classic evasion manoeuvre. Unfortunately, within seconds, the Mercedes had replicated my move, and was again tucked in right behind me, clearly demonstrating that this wasn't paranoia. We really were being 'tailed.'

I reasoned that as long as we kept driving, it was unlikely the bandits would force us off a busy main road, so we just needed to make sure we didn't take a wrong turn down a quiet side street. We carried on for another mile with the Mercedes virtually hanging off our rear bumper, headlights flashing and horn occasionally sounding, the dark tinted windscreen making it impossible to see the faces of our pursuers. Suddenly, on a long straight stretch of road, the driver made his move and accelerated to pull alongside us, maintaining his position as I attempted to accelerate away. Slowly, the passenger window opened, and a blood-stained hand slowly emerged, closely followed by the familiar, grinning face of one of the roadside butchers. As Kirsty and I breathed a huge sigh of relief, the smiling youth signalled that we were to follow their car, and swerved in front of me. A hair raising ten minutes later, after we'd car-chased the Mercedes on a complicated, high speed route, we reached a large intersection, where the kindly boy-racer butchers pointed us in the correct direction. They then executed a spectacular U-turn and screeched back the way they'd come, with a final blast on the horn and smoke pouring from their rear tyres.

It was another chance encounter which turned into a memorable experience, typical of the type of interaction with locals that self-driving can provide, and one of the reasons I always choose to drive myself if I can. That's not always easy to arrange though, as I found when trying to plan our Sri Lankan trip.

Despite being strongly advised to rent a car with a local driver, I persevered and eventually located a small local rental company near the airport in Negombo, with a handful of self-drive cars, all bearing the welcome, tell-tale scars of a few years active service on the roads of the Indian Ocean island.We'd been in Sri Lanka for over a week when we collected the car, having travelled by train and local bus, so had chance to observe the local driving style, which, as in most places, actually did follow some form of driving etiquette, though one which was obviously markedly different from that in Europe. The main difference was that, as in most parts of the developing world, you needed to remember that the most important function of your vehicle is the horn. This must be used every time you pass another vehicle, or pedestrian, and as soon as a red light turns green. Having quickly mastered the basic local rules, driving in Sri Lanka wasn't difficult, and despite the warnings of death and disaster on the Lonely Planet forum, we came home from the trip unscathed. Although, that isn't strictly true.

We had an enjoyable few days exploring the cave temple complex at Dambulla, the ancient City of Polonnaruwa, and the two hundred metre-high rock fortress at Sigiriya, fully enjoying the freedom afforded by having our own car. Unfortunately, our visit to Sigiriya, the spectacular column of rock which housed the 5th Century court of King Kasyapa, was to prove costly. With two days of our trip remaining, we decided to hike the steep staircase carved into the rockface, to see the ancient painted frescoes and 'mirror wall' at the summit. The mirror wall is adorned with some of the oldest 'graffiti' in the world, with poems, messages and etchings from visitors going back as far as the 8th century, but scaling the rock proved a long, steep climb in the searing midday heat. We'd underestimated the challenge and hadn't taken enough water, meaning we arrived at the rock's plateau sweating profusely, red faced and thirsty, though we agreed that the view across the surrounding jungle was well worth the climb.

Whether it was delayed heat exhaustion, the result of a dubious prawn curry or the amount of Lion Beer we consumed at our lakeside hotel that evening, both Kirsty and I were suffering the following day. Shivering, sweating and feeling lethargic, plus being troubled by violent intestinal disturbances, it was a rare occasion where we were both confined to our room for the whole morning. In the afternoon, I felt a little better and having forced myself to get up, borrowed a cycle from the hotel, leaving Kirsty slumped in a chair on our balcony, swatting at mosquitos while overlooking a lily-covered lake.

I set off to explore the ancient ruins of a scattered temple complex in the forest close to the hotel. After pedalling in the heat for around half an hour, I began to regret leaving my sickbed. Sweat soaked my t-shirt and poured down my burning face, yet I'd began to shiver uncontrollably, and my whole body ached. The lack of suspension on the bike didn't help and as I bumped along into a wooded clearing, I was overcome by a terrible wave of nausea. I dropped the bike, sank to my knees and vomited spectacularly into the undergrowth. After ten minutes of prolonged retching, then dry-heaving, I was exhausted. I crawled a few feet to escape the colourful mound of puke I'd deposited, rolled onto my back and closed my eyes. My face was shaded by the forest canopy, but the dappled rays of early afternoon sun poured through the branches high above, to warm my fever-chilled body. The wind rustling the leaves and surround-sound of forest birdsong were better than any 'chill-out' relaxation apps. I was soon asleep.

I was woken by the sensation of movement close by, and blinked open my eyes as I tried to work out where I was. The sun had shifted, leaving me in the shade, so I guessed I'd been asleep for around an hour. My mouth was dry and my body still ached, though my shivers had subsided. I slowly turned my head to the left to see what had woken me, and my gaze was met by a pair of large brown eyes staring back at me from around five feet away. It was a male Chital deer, sporting an impressive set of three-pronged antlers. Grazing close by were a female and two fawns, their golden coats flecked with bright white spots, explaining the species' other name, the Ceylonese Spotted Deer. The deer family seemed unworried by my presence, and I remained still, watching the adults graze on buttercups, as their offspring amused themselves skipping about the clearing, chasing butterflies. Lying in the shade of a thousand-year-old ruin, in a peaceful sunlit forest, with only the forest creatures for company, I reflected that there were much worse places to be ill.

Then to emphasise that point, I was suddenly transported a few thousand miles to the west, by that familiarly annoying soundtrack of the new millenium– The Nokia ringtone. I'd brought my phone in case Kirsty needed to reach me, and now it was vibrating and beeping out its shrill tune in in my pocket, to shatter the woodland tranquillity. The deer family bolted as I scrabbled in my shorts to see which colleague didn't understand the meaning of an international ring-tone. The unanswered call was from Simon, one of our company's sales managers, and I pictured him crawling along in the drizzly gloom of a morning M62 rush hour, as I reclined in a sunlit forest clearing, communing with wildlife like a sick-spattered Dr.Doolittle. I rose unsteadily to my feet, just in time to see a skinny black dog greedily devouring my now congealed pile of vomit. I retrieved my bike and began a shaky journey back through the woods to the hotel.

A day later I was negotiating the chaotic roads of Negombo, as we attempted to locate the sidestreet office of the car rental company. As rickshaws, scooters and cycles buzzed around us like annoyingly persistent flies, I decided that I'd still rather be driving in Sri Lanka than joining Simon on that dismal trans-Pennine motorway commute. It was hard to believe that I'd be back there in a couple of days, trying to adjust back to European driving, and hopefully remembering not to sound my horn every time I overtook a lorry on the M56!

9 PLANES, TRAINS AND AUTOMOBILES. AND BOATS.

"Daddy, I need a wee-wee. Please can we stop?" Our driver had been wriggling in his seat for a few miles, and now he looked at me in the rear-view mirror with pleading eyes. He tugged at his wispy goatee beard in agitation, and his discomfort was obvious. I sighed impatiently and scanned the road ahead.

"Okay. You can stop next to those trees. But be quick."

"Oh, thank you daddy, I am so grateful." He beamed a thankful smile into the mirror.

We were in a taxi travelling between the Ghanaian Capital, Accra, and the border with neighbouring Togo. In West Africa, familial titles are used in everyday speech as a friendly term. Therefore, a person of the same age will refer to you as brother or sister. An older person will be called mother or father, or the less formal mummy and daddy. My role as 'father' to William, our twenty-something taxi driver, had been firmly established in the initial miles of open road beyond the traffic choked boundaries of the city. William was soon displaying the worrying driving style typical of taxis and mini-buses in that part of the world. High speed overtaking whilst checking his phone, passing slow moving vehicles on blind bends and hills, and looking at me in the passenger seat, rather than at the road, as he waved his arms and pondered loudly whether Arsene Wenger would ever lead his beloved Arsenal to another league title.

After repeated ignored warnings, I'd had enough, and decided that William had to be 'grounded.' After making him stop the car, I administered a severe ticking off, which caused him to gulp and hang his head in contrition. I actually thought he was on the verge of tears, as I told him that any more dangerous driving would result in his immediate dismissal. (Though how that would work in the middle of the Ghanaian bush was unclear). In order to monitor his performance, I would join Kirsty in the back seat, where I could keep a close eye on the road, and on his driving. William would need to seek my approval before any further overtaking.

"I'm sorry, Daddy." William had looked mournful at the prospect of losing his best fare of the year, and his driving unsurprisingly improved from that point. Proceeding at a more sensible pace, a truck on the horizon would elicit a glance in the mirror from William, and a quizzical raised eyebrow. I'd survey the situation and either advise caution with a shake of the head, or grant permission to overtake, with the air of a parent allowing a child a ride on a merry-go-round.

"Go on then William, but be careful."

"Thank you, Daddy!"

I'd like to think William learnt something from my fatherly advice that day, which has enabled him to stay safe on the often lawless roads of Ghana. I also wonder if he remembers the day he experienced the absolute definition of a backseat driver, with a traveller who hates having someone else in the driving seat!

Whilst self-drive is always my preferred method of travelling, other forms of transport are sometimes necessary or preferable. As was the case in Ghana, crossing international borders can be expensive, or forbidden in a rental car, and distance, timescales and the geography of a country may mean that driving yourself is simply not practical.

Often though, the journey becomes an essential part of the trip, and although using a particular mode of transport may not be the quickest, or most comfortable option, it's likely to result in exposure to greater adventure, removed from your comfort zone, whilst travelling like the locals.

Travelling by rail, especially on overnight sleeper trains is a great way to cover long distances. I love train travel in India, legs dangling from an open carriage door, as you trundle through the mist shrouded countryside at dawn, waving to the crowds of sleepy-eyed, smiling locals crapping by the trackside. Generally, I sleep well on trains, but an Indian six berth sleeper compartment, separated from the busy corridor by a curtain, isn't conducive to a restful night. It's a strange experience to nod off with your face feeling the gentle caress of pungent breath from an elderly, handlebar-moustachioed Sikh book salesman sleeping opposite. Then to wake up, seemingly minutes later, to find two giggling newlyweds snuggling up in the bunk in front of you in his place. On one occasion, as can easily happen in India, Kirsty had fallen ill when we took an overnight train from Kochi to Mumbai. After spending a listless, fevered day without food, the last thing she wanted was a journey on a crowded, delayed overnight train. She slumped on the floor of the station with our backpacks while I went to seek out water, and fell asleep. I returned to find her laying amidst a depressing floorbound assembly of mutilated beggars and mange riddled stray dogs. Predictably, I couldn't resist taking a photo, which I don't think she's ever fully forgiven me for. The upside of being ill was that she fell into a deep state of semi-consciousness once on board the train, and slept all night, while I was disturbed by a constant conveyor belt of cabin mates.

Eastern European night trains are a great experience too, allowing you to visit multiple countries on a short trip, using the train as a mobile hotel, though the formidable, and often muscular, female carriage attendants are often a little short on customer service skills and leave you in no doubt over who's in charge of their specific carriage!

Travelling by boat can also be an interesting experience, though it's important to check out the size and reliability of the vessel you intend to catch. We arrived at the port of Entebbe in Uganda seeking the 'comfortable car ferry' which was to take us across the choppy waters of ocean-sized Lake Victoria to the Ssese Islands. I thought the harbourmaster was joking when he told us the ferry was 'broken' and pointed us towards an aging wooden pirogue canoe, powered by two huge outboard motors, and already crammed full of locals and their colourful cargo. The journey by ferry across the huge body of water was supposed to take around three hours, and the youthful skipper assured me his boat was 'very fast' and wouldn't take longer than four, as he baled alarming volumes of water from the canoe with a plastic bucket.

Not one of the glum looking passengers had a life jacket, and the boat already seemed dangerously overloaded. We surveyed the situation, and considered our slim chances of survival if the boat were to hit a submerged object or spring a leak. Less dramatic, but almost as important, we had four days left of our two-week trip, and it was the rainy season when storms were frequent. The ferry would sail whatever the weather, but if this small boat couldn't make the return trip, we'd be stranded. Our decision to turn down the last two seats on the boat was vindicated when we heard a few days later that the same boat had broken down during a storm, and the terrified passengers were left drifting amidst high seas for two hours before being rescued by a passing fishing boat.

Sometimes though, travelling by slow-boat is the only way to go and can prove to be a highlight of a trip, as was the case when we travelled down the Irrawaddy River from the former Burmese capital of Mandalay to the ancient city of Bagan. It was 2009, Aung San Suu Kyi was still under house arrest and Myanmar was subject to a boycott by most western travel companies. I loved South East Asia though, and was intrigued by the mysterious pariah state, ruled with an iron rod by a cabal of billionaire military generals. I did my research and decided that by avoiding certain travel agents, airlines and hotel chains, it was possible to travel independently in the country without putting any of my dollars into the pockets of the ruling junta.

We'd therefore forgone the fast Government funded 'tourist' boat to take the slower local option - an ancient, wooden two-tiered vessel with open decks. Our journey began in the dark 4am chill of a Mandalay morning, as we headed towards the pungent city docks. We'd read on the Lonely Planet forum that the journey should take around twelve hours, but regularly took fifteen, and one unfortunate couple informed the Burma message board that they'd staggered ashore in Bagan a full twenty six hours after departing Mandalay.

The pre-dawn air was thick with the smell of drifting smoke from the day's first breakfast fires, as we teetered aboard along creaking planks, and stepped over blanket-covered locals snoring on the wooden deck. First light revealed a floating microcosm of Burmese life. Peasants with trussed poultry; teenage girls, faces smeared with yellow thanaka paste for protection against the sun; monks and shaven headed novices; old women with bright red betel stained teeth; Government spies and itinerant junior salesmen in shirts and ties and llonghi robes; blind beggars and their child guides, and all manner of hawkers, including an old woman selling baby owls from a basket, shared the cramped upper deck with us. Downstairs was a deck bulging with crates of produce, scooters and cycles, cowering livestock and the occasional slumbering stevedore.

There were around a dozen western travellers on board and as we departed at 6am, a crimson sun appeared over the pagodas on the far bank, and an onboard party of national stereotypes broke out. A French family of middle aged parents and two teenaged offspring cracked open a bottle of wine, and began tucking into a parcel of cheese. The three Polish students slammed down shot glasses of Vodka with their mohinga fish noodle soup, and an elderly American couple handed out fruit muffins and paper cups of coffee from a flask, as we chugged along to the sound of temple bells calling monks for morning meditation.

By eleven the sun was high in the sky, and passengers and crew were visibly wilting in the sticky heat. Everyone manoeuvred into a shaded space and dozed fitfully on the deck. We stopped at every village en-route and our arrival would generally be heralded by a child's shouted alert, which would propel every merchant into a frenzied race towards the muddy banks of the river, their wares balancing precariously on their heads as they stumbled to meet us. Wooden carts drawn by white hump-backed oxen would be despatched to the water's edge, to be loaded with bags of flour by perspiring stevedores, their ripped frames and thick coating of white dust making them look like ghostly bodybuilders. A stern faced, one eyed boatman prevented the hawkers from getting onboard, so all business was transacted via an exchange system of tossed produce and bundles of tattered kyat banknotes. Enterprising kids waded in the shallows to retrieve badly aimed bananas and raffia baskets, before selling them back to their original owners.

A blast of the boat's horn would signal our departure. Gangplanks would be withdrawn, and we'd drift back out into the slow flowing Irrawaddy. The somnolent air on board would soon return. Cheroot cigars would be lit, betel wrapped and chewed, hats pulled over faces, and the onboard community would lapse into another period of lethargic dozing, and bank-gazing silent reflection as the boat chugged on towards Bagan.

I'd spotted a wooden cabin at the stern on the top deck, and went to investigate who could be travelling in this hut-like 'VIP Lounge.' I poked my head round the door and was greeted by the smiling faces of six monks, clad in maroon robes and ranging in age from late teens to early eighties. Accompanying them was a young novice, aged about six, his little head freshly shaved to a 'Grade 1' sheen for the journey. This separate travelling space is designed to provide monks with a tranquil space to meditate and also to prevent any contact with women, one of the 227 rules which make up the Patimokkha, or strict code of monastic discipline in Theravada Buddhism. Only on this occasion, the cabin had the feel of a lads' coach trip to the seaside, with a fug of aniseed scented smoke from the eldest monk's loosely packed cheroot, and the crackle of a small transistor radio, its aerial extended out of the window to maximise the weak signal. With no shared language, our meeting was limited to smiles and handshakes, and a photo of the little novice eliciting a gap-toothed grin upon seeing his own image in my camera's viewfinder.

At around 6pm, the sun dipped quickly towards the horizon and we were treated to a kaleidoscopic sunset perfectly reflected in the inky waters of the river. Soon, the banks disappeared into the blackness of a moonless night, and an elderly Englishman with eyebrows like squirrel tails approached us.

"Have you noticed that light?" he asked, pointing out a lantern flickering on the shore on the port side of the boat. "Keep watching it."

We stood and stared into the gloom, with the slow moving light our only point of reference. We tracked it as it edged towards the front of the boat, then to the starboard side, then to the rear, and finally back to the port side where we'd seen it originally.

"I knew it! We're going in circles...we're lost!" Our fellow traveller exclaimed triumphantly. I decided to investigate, and picked my way carefully through an obstacle course of passengers lying on the decks to arrive at the bridge, where I found the crew desperately trying to navigate through a section of treacherous sandbanks. With no radar or sonar, the aged craft's navigational technology stretched no further than a skinny twelve year-old boy in a ragged vest, standing at the bow of the boat, prodding the river bed with a bamboo pole. Peering into the darkness and clutching the wooden rail in front of me, my eyes followed the powerful beam of a lamp scanning the featureless banks of the river. The captain and first mate stood behind me, the tips of their cheroots glowing in the blackness as they desperately sought an identifying landmark. No one spoke, and the tension was palpable. Misreading the treacherous shoals in this part of the river would likely result in grounding, then stranding of the vessel. The twenty six hour marathon journey mentioned on the Lonely Planet forum, wasn't a record we wanted to break.

Suddenly the beam of light flashed across a ruined temple stupa, the first mate yelled a warning and the captain's cheroot fell from his mouth as he began to furiously spin the ancient wooden ship's wheel. The pole-prodding boy was almost propelled into the water as the boat listed suddenly, and we heard crates sliding along the deck above us. I cringed and waited for the sound of the wooden hull crunching into sand, but the boy prodded the water in front of us and gave his boss the thumbs up. The sighs of relief were audible, grins flashed and backs were slapped as the three Burmese congratulated each other on their navigational skills.

Eventually clear of the hazardous shallows, the captain sounded a triumphant blast on the horn, and we steamed on towards Bagan. Around sixteen hours after departing Mandalay, we arrived at a muddy foreshore crammed with a rambunctious gaggle of would-be porters, hotel touts, horse carts and market stalls illuminated by paraffin lamps. We hauled our packs onto our backs and wobbled across creaking planks to try and find a lift to our hotel. A succession of locals with their ubiquitous red betel stained teeth informed us that there were no motorised taxis, and that a cart hauled by an aged pony with protruding ribs was our only option. Suddenly our choice of hotel, five miles away, didn't seem such a great idea. However, laying in the back of the cart, heads resting on our bags, as we rattled along rutted country lanes, we enjoyed an amazing celestial light show with more stars than we'd ever seen illuminating the inky black sky, and suddenly we were glad there were no taxis.

We eventually arrived at our hotel, which I'd been told faced onto the Bagan Plain, site of the ruins of two thousand temples and pagodas, constructed in the eleventh and twelfth centuries. After being led to our room by two tiny, ten-year-old twin bell-hops, I optimistically opened the patio doors, hoping to spot some ancient Buddhist architecture in the darkness. Our room opened onto a small, raised section of wooden decking, overlooking what I assumed was a grassed area leading to the plain. It was pitch black and I couldn't see a thing, so stepped off the decking to explore.

Kirsty was in the room, starting to unpack her bag when she heard the splash. She dashed outside to see my head bobbing just above the surface of the green-slime filled pond into which I'd just plunged. The air was filled with a cacophony of croaking from the thousands of frogs I'd disturbed with my unintended exploration of their natural habitat. Kirsty was momentarily speechless before coming out with the predictable comment of "What are you doing in there?"

I managed to propel myself through the filthy quagmire and dragged myself back onto the decking, caked from head to toe in pond filth and smelling like a Rangoon sewer. As I headed to the bathroom to clean up, there was a knock at the door. I opened it to find the two twin boys bearing towels. Four eyes widened and two little mouths fell open at the terrible apparition which greeted them. Less than five minutes earlier, they had delivered their guest safely to his room. I now stood before them dripping wet and caked in stinking, aquatic slime. I took the towels from them as they recoiled nervously, gave them a big smile and told them that I thought the pool might need cleaning. Not surprisingly they went out of their way to avoid me for the remainder of our stay!

Whilst I have some amazing memories of trips undertaken by boat and train, I have little enthusiasm for road travel where I'm not in control of the vehicle. Long distance journeys by taxi and bus are to be avoided at all costs as far as I'm concerned.

One of the problems with renting a taxi or private hire vehicle, aside from poor driving ability, is that the driver often tries to expand his role, in order to increase his earnings by becoming an impromptu tour guide. Anyone who has been unwillingly taken on an unexpected detour to 'my brother's shop,' only to spend two hours being harangued into buying carpets, precious stones, herbs and spices or other unwanted local produce, by a high-pressure salesman, knows how tediously soul destroying this can be.

'Owning the passenger' in order to ensure further custom can also be a problem, with persistent drivers hanging around outside your hotel waiting to ambush you every time you attempt to leave, then acting like a distraught, betrayed lover when you tell them you'd prefer to walk. Our most dramatic encounter with a spurned taxi driver occurred in the mysterious Balkan nation of Albania.

Albania is a fascinating land, governed by a complex series of ancient laws known as the Kanun. These cover all aspects of life, and are largely based around a code of honour, the Kanun of Lek Dukagjin, which, amongst other laws and traditions, defines the rules of 'Gjakmarrya,' or blood feud. This Kanun states that 'If a man is deeply affronted, he has the right to kill the person who insulted him. However, he will then become a target for revenge by the victim's family. The victim's closest male relative is obliged to kill the murderer of his family member.'

This ongoing, tit-for-tat cycle of honour killing often spans multiple generations and can result in the eventual annihilation of whole clans. The importance of honour and not 'losing face' cannot therefore be understated in Albania. The Kanun states that 'A man who has lost his honour automatically becomes a dead man.' In other words, it's not the sort of place you want to spill someone's pint on a night out.

It had been made very clear when I collected my hire car in Croatia, that on no account could it be taken into Albania. When I asked why, the desk clerk cast a furtive glance over her shoulder and hissed 'bandits!' We therefore decided to park at the border post in neighbouring Montenegro, and walk across into Albania, where we could pick up a taxi to the city of Shkodër. The border was a low-key affair in scrubby countryside. A disinterested customs official waved us through the barrier, towards a small group of taxi drivers dozing in the sun. None looked particularly eager to transport us the ten miles into town in their rusting Ladas.

One vehicle stood out amongst the rest. A gleaming red 1980's BMW, with leopardskin seat covers and sporting an array of Bayern Munich merchandise. Its driver snored in the front seat, a full head of greying curls evoking memories of the Keeganesque late 70s perm. The driver's drooping walrus moustache twitched in time with each loud exhalation.

I tapped on the window, and he lazily opened one eye, before leaping to attention as he registered the fact that a foreigner was seeking a ride. In a flash he was on his feet, grinning and ushering us into the backseat, whilst chuckling and taunting his snoozing colleagues at missing out on a lucrative payday.

His name was Erjon, and his eagerness to become our driver, fixer, tour guide and general Albanian tourism one-stop shop, was only mildly tempered by the fact that he spoke hardly a word of

English. Undeterred, he happily chattered away to us in a hybrid language of Albanian and German, with a smattering of English, supplemented by flamboyant hand signals. The latter were particularly unnerving as we tore along the country lanes at breakneck speed. Erjon seemed to know the road so well that he generally found it unnecessary to look through the windscreen, allowing him to keep his eyes fixed on me, in the rear-view mirror, as he attempted to negotiate a price for his services for the day.

If any slow-moving locals or livestock happened to stray into our path, Erjon flicked a switch beside the steering wheel to employ a high-tech horn system, which blasted out a sudden, terrifying, ear splitting burst of Beethoven's Victory Symphony. We cringed as we looked back at elderly ladies on cycles sent spinning into ditches, yelping dogs scampering for cover and, on one occasion, a distraught toddler forced to watch a favourite toy truck reduced to shrapnel beneath Erjon's wheels of steel.

Eventually we arrived in Shkodër and Erjon's hand-signalled negotiations to become our guide descended into a blur of fingers, knuckles and palms. Anticipating an awkward day of being shown the limited sights of the city by a frustrated rally driver who spoke little English, I attempted to call a halt to the proceedings by paying. Seeing his opportunity for further monetary gain vanishing, Erjon reluctantly accepted my payment, but thrust his business card firmly into my hand, to which he applied a steely grip, whilst staring hard into my eyes, and nodding slowly. The message was clear - I may not be your guide, but I alone am your driver. You WILL use me to return to the border. I nodded and put the card in my back pocket, patting it and nodding solemnly to reassure Erjon, who looked close to tears.

Shkodër was somewhat underwhelming, and it was no surprise that we seemed to be the only tourists in town that day. Possibly that year. There was a litter strewn, ruined castle and a dirty river, where we saw an old man hanging a large and depressing collection of post-wash underpants on a bush to dry. There were long, dusty roads and shops with curious window displays of plant pots and paint brushes. My abiding memory though, is of a spectacularly tattooed child of around eleven years old, smoking a small cigar, who met my surprised gaze and returned it, accompanied by a slowly raised index finger. I ducked my head and hurried on, eager not to offend his honour in any way.

By late afternoon, the heat had sapped our energy and we decided to make our way back to the border. We plodded along a non-descript, signless main road, sweating, thirsty and lost. A car horn sounded behind me, and I turned to see a taxi slowing down and flashing its lights. Not Erjon's gleaming München-mobile, but a taxi nonetheless. I guiltily touched the business card in my pocket as we climbed into the back seat. "We'd never be able to explain to Erjon where to pick us up anyway," I reassured Kirsty unconvincingly as we pulled away from the kerb.

We soon left the city centre and headed out into the open country leading to the Montenegrin border. I began to relax as the Soviet era apartment blocks retreated in the rear-view mirror. We crossed a rickety wooden bridge over a river and turned left at a cafe on the far bank. As we passed, I glanced to my right and made fleeting eye contact with a customer sat at a pavement table. I tried to convince myself that curly perms were still highly popular in Albania that summer, and the walrus moustache was far more common than it had been in the rest of Europe since the mid seventies. However, I couldn't help turning and scanning the road behind me. Empty. I breathed again and stared ahead.

It was the reaction of our driver which told me something was amiss. A furrowed brow and a muttered curse as he glanced in the rear-view mirror. I sank low in my seat, fearing the worst, but hoping I was wrong. That vain hope disappeared altogether, with the first unmistakable blast of Beethoven's Fifth Symphony. We turned in our seats to see the red bonnet of Erjon's Beamer, around three inches from the rear of our vehicle. Erjon was clearly not happy, arms flailing and shouting angrily, he seemed to be engaged in a very violent argument with an invisible passenger. Our driver continued to monitor the pursuit in his mirror. His verdict of 'he a crazy man,' wasn't cheerfully received on the backseat, where I contemplated the uncomfortable fact that, having offended Erjon's honour, I seemed to have instigated my very own Albanian blood feud.

Erjon blasted his horn and pulled alongside us on the single-track road, while spitting threats as he raced along beside us. We all react in strange ways to fear and for some reason my own defence mechanism was to smile and wave to our pursuer. Not surprisingly, this enraged him further and he swerved in front of us, causing our bemused driver to come to an abrupt halt.

Erjon's car was parked across the road and he sprang from the driver's seat and strode towards us. Kirsty sank low in her seat and our driver turned to me and uttered the reassuring words, 'he a very bad man.' After quickly taking in our surroundings and deciding there was no escape route, I decided that if I was to meet my end, cowering in the backseat of a taxi would be a less than honourable exit. I got out of the car and employed my usual smiling face tactic, and a friendly "Hi Erjon, how are you..."

Before I had chance to lie that I'd somehow lost his business card, or that my phone battery had died, he launched into a frightening tirade of Albanian abuse, whilst thumping his heart with his fist, his nose positioned around an inch from mine. After a couple of minutes of incomprehensible profanity, his parting gesture was to hawk up a throatful of phlegm, which he deposited loudly by my feet, before stalking back to his car, and firing up the engine.

Erjon's tactic was now to drive at around 5mph in front of us, swerving occasionally to prevent our taxi overtaking him. He seemed to be weighing up his options. Our driver shook his head and muttered a curse in Albanian, before meeting my eyes in the mirror. "Very, very bad man," he confirmed again. We eventually arrived at the border and Erjon pulled up in front of us. We paid our driver and exited our vehicle at pace, trying to appear nonchalant as we strode towards the Montenegrin border, and safety. Unfortunately, I couldn't resist the urge to look back, and saw Erjon scrabbling in the glovebox of his car, with our driver seemingly remonstrating with him.

Suddenly, all became clear, as every psycho-thriller stalker movie and cold-war spy flick morphed into a nightmare vision in my brain. Erjon would obviously exact his revenge by shooting us at the very point we entered the no-mans-land between Albania and Montenegro. The murders would therefore take place between countries, and the bureaucratic judicial confusion would enable him to avenge the insult to his honour, but remain free. The perfect crime.

I've left countries in a number of unusual ways, but none so strange as that day. The two young Montenegrin border guards stood open-mouthed as Kirsty and I sprinted towards them, lurching from side to side as I yelled 'Zig Zag!!' and employed my best bullet evasion technique.

Our passports stamped, I felt it safe to look back towards Albania. Erjon was leaning on his taxi, munching on the large baguette he'd retrieved from his glovebox. Catching my eye, he began shouting some undecipherable insults, accompanied by an array of hand signals which definitely traversed our previous language barrier. I waved him goodbye, grateful that I'd seemingly offended the honour of an Albanian and survived, although I never have dared to revisit the country since!

Whilst travel by taxi is by no means my favourite mode of transport, I would have to say it's preferable to my absolute nemesis - travel by bus. Correction, travel by long-distance bus. Using local buses to get around cities can be great fun, and a good way to interact with the locals. The 'Reggae-Reggae' buses of the Caribbean with their huge, ear-splitting sound systems are an incomparable way to start a night out. I love sitting at the back of the bus with a classic roots reggae track blasting through the speakers, watching the heads of all on board – grannies in church bonnets, schoolkids in uniform, smart suited secretaries, ganja toking rude boys, all nodding in unison to the bone-jarring beat.

A similar mobile musical journey can be experienced at the other side of the world, while riding in the jeepneys of the Philippines. Originally converted from US Army jeeps, left in the country at the end of World War 2, the jeepney is the main public transport option in Filipino cities and an icon of the country. Carefully customised with garish paintwork and a surfeit of chrome, jeepneys proudly display their name -'King of the Road,' 'Driving Machine,' 'Business Man,' alongside Catholic religious imagery, and multiple mirrors, horns and mascots, making each vehicle totally unique. Passengers sit on bench seats in the rear and fares are passed down the line to the driver. How he knows where each passenger got on, is getting off, and how much cash they passed him is one of the great mysteries of travel, but they always seem to get it right. As in the Caribbean, the music system is a vital component of the jeepney, though the musical style is quite different, with a tendency towards tinny Pinoy pop and western eighties classics. I recall a memorable journey in one of Manila's fifty thousand jeepneys, with every passenger jigging in their seats and singing along to Rod Stewart's greatest hits. We were enjoying ourselves so much that we decided to stay on board long beyond our intended stop, and spent an hour rocking out to a soundtrack of 'Maggie May' and 'Do ya think I'm sexy?' Joining fifteen Filipino commuters in an arm waving chorus of 'I am Sailing,' as we roared through the steamy, neon-lit streets of the Philippines capital city, is an experience I'd love to repeat some day!

I have few such fond memories of any long distance bus journey I've been forced to endure though. I've travelled on enough buses in India to know that you should always sit in the middle of the vehicle, so you are afforded maximum protection from any impact, though seat position is unlikely to save you if the bus goes over a cliff edge. In Southern India, I watched in horror as our driver tore through a busy town on the wrong side of the road, in a kamikaze overtaking manoeuvre which forced oncoming vehicles to swerve off the road and onto the footpath. The culmination of this deadly driving display was to run down a pedestrian who was stupid enough to be walking along the roadside, whilst only monitoring the oncoming vehicles. Clearly not expecting a fifty two-seater to be approaching from the rear, he was taken by surprise as we clipped him at speed, and sent his limp body spinning into a swampy ditch. The incident was horrific to witness but didn't deter our driver, who ploughed on regardless, scattering scooters, rickshaws, tuk-tuks and pedestrians to the soundtrack of a continuous horn blast.

The worst bus journey of my life though, was an inter-country journey in Eastern Europe, between the Moldovan capital of Chisinau, and the West Ukrainian city of Chernivtsi. The day had started badly. Correction – things had started to go wrong at the trip's planning stage, when I found it wasn't possible to rent a car in Moldova and return it in Ukraine, probably due to a lucrative cross border trade in stolen vehicles which the authorities were vainly trying to control. As the Lonely Planet put it, 'in the country which ranks as the poorest in Europe, you may be tempted to question why every second car in Chisinau is a BMW, Mercedes or Audi. Answer - Don't ask.'

Car rental therefore wasn't an option, and the train from Chisinau to the historic, cobble-stoned city of Lviv, took at least twenty hours to rattle along two hundred miles of track, with no sleeper compartment. I therefore decided that our best option would be to catch the overnight bus to Chernivtsi, the first large town across the Ukrainian border where I could rent a car, and then self-drive the remaining distance to Lviv. Nine hours by overnight bus didn't seem too bad when I was sat at home planning the trip. It seemed less appealing as we trudged back to our Chisinau hotel at 6pm, eager for a cold shower after a sweltering, thirty two-degree day, spent exploring the intriguing city of Soviet architecture and pavement café's, peopled by an unusual mix of headscarf-clad babushkas and blonde barbie-dolls in hot pants.

Our hotel had kindly allowed us a late check-out, in order to have a shower and change of clothes in advance of our journey. We were therefore surprised upon returning, to find our bags lying next to the front desk, open and with some familiar undergarments poking haphazardly from the half closed zips. The friendly desk clerk who'd agreed to our late check-out had been replaced by a moon-faced blonde woman, with eyebrows tattooed into an expression of permanent shock. A thick layer of make-up emphasised a pronounced moustache ,which, caught in the sunlight streaming through the windows, was as fluffy as a baby rabbit's tail.

"Room is taken. Late reserving by German Businessmans." She snapped at my enquiry as to why we'd been unceremoniously 'bounced.'

With the sun setting, and the temperature still in the high twenties, my shirt was sticking to my back, and the prospect of leaving without a shower to face an overnight bus journey was less than appealing. After ten minutes of unsuccessful pleading for access to some form of washing facility, I resorted to removing my shirt, and shaping up to perform an elaborate clothes change and 'freshening-up' exercise, in full view of the reception desk. Obviously fearful of the important German businessmen being greeted upon arrival by a half-naked, sweaty Englishman, the desk clerk wiped the sweat from her moustache with a hairy forearm and thrust a key in my direction.

"You may use sauna shower, but must be quick." She narrowed her eyes and added mysteriously, "We have sauna party this evening."

Kirsty and I gathered our bags and headed down a narrow staircase into a subterranean world of brash gold fixtures and fittings, rendered even more lurid by dark, navy blue paintwork covering the walls and ceiling. The lights glowed orange, and there was an unsettling aroma of stale human in the labyrinth of small cubicles, with incongruous furnishings ranging from massage tables to faux antique chaise-longues. It felt like a sex dungeon designed by Donald Trump. The floors were tiled throughout, and we showered quickly, shuddering at the thought of the fluids that had probably been sluiced down the drains here. There was no ventilation whatsoever, and I was dripping with sweat again as soon as I'd stepped from the hissing steam of the unadjustable shower. I spotted a green-lit exit sign, and emerged blinking into the car park at the rear of the hotel.

The early evening air felt pleasantly cool on my hot, wet skin and I stood only in my shorts, allowing a faint breeze to dry me naturally. I noticed an electric gate click open to my left, and a mini-bus entered the car park. Assuming it to be the arriving German guests, I wondered why it was heading towards me, rather than the reception at the front of the hotel. The reason soon became apparent, as the rear door slid open and a hideous procession of heavily made-up, middle-aged women began to disembark. As they teetered towards me on cheap high heels, supporting muscular, fake-tanned legs, I realised that they were actually probably only in their late twenties, but a combination of cheap, local market make-up and their choice of profession had aged them prematurely. Clearly, these ladies were to provide the local entertainment at the eagerly awaited sauna party. Bizarrely, I hastily put on my t-shirt as they approached, feeling underdressed as they critically sized me up, assuming I was a fellow party-guest. Their sneers suggested they were unimpressed by my potential contribution to the evening's events, both financial and physical!

Kirsty received a similarly cool reception as the women clip-clopped into the sweat soaked dungeon, as she finished getting dressed, and she was bundled out of the exit door behind me, to a fanfare of hissed insults. We packed our bags and headed to Chisinau bus station.

I hadn't dare allow my mind to conjure up an image of the bus. It was too tempting to drift towards reclining seats, air conditioning, ample leg room, a toilet and maybe even a reading light, on board a modern coach, gliding smoothly through the warm Eastern European night. Had I tried to prepare myself for disappointment with a 'worst case' scenario however, it would have fallen some way short of the grim reality.

The vehicle seemed to be of early 1980's vintage, and was clearly designed to carry around thirty commuters on short hops around Chisinau city centre. It therefore had no toilet, the seats had fixed, stiff backs, and the leg room was fine for anyone under five feet tall. There was air-conditioning though, only it didn't work. To compound the impact of this on a stifling, humid night, the bus had clearly been parked all day in a position to soak up the maximum amount of sunlight, and every single window, except the driver's, had been glued firmly shut. I was soaked in sweat, from my head to my toes, within a minute of sitting down.

The bus was full of mostly elderly locals, who were clearly reluctant to store their baggage anywhere they couldn't see it, so rammed it into the small overhead racks, placed it on their knees or positioned it in the aisle, making it impossible for anyone to stand up. With the doors closed, the vehicle stank of onions and cabbage. As the driver started the engine, the whole bus filled with diesel fumes, and as we lurched and stuttered out of the bus station, he cranked up a cassette player which blasted out Euro-pop from a tinny speaker above our heads. Our fellow travellers dealt with the wilting heat and increased noise stoically. They fanned themselves with books and magazines. They occasionally let out a deep sigh, but mostly they just sat, eyes closed, sweat pouring down their red faces, resigned to a night from hell.

Travel can throw up a variety of challenges, which cause you to think and act quickly, to make rapid decisions and react to changing circumstances. I like to think I can generally rise to those situations, to achieve a successful outcome on most occasions. This was different. A slow drip-feed of torture.

The night was black, and the windows seemed to have been tinted using orange cling film, so it was impossible to see through them. The interior lights didn't work, and our torch was flickering with a semi-dead battery so we couldn't read. In those days, mobile data had yet to be invented, so we couldn't peruse our phones. Sitting in the stifling heat, in inky blackness, amidst the stench of thirty similarly trapped souls, ears being subjected to a repetitive tinny disco beat, and the whole structure you're travelling in being repeatedly shaken enough to induce nausea, is a very special kind of hell.

I tried playing some soothing tunes on my iPod but the tinny beat from the speaker above my head merged with my chill-out tracks to produce a brain frying dissonance. My attempts at deep-breathing and meditation failed, though I doubt a Zen master could have relaxed on that bus. Never in my life have I experienced time pass so slowly. I resisted turning on the torch to check my watch, and closed my eyes, focusing on the bumping, swaying motion, with the occasional variation of a jolt and accompanying loud bang, as the driver failed to spot a concealed pot-hole on the dark road. I tracked a slow moving rivulet of sweat, as it picked a course through my hair to emerge on my forehead, where it paused momentarily before pushing on with speed towards my right eyebrow. I enjoyed the welcome distraction it provided as it rested there for a few seconds, before tracking slowly south, to nestle in the corner of my eye. I breathed slowly and deeply, imagining the minutes which were ebbing away as we edged closer to Chernivtsi.

Eventually, I could wait no longer and scrabbled in the rucksack at my feet to locate my torch. I flicked it on and directed its flickering beam towards my watch. I almost daren't look. My most optimistic guess had been that we'd been on the road for three hours, though I guessed it was nearer two. To prepare myself for disappointment I told myself it would only be one and a half. I almost cried when I realised we'd only been travelling for fifty minutes. Fifty minutes! The realisation that we had around eight hours left to go, caused me to fight an overwhelming urge to emit a blood curdling scream, and propel myself towards the door, to hurl myself into the dark night, and freedom.

Two hours later, I was sat, soaked in perspiration, red eyes open wide, as I strained to make out shapes through the windscreen ahead to relieve the monotony. Our fellow passengers had somehow found what for me was the impossible nirvana of sleep. Our fetid travelling compartment was now filled with the sound of their snuffling, snorting, coughing, farting and groaning, as we rumbled on through the night. Kirsty's eyes were closed, and she was breathing deeply and slowly, but would occasionally jolt forward with a start to exclaim that she hadn't slept a wink yet. With any sense of modesty long departed, I removed my sweat soaked t-shirt, and felt the perspiration course down my torso and gather at the waistband of my shorts. I shifted in my seat and Kirsty sensed the movement. 'Don't even think about it,' she murmured without opening her eyes. Sitting in my underpants was a step too far, even for this journey.

After travelling for four hours, at 2am, I was staring ahead through the windscreen, transfixed in moth-like fascination of a distant light which we seemed to be heading towards. The slowing of the vehicle, the crunching of the gears and familiar scent of diesel fumes confirmed my hopes - we were stopping!

I'm unaware of the name of the Moldovan/Ukrainian border post where we stopped, but for me it was the most welcome oasis imaginable. I was already at the door when we drew to a halt, and as it opened, I leapt forth into the warm night, gulping at the fresh air like a fish on a river bank. As the other passengers disembarked, I laid on the cool, chewing-gum spattered pavement, enjoying the chill of the concrete on my skin. Kirsty joined the other passengers in search of water as I lay staring at an orange street light above me, and within seconds I was asleep.

I woke to a nudge in the ribs from the driver's white, eighties style training shoe, and looked up at the puzzled faces of my fellow passengers, who were wondering why the Englishman was lying half naked, spread eagled on the filthy border post pavement. Not for the first, or last time, Kirsty seemed to be trying to distance herself from me, and sat on a bench, drinking from a bottle of water, while looking at the bus with wide-eyed dread.

We trooped back on board and located our damp, sweat-soaked seats, and were soon once again rattling along through the impenetrable black night. My eyes would occasionally fall shut and my head would dip, dip, dip as I teetered on the brink of sleep, only to lurch forward with the shock of a loud bang and jolt as we plunged into another pot-hole. I began to wonder if extreme boredom could induce a trance-like state of coma, and if so, willed it to happen as soon as possible.

Three hours later, every bone in my asphalt-jarred, sleep

deprived body ached. My mouth felt like I'd been chewing sandpaper from the bottom of a budgie cage, and I could sense the blood vessels pulsing in my eyeballs. My naked upper half felt strangely cool and damp to the touch, like a recently deceased corpse, and the air on the bus, like old veg soup, reminded me that my fellow passengers had also spent the last six hours expelling all their bodily toxins in this mobile sauna. And now it seemed I was hallucinating. Straining to see through the orange tinted glass, I was sure I could detect a subtle change in the light out of the right hand window, and hardly dared to believe that what I was witnessing, was the first glow of sunrise. The beginning of a new day, and the end to this intolerable journey. I pressed my nose to the glass like a child on a long car journey, and willed the sun to appear. As it slowly appeared above the low hills on the horizon, it filled the bus with a warm, apricot glow and my fellow passengers, Kirsty included, began to stir from their fitful sleep. She was surprised to find me, wired and grinning manically, as I jabbered a detailed commentary on the sun's ascent and my estimate of how many miles, and hours we had left on the bus. I'd moved beyond exhaustion, and extreme physical discomfort to a place where anything was better than another hour sitting hunched, sweating and sleepless in this steel capsule of torture.

I was bordering on euphoria as we approached Chernivtsi. The other bleary eyed passengers regarded me with baffled expressions, as we negotiated the 8am traffic, crawling through the city's nondescript outer limits. I bobbed around excitedly in my seat, mentally urging the driver onward towards the bleak Ukrainian bus station which to me, was the most welcome destination on the planet at that moment. I resisted kissing the oil stained concrete as I alighted the bus. All I wanted was a shower and a comfy bed. Unfortunately, I had to pick up a rental car and drive 175 miles to Lviv.

Lost again, while attempting to find the correct road out of town at 9am, I pulled up beside a bench where two old soaks were making inroads into the day's first bottle of vodka. As is usual, they regarded me with the sort of open mouthed, befuddled expressions which would have befitted a nun riding down their street on an ostrich. They looked at my map upside down and pointed some vague directions, before one made a comment to his pal, and they both doubled up with laughter, which was obviously at my expense. I smiled and returned to the car, where I pondered aloud what the joke could have been. Kirsty raised a critical eyebrow as she looked me up and down and left me in no doubt – the Night Bus to Chernivtsi had left me in a physical state which was visibly hilarious even to a couple of alcoholic tramps!

Apart from the potential for physical discomfort, another hazard the long distance bus presents to a two-week-traveller is the loss of control over your schedule. In many countries, timetables and routes change regularly, multi-hour delays are common, and bus stations and ticket buying processes often represent a mysterious dark art, particularly in regions where signs aren't written in the Roman alphabet. I always view a long distance bus journey as a 'red flag' in any travel itinerary, with the potential for knock-on impacts which can obliterate a well planned schedule. Such was the case, when we planned to travel by bus from the Chilean capital, Santiago, across the Andes to Mendoza in Argentina. I'd researched the timetables and knew that a daily 7am bus would arrive in Mendoza at 2pm, allowing us a day and a half to explore the city and surrounding wineries, before catching our flight to Buenos Aires.

As soon as we arrived at the bus station, it was clear our plans wouldn't run smoothly. Crowds shuffled and slunk and slumped on their luggage; red faced officials shouted and pointed; people queued, waving scraps of paper; sporadic announcements were made by men in hi-vis vests, causing voices to be raised and arms to flail. And most ominously for us, a long row of buses stood parked in a line, their engines silent. I left Kirsty with our bags and elbowed my way into the melee, questioning anyone who caught my eye with a plaintive 'Perdon, que pasa?' The response was a word I was unfamiliar with at that point, but which is now embedded in my Spanish vocabulary. Huelga. Strike.

Some unknown grievance had enraged the Chilean bus drivers' union, to the point that they'd all downed keys, and walked out.

No one seemed to know how long the strike would last, but it had begun the previous day, and a helpful English speaking traveller provided the unhelpful answer I didn't want to hear - definitely no buses today. Maybe none tomorrow. For us, this was a big problem. At best, we would miss the delights of the Mendoza region and arrive just in time to catch our flight to the capital. At worst, we would miss that flight. (Booked well in advance, at the cheapest fare, and obviously totally non-refundable). Had we been on a longer trip, the obvious response to the situation would have been to return to our hotel and check-in for another day or two, then continue to enjoy our time in Chile's laidback capital. For us though, on a tight two week schedule, we had to cling to any faint hope that the dispute would be resolved quickly. That meant hanging around the bleak compound with the other stranded hordes, resting on our bags in a dusty corner, monitoring the expressions of the hi-vis officials, and trying to decipher the latest rumour with our limited Spanish. I'd spotted a party of around forty eleven-year-olds with their teachers, all wearing matching red baseball caps emblazoned with their school name, and guessing correctly that the teachers would speak better English than I speak Spanish, I sidled over and engaged a bearded, red-capped Geography teacher in conversation.

Estaban explained that the children were embarking on a combined football and educational tour of Argentina. They'd play matches against teams from the neighbouring country, then the two groups would socialise together and swap information on their lives and the areas they lived in. A nice idea, but one which seemed to have been thwarted by the fact that their charter bus driver was a union member, and was prevented from driving during the Huelga. However, Estaban had a cunning plan. As the teachers' union rep, and an avowed left-winger, he had much in common politically with the militant bus drivers, and had been engaged in back-channel discussions with the top man on the bus station picket line.

"I explained that these are poor kids. Their families saved a long time for this trip. Maybe he can help us, I hope..."

I wished Estaban luck, and headed off to join a jostling group of travellers listening to a hi-vis orator barking out rhetoric that I didn't understand, then perused the impromptu snack stalls which had gravitated towards the bus station and its enforced population of hungry travellers. Returning to Kirsty at our shaded base station of bags, I was stopped in my tracks by a small boy in a red cap, who jabbered an incoherent, but obviously urgent message, and took my hand to lead me through the crowds to the opposite side of the bus station, where the other red caps were gathered. Seeing me approaching, Estaban motioned me to hurry, whilst looking furtively over his shoulder.

"Good news!" He grinned. "They're letting us go. We'll be the only bus crossing the Andes today, maybe even this week. And you can come too!"

Before I could ask for an explanation, he despatched two of the bigger boys in the team to collect Kirsty and our bags.

"We must be fast." Estaban urged. "I don't want the big union boss to find out and overrule the guy here."

I spotted Kirsty approaching through the crowd, looking confused, being led by a phalanx of red cap wearing boys, lugging our rucksacks between them.

"Only two conditions to you coming." Estaban looked serious. "One is you can teach the kids some English on the way. Two, is you have to wear these." He thrust two red baseball caps in my direction, and I laughed.

"No. It's serious. You must wear them. I've said that you're English teachers attached to the school, so it's important you look like the rest of us."

And so it was that Kirsty and I took our seats on the only bus to cross the Andes from Chile to Argentina that day, wearing bright red caps, and sitting at the back of the bus, trying to amuse a rotating group of eleven year olds, who took turns to lean over the seatbacks in front of us, demanding to be entertained. After exhausting my usual English lesson of animal names accompanied by a vocal impression of each beast, I resorted to picking random words from our Spanish phrase book (this was a few years before Google translate!), to construct unlikely sentences to keep the kids amused.

"Mi tortuga perdió su maleta en la piscina" My tortoise has lost his suitcase in the swimming pool.

"El maestro monta a su tío a la iglesia el Jueves" The teacher rides his uncle to church on a Thursday.

Each bizarre sentence was met with squeals of laughter as the phrase was passed down the bus. After a couple of hours, this game lost much of its appeal, at least to Kirsty and I, and we tried pausing the 'lesson', hoping the kids would lose interest. We even feigned sleep, but every time we opened our eyes there was a different set of red cap topped faces, peering at us over the seatbacks, pleading for more ridiculous phrases.

The eight hour journey turned into a full childminding shift, and I began to suspect an ulterior motive in Estaban's supposed favour in smuggling us aboard! We got off the bus in Mendoza feeling exhausted and waved our new friends off with best wishes for their trip, as we set off to find our hotel, receiving a few strange looks in our matching red caps.

Modern travel most often necessitates the use of an aircraft, and anyone who has travelled abroad to any degree could write a book detailing airport delays, nightmare passengers, aborted and rough landings and lost luggage. Generally though, air travel is viewed as being the safest mode of transport. We expect the highest standards of professionalism and safety in every aspect of the industry, wherever in the world we fly. It therefore comes as something of a shock when we're exposed to the unfortunate fact that airlines are only as efficient as the people who work for them, and sometimes those people aren't always hugely efficient.

No matter how frequently you fly, it's always reassuring to hear the calm, confident, BBC newsreader-like tone of a mature, experienced pilot before take-off. The voice from the cockpit of a young woman with a regional accent, does still tend to elicit a few raised eyebrows, and nervous jokey comment from passengers of a certain age, who remember when pilots were all distinguished chaps with silver hair, who went to school with Prince Andrew. Those passengers wouldn't have enjoyed my experience in the Caribbean U.S state of Puerto Rico.

We were flying to Vieques, an island idyll with a dark history of being used to test missiles, which have reputedly led to contamination of the seas and food chain of the island. Vieques has some of the highest rates of diabetes, heart disease and cancer in the Caribbean, and the US military has admitted to using toxic chemicals such as napalm, depleted uranium and agent orange on the island, but to the anger of the nine thousand population, it rejects claims for compensation. It's a tiny place where everyone knows everyone else, and wild horses roam the streets. Local youths don't need to call a cab to get home after a night out. They simply mount a passing horse and ride it, bareback, and usually at breakneck speed, down the main street of the village. An interesting place, but first we had to get there.

The flight from the small town of Ceiba on Puerto Rico's North Eastern coast was only scheduled to take twenty minutes, and we turned up at the tiny airport thirty minutes before our 9am departure. There were few other passengers around, and one unmanned check-in desk. I fell into conversation with Phillipe, a late middle-aged Frenchman in grubby cargo shorts and a Hawaiian style shirt. He was unshaven and ruffle haired, with a ruddy complexion and the lingering aroma of last night's rum, forty Gauloises and someone else's bed. He had a sizeable paunch and scabby, stick legs, and I immediately categorised him as one of those slightly louche and dissolute European men of a certain age, who you frequently encounter whilst travelling around the Caribbean. We chatted about English and French football before he excused himself for a cigarette, whilst bemoaning the fact that it was now illegal to smoke on planes. Phillipe had a rather sickly, sweaty pallor, and I remarked to Kirsty that he looked well hung over, and it would be just my luck for him to be sat puking behind me on the flight.

A couple more passengers arrived, and there were now five of us waiting at the check-in desk, with ten minutes to go until our scheduled departure. A door opened behind the desk, and the check-in clerk appeared wearing a white shirt. I was surprised to see that it was Phillipe. I was even more shocked when I noticed the pilot's epaulettes on his shoulders and realised that, in addition to his check-in duties, Phillipe would actually be flying our plane!

After weighing our bags, we each had to stand on some ancient weighing scales, while Phillipe recorded our weights and carried out some calculations, literally on the back of his fag packet. He then handed each of us a piece of card with a seat number on.

"Must get the weight balance right." He informed us loudly. Then under his breath to me "You sit with me, we can talk soccer!"

We all carried our own bags out to the tiny six-seater aircraft, and I clambered in alongside Phillipe. I was somewhat surprised to see that the aircraft had dual controls, and in front of me was a joystick, which moved in tandem with the one Phillipe was, hopefully, controlling. We taxied down the runway and paused while Phillipe had a coughing fit, opened a squeaky window and deposited a mouthful of mucous on the runway.

"Excusez moi, ladies and gentlemen. I 'ave ze bronchitis." He didn't sound like he'd been to school with Prince Andrew.

I commented on the fact there seemed to be no communication with air traffic control, and Phillipe dismissed this with a shrug.

"Eeet's quiet today. We're ze only plane in ze sky. Plenty of room, non?" Worryingly, as he said this, he did seem to scan the airspace above us, in an air traffic equivalent of checking a side mirror before pulling out from a parking space onto a busy road.

Then we were bumping down the runway, as Phillipe told me why Nantes would never win La Ligue 1 again in his lifetime, and were quickly airborne, banking steeply to the left, the joystick in front of me jerking and turning, in response to Phillipe's manoeuvring. As we straightened out, Phillipe suddenly gripped the left side of his chest with his right hand. I turned in horror, expecting to see his head tilted back, glassy eyes staring to the heavens, mouth wide in a rictus grin, mocking me in death for never learning how to land a six-seater aircraft.

Instead, his brow was furrowed. "My sunglasses. I think zey are here?" He motioned to the incomprehensible dashboard in front of me and I gratefully located and handed them over. Shades applied, Phillipe morphed into a low rent 'Top Gun' pilot, as we skimmed over the ocean and he explained how he flew between the mainland and Vieques continually throughout the day. He was an aviation jack-of-all-trades, with his piloting duties supplemented by his job as check-in clerk and ticket salesman for the small, three plane airline he was employed by.

"Eeet's a great life, no one checks up on me." He enthused as we bounced through a bank of fluffy cloud, and I could only imagine being sat next to Phillipe on a runway approach in inclement weather, at the end of a ten-hour shift including a three hour, rum-fuelled lunch break. As we banked sharply on approach to the small airstrip at Vieques, I half expected Phillipe to ask me if I wanted to land the plane. Again, our conversation seemed to take precedence over any communication with air traffic control, and I found myself anxiously scanning the surrounding skies as we approached, like a driving instructor with a nervous learner at a tricky roundabout.

As we came in to land, Phillipe's phone bleeped and he checked a text message while deftly manoeuvring the aircraft with one hand. I think we all breathed a sigh of relief as we bumped along the runway, and Phillipe brought the plane to a halt by the small shed, which was Vieques' arrivals terminal. Phillipe shook my hand and recommended a bar in Esperanza town for later that night.

"Maybe I see you there, depends where I finish," smiled the old pilot, lighting a cigarette as we walked back to the terminal. A typically Caribbean airline experience, unlike anything that could happen in Europe. Or could it be that it's just better hidden from the paying public?

A somewhat 'laid back' approach from the pilot of a small Caribbean airline is perhaps to be expected. Lax security at an international airport which was the departure point for one of the world's worst airborne acts of terrorism is more alarming. On 27 November 1989, Avianca Airlines Flight 203 took off from El Dorado International Airport in the Colombian capital of Bogotá, heading for the southern city of Cali. Five minutes into the flight, a bomb planted by associates of drug lord Pablo Escobar exploded, killing one hundred and seven passengers and three people on the ground who were hit by falling debris. It could therefore be expected that, even though over twenty five years had elapsed since this atrocity, Colombia's reputation as the cocaine capital of the world would ensure watertight airport security. To our good fortune, we found this wasn't exactly the case.

We'd committed one of the cardinal sins for a two-week traveller on a strict time budget, when arranging our South and Central American trip, by booking connecting flights on the same day with different airlines. Booking multiple flights with one airline on a single reservation removes the potential impact of any flight delays or cancellations - the airline needs to 'own' the problem and get you on their next available flight. Making separate bookings with two airlines, places the problem squarely on the toes of the traveller, with a missed connection simply resulting in the cost of the ticket being forfeited and a new booking required.

We reflected on this as we sat on the runway in the Colombian coastal city of Cartagena, listening to distant rolls of thunder and watching through rain spattered windows, as sheet lightening illuminated the end of the runway. We were at the back of a traffic jam line of five planes, all sat on the tarmac, prevented from take off by the electrical storm which had now being flashing around us for thirty minutes. At the time of booking, our schedule seemed to build in enough time to cover any delays. An 11am flight with Colombian airline Avianca from Cartagena would land in Bogota at 12.30pm. Our connecting flight to Panama City with Copa Airlines was scheduled to depart at 2.15pm. However, we hadn't factored in that our first flight would land at the domestic terminal, and the Panama flight would depart, not surprisingly, from the international terminal. We'd also not factored in a morning of violent electrical storms, which had delayed the arrival of our inbound aircraft, and also now delayed our outbound flight for nearly an hour.

We were eventually given clearance to depart and began to slowly taxi along the runway, as the planes before us lifted off into a glowering black sky. Realising that it was looking highly unlikely we'd make our second flight, I summoned up the Skyscanner app on my phone to see how much a ticket on the next Panama flight would be. I immediately wished I hadn't, as the equivalent of £450 flashed up on the screen. £450 each. Our flight home was from Panama, so not going at all wasn't an option, and the only alternative to a bank-busting airline ticket, was a treacherous trip by boat and car through the dangerous and largely unexplored Darien Gap. I gulped and hid my phone from Kirsty.

The duration of the flight was taken up with discussions on tactics for exiting the plane quickly, and attempting to reach the probably closed check-in for our second flight in the minimum amount of time. Economy class was full, and we were seated midway down the plane, with potentially one hundred passengers to disembark before of us. I pleaded with a cabin attendant to let us move to Business Class for the last ten minutes of the flight, and at first thought he was considering the possibility. The realisation that our connecting flight was with a rival airline soon put paid to any optimism though, and he returned me to my seat with a cold smirk.

I usually sneer at those passengers who spring to their feet as soon as the seatbelt light goes out, and start tugging bags frantically from overhead compartments. On this occasion, Kirsty and I were those passengers. Bags recovered before most passengers had even vacated their seats, we set off down the aisle, elbows to the fore, yelling "Perdon! Perdon! Disculpe! Perdon!" in order to get pole position at the front of the queue when the doors were eventually opened at 1.55. Our flight to Panama was due to depart in 20 minutes.

Thankfully, it wasn't a bus transfer to the terminal building, and we clattered down the metal stairs and sprinted across the tarmac into the domestic terminal. We'd agreed our tactics, and Kirsty set off at pace to the international terminal to locate the Panama check-in desk, while I headed to the baggage reclaim. If we'd had any real hope of making our connection, we'd have abandoned our checked-in bags and hoped to have been reunited with them at some point in Panama, but this already seemed a lost cause, and that was confirmed as my phone buzzed, just as the baggage carousel sprang into life.

"Check-in closed half an hour ago." Kirsty's text confirmed what we already knew. Ironically, our bags were two of the first to emerge, and I lugged the two rucksacks onto my shoulders, and set off for the International Terminal. It was approaching 2.15 when I arrived and found Kirsty standing next to Passport Control.

"That's annoying," she observed, nodding towards a display screen. "It hasn't actually taken off yet."

'Last Call/Ultima Llamada,' flashed intermittently in red alongside our flight number. There were no other passengers at passport control. Four desks were manned, and the customs officials chatted amongst themselves or tapped away on their keyboards. Beyond them, the security control staff were similarly underemployed, loafing around, checking their phones as they stood by stationary conveyor belts. We'd checked in online so had boarding cards. The thought that we were so near, yet so far, was incredibly annoying, to the point that I found myself wondering "What if...?"

"Come on." I said with a rekindled sense of urgency. "Let's try it."

"Try what?" Kirsty was understandably confused as I headed towards passport control. My newfound optimism that we could maybe still make the flight, had failed to consider the fact that we were carrying our large check-in bags on our backs. We breezed through passport control and the security staff stirred into life as they saw us approach, each carrying standard hand luggage, plus a 20kg rucksack.

It was at this point that I realised we were about to pass through the security scanner carrying all manner of forbidden items, including my trusty swiss army knife, a pair of scissors and numerous bottles of liquid, all exceeding the 100ml limit. Too late. We selected the closest conveyor belt, which was being operated by a beak-nosed, middle-aged woman with dyed black hair, accompanied by a frail and nervous looking youth. They seemed surprised at the size of our carry-on luggage, but allowed us to feed the bags into the X-Ray machine, with the woman hunched over her monitor, beady eyes scanning the screen like a crow searching for worms on a wet lawn.

'Last Call' was still flashing on the monitor, so as the bags passed through the X-ray machine, I urged the young official on with cries of "Prisa! Vamos!" He wore a badge to inform us that he was Jorge, and was an 'aprendiz' or trainee, and my increasing agitation seemed to transmit to him like a virulent contagion. His eyes flickered nervously, and he licked his lips in anticipation as the first of our bags emerged.

What happened next has been the source of much discussion between Kirsty and I, and to be truthful, we're still unsure as to what actually happened, and how it happened. Unsurprisingly, the security scan identified a veritable treasure trove of confiscatable items. The crow's eyes lit up and she began frantically pointing at my bag as it emerged first from the machine. Fifteen feet away, Jorge responded and my rucksack, complete with multi-bladed swiss army knife, was removed and I was ordered to open it. At this point, Jorge was unsure what he was looking for, and sought clarification from the crow, who was now in an advanced state of excitement, having spotted even more illicit items in Kirsty's bag, and was gesticulating wildly towards it. Other passengers had by now arrived behind us and were already feeding their bags onto the conveyor belt. Kirsty's bag emerged from the X-Ray machine and Jorge looked confused as he yanked it from the conveyor belt. My bag was still open on the desk in front of us, but otherwise untouched, so I took the opportunity to stealthily remove it from his line of sight, and placed it on the floor. Jorge began rummaging in Kirsty's bag, while his now harassed colleague shouted impatiently that there was 'mucho liquido' in the bag, as images of the new arrivals' bags began to flash across her screen.

Urged on by my increasingly agitated shouts of 'mucho prisa! Jorge quickly located a number of bottles containing suntan lotion and other assorted toiletries, plus the scissors, all of which he inexplicably passed to me, one by one, as the crow screeched incomprehensible instructions while hunched over her screen. I slowly and deliberately took each item that Jorge passed me and placed it in my own bag on the floor, which I then refastened, leaving a single bottle of shampoo on the counter as a consolation prize.

'Puerta Cerrada/Gate Closed', was flashing next to our flight number, and Kirsty and I now began stuffing items of clothing back into her bag almost as quickly as the sweating, fast-blinking Jorge was removing them. By this stage, the security staff seemed more stressed than we were, and we left Jorge twitching and scratching his head, no doubt wondering how he would explain to the crow that our obviously illicit luggage had yielded no more than a single bottle of Head and Shoulders.

We heaved our bags onto our backs and set off running at speed through the terminal, looking for departure gate thirteen. Panicked passengers scattered, and security staff momentarily twitched towards their guns as we careered through the departure lounge, teetering under the weight of our rucksacks, yelling "Trece! Donde esta la puerta trece!?" We eventually located the gate, manned by a very camp Copa airlines employee, who gave us a bemused smile as we arrived at the desk where he was checking the boarding cards of four passengers from a late arriving Copa flight, which had fortunately caused the delay of the Panama departure.

"What....? How...?" He shook his head in confusion as he looked at the large bags we planned to carry on board.

"Oookaaay. Well you somehow got this far, so I guess we'll have to find room somehow." He was still laughing as he led us out to the aircraft, where our rucksacks were taken by the equally baffled flight crew, and consigned to the only space onboard which could accommodate their sizeable volume - two unallocated Business Class seats.

The doors closed immediately, and we began taxiing for departure. Kirsty and I flopped, sweating and exhausted in our seats, realising we'd dodged a huge financial bullet, but also slightly concerned that we'd seemingly breached the supposedly strict security of a modern airport, simply by creating a rolling ball of noisy confusion!

Using planes, trains, buses and boats can lead to some memorable travel adventures, but the less control you have over your mode of transport, the bigger the risk of exceeding a two week trip schedule. You have to quickly assess the situation, and be prepared to adapt, change plans and maybe even cancel elements of your journey, if there's a risk you won't make that all important flight to get you back to work on time. Deviating from a well-planned route can seem a disaster at the time, but has to be weighed up against the consequences of a late return, or if safety becomes a real concern, potentially not returning at all!

In a strange and sometimes hostile environment, under time and financial pressure, being subjected to misleading and contradictory information, it's easy to make a rash, and costly, decision. Such situations require clear thought and calm objectivity. Amidst the chaos and confusion, I usually find it's well

worth pausing for a moment to ask the all-important question –
'Well, what's the worst that could happen?'

10 WHAT'S THE WORST THAT COULD HAPPEN?

You've worked all year. Saved your hard earned cash. Bought the latest Lonely Planet, and identified a rough itinerary. Spent countless hours researching flight and accommodation options. You've asked questions on travel forums, then endured tortuous hours using Google Translate, deciphering an email trail in a strange language, in order to arrange transport or glean some important snippet of local knowledge. You've entered your credit card details and pushed submit. You've committed to the trip.

And now you're in the country. Those places you've imagined for months have sprung into vivid life around you. The hotel you read a baffling array of conflicting reviews about on Trip Advisor, is now your temporary home. You've tracked down that out-of-the-way bar that was recommended, that secret beach or undiscovered village, which you furtively read about on your phone during a boring team meeting. After months of thinking, planning and dreaming, you're in the middle of the best two weeks of the year. Maybe even the best two weeks of your life.

Then it happens. Perhaps via a late-night phone call, or an email picked up using a restaurant's patchy Wi-fi. An evasive fixer in a hotel foyer shrugs and talks about 'big problems.' Or maybe you're stranded on a rural dirt road, confronted by a landslide or a flood, blocking the only viable route to your destination. Or sat in an airport terminal, staring at an agitated queue of fellow travellers responding to a 'flight cancelled' announcement. Maybe that comfortable car ferry you booked turned out to be an overcrowded canoe!

Your careful planning goes out of the window. That well-structured two week schedule lies in ruins. There are options, there always are. But what are the compromises to be made?

Missing out elements of the trip that you've dreamt about for months? Uncomfortable alternative transport arrangements? Handing over a wad of cash to that evasive fixer? Taking risks that mean you return home, and to work late. Or not at all.

Or maybe the situation requires an immediate, split second decision. Walk across the rickety wooden bridge over a fast-flowing river gorge, or turn back. Hand over the 'fine' at the impromptu roadblock on a dusty African road, or call their bluff, and risk a comprehensive shakedown, or worse. Walk that unlit street in a sketchy part of a strange city, or wait another hour for a taxi.

In a strange environment, under pressure, and with everything seemingly riding on the outcome, it can be all too easy to panic, and make a rash decision. In such a situation, I find it pays to pause and ask the all-important question – if I get it wrong, then what's the worst that could happen?

If I make the wrong choice, are we looking at discomfort, inconvenience and additional expense? And if so, is that something I can tolerate?

Or could that flawed decision result in something much more serious – a significant delay, meaning you miss your flight home; a very serious financial impact, which eats into your resources for months or years to come; a serious brush with a corrupt judicial system that sees you incarcerated in a filthy cell for years; or even worse, serious injury or death by accident, or at the hand of others.

In addition to helping make difficult decisions, asking 'What's the worst that can happen?' can also be a useful tool to put the brake on a rising sense of panic, a feeling that a situation has got dangerously out of control. A sense check that, yes, things are bad, but not horrifically so, in a life altering way.

That was certainly the case when Kirsty and I embarked on a hiking trip in the principality of Andorra, in the Eastern Pyrenees mountains between France and Spain. It was September, well out of season for the ski resort town of Andorra la Vella, meaning most of the bars and restaurants were closed. Those that were open were sparsely populated by a smattering of locals and visitors like ourselves, there to walk in the surrounding mountains. We'd struggled to purchase detailed maps in the UK, so settled for a 'Walking in Andorra' book, thinking, incorrectly, that we'd be able to purchase more detailed walking maps when in the country.

And so it was, on a bright Monday morning that we parked our rental car on a gravel track leading to a trailhead north of Andorra la Vella. Our intention was to use our book to follow a circular eight mile route, which we expected to take around six hours. The weather was perfect for mountain hiking, with a refreshing breeze, and we set off in our walking boots, clad only in shorts and t-shirts, with a backpack containing thin waterproofs and water, plus a packed lunch of two cheese rolls, a large packet of crisps and two Kit Kats. The sun was shining, and the mountain views were magnificent – what could possibly go wrong?!

Our guide book had a hand drawn map, and step-by-step instructions which seemed pretty straight forward – 'After two miles, the path leaves the river and climbs to a shepherd's hut. Here the path forks. Take the left branch.' Easy, we thought as we strode confidently onwards. It was great walking country. Rough terrain, but easy to follow tracks, through an alpine valley surrounded by cloud shrouded peaks. We ate our packed-lunch next to a walker's refuge, a deserted stone hut high on a mountain pass, with a fireplace and raised wooden ledges to accommodate the sleeping bags of long distance hikers. An eagle soared above us as we tucked into our cheese butties, swooping low, as if to assess the chance of an airborne smash and grab raid on our lunch.

We pressed on, and by early afternoon, after four hours of walking, were scrambling across a rocky field of boulders, before crawling up a loose scree slope, to arrive at a high altitude alpine lake. We were now in the cloud line, and visibility was reduced to around thirty metres. The air grew chill and we shivered and rummaged in our rucksack to retrieve our waterproofs. I'd been carefully following the guidebook's step by step instructions, but unfortunately hadn't thought to read the whole walk from start to finish before we embarked upon it.

The potential problem this could cause only became apparent as we stood at an intersection of four paths, at a height of around one thousand five hundred metres, in a swirling fog of cloud which reduced visibility to around ten metres, and dropped the temperature to five degrees centigrade. Shivering in shorts and thin anoraks, I read out the next instruction from the book.

'You will reach an intersection of paths. The 2900 metre Pic de la Serrera is clearly visible ahead. Take the path towards it.' Obviously the author had completed the hike on a bright, sunny day, because the peak of La Serrera wasn't clearly visible ahead. In fact, nothing was. All we could see in the drifting mist were the first ten metres of four paths, all heading in different directions. We didn't have a clue which way to go.

We decided to wait and see if the cloud cleared, but after ten minutes of shivering, and peering in vain into the swirling abyss, hoping to spot a glimpse of the elusive peak, we accepted that our waiting game was unlikely to pay off. The onset of darkness in around five hours was likely to occur before the mountain came into view. We had to make a decision. Based on the map in our book, two of the paths seemed to be heading in totally the wrong direction, so we discounted them immediately. One path seemed to be heading upwards, whereas our route was supposed to head to lower altitudes, so I felt fairly confident that I'd identified the correct route, and we set off along a thin, winding track heading in a vaguely downhill direction.

My level of confidence reduced as the path became less defined and the cloud closed in, and twenty minutes later we were blundering across marshy ground, with thick tussocks of reedy grass slowing our progress in the ever thickening fog. As a soaking drizzle began to breach our thin waterproofs, Kirsty and I both knew we were hopelessly lost, but also knew that voicing that fact would make things feel worse, so we blundered on, hoping for a miracle which would reveal the peak of Pic de la Serrera rising majestically before us. When lost in zero visibility conditions, the cessation of a distinct path should be the point you immediately call a halt. Once the path is gone, any chance of backtracking and retracing your steps is lost with it. Unfortunately, the termination of a clear path is usually a gradual event, and you tend to try and convince yourself that you're still on the right track, until you've blundered well beyond the point of no return, as was the case on this occasion.

We were now wet, cold, hopelessly lost and high up a mountain. Our supplies comprised of a litre of water and a single Kit Kat, which we'd fortuitously saved from our lunch. It was hard to see how things could get worse. But, predictably, they did. We could hear the distant sound of running water. We knew that our intended path tracked downhill to the valley bottom, and that water travels downwards. Therefore, I reasoned, using mountain skills honed via considerable experience of watching Bear Grylls, that if we found the river and followed it, we'd eventually reach our destination. We slogged across the boggy ground, at times up to our knees in slimy mud. The waterproof qualities of our walking boots now punished us by retaining water rather than repelling it, and we squelched, slid and stumbled towards the river, which turned out to be a small, fast flowing mountain stream.

The river's banks were boulder strewn and muddy, and we found we made quicker progress walking in the icy water as the river meandered down the valley. The chilly, swirling mist continued to surround us, and we had no idea where we were, as we suffered a miserable, hour long descent, tempered only by the thought that we would soon reach the valley bottom, and the path back to our car.

A series of waterfalls indicated that the descent was becoming more pronounced, and we were soon clambering over tricky moss-covered rocks, the cold mountain water soaking us both. Kirsty slipped a couple of times and I became concerned that one of us could easily break an arm or leg before we reached the valley floor. As we scrambled down, the sound of the river seemed to grow louder, and we wondered if we were finally close to the bottom. At the foot of one fifteen metre drop, the banks of the river widened, and I wondered aloud if we'd reached the valley floor. The sound of the water's flow was much louder now, and I guessed that the mist may be concealing a stretch of rapids ahead. I was up to my knees in the river and picked my way carefully forward, willing the valley to appear before us through the cloud.

I peered into the mist, and couldn't understand why my field of vision along the river didn't seem to be increasing beyond a large boulder which split the fast flowing current ahead. Kirsty was around twenty feet behind me when the shocking reality of our location hit me. I couldn't see beyond the boulder, because at that point the river disappeared, and transformed itself into a roaring cascade which plunged over a precipice to the valley bottom far below. A shocking sense of altitude hit me as I realised that our slow descent of the past hour had delivered us only to a plateau, still seemingly hundreds of metres above the valley floor. Following the river would indeed take us downhill, but only via the sheer drop of a huge waterfall.

I turned to face Kirsty and shook my head. Whatever difficult situation we face, Kirsty reacts with an outward calmness. She rarely shows fear, though I've learnt to recognise it by her stony expression and sometimes snappy conversational responses. On this occasion though, it was unmistakeable, as her face fell and she became tearful. The fact that the tortuous, rain soaked, treacherous scramble of the last hour had actually worsened our situation was tough to take, and I felt a knot of tension in my stomach. Strangely, the first thought that crossed my mind was the likely cost of a mountain rescue helicopter. This could prove to be an expensive walk.

My own sense of panic was increasing. We were well and truly lost, in zero visibility conditions, high on a mountain plateau, with no food and wearing inadequate clothing. We had no GPS transmitter, there was obviously no cellphone coverage, and no one knew where we were. Kirsty had slumped on a rock with her head in her hands.

Luckily, I realised that this was a perfect moment to ask myself the all important question – 'So, what's actually the worst that could happen?' It was September, there was no snow or ice and temperatures would likely fall no lower than around five degrees overnight. We had a lighter in our rucksack, and could maybe find some kindling to light a fire. If we found some shelter, our light clothes should dry fairly quickly. In short, we wouldn't die of hypothermia. We had a Kit-Kat and water. We'd be hungry but wouldn't starve. I'd read there were wolves in these mountains, and a small number of reintroduced brown bears, but it was highly unlikely we'd be viewed as prey, especially with a fire lit. (I did decide not to mention this particular point to Kirsty though.) The following day, the cloud cover may clear, revealing the hidden peak, and the path to safety. If it didn't, our hotel would realise we were missing, and our car was parked at the trailhead. It wouldn't take long for a rescue team to locate us. Therefore, I concluded that the worst that could happen was for one of us to break a limb in a rushed scramble down the mountain, and go into shock. Coupled with low temperatures, that would represent a serious risk. If, however, we slowed our pace, and found some shelter, the worst scenario became a cold and uncomfortable night, rescue the following day and a potential bill from the mountain rescue team.

Stating this out loud had a remarkably positive effect on us both. The panic which had threatened to consume us, immediately dissipated in the face of the common-sense facts. We rested for ten minutes, then set out to try and find somewhere to spend the night. It was clear we would be unable to retrace our steps back uphill in the deteriorating conditions, so we resigned ourselves to a night on the plateau. The landscape was totally featureless in the swirling grey mist, as we slogged along through muddy marshland, unable to see the path above us from which we'd descended, or the valley below where we needed to be. There were no large rocks to provide overnight cover, and no foliage to use for firewood, so we plodded on for around forty five minutes, both lost in our own thoughts, but at least now reassured by the fact that death was highly unlikely.

My train of thought was suddenly broken by an unexpected and totally alien noise ahead. The faint clanging of a bell, transported me back to the previous day in Andorra la Vella, where I'd seen an old man on a bicycle cart selling donuts, advertising his wares by ringing a bell. 'Great!' I thought. 'A couple of donuts to supplement the Kit Kat!' My brain then began to function, and I wondered how he'd pedalled a three-wheel cart up the mountain without spilling his load. I turned to Kirsty, who had heard the noise too.

"Cow bells!" She was a step ahead of me.

It sounded like the cows were on the plateau ahead of us. There was no way even the most sure-footed mountain cow could have handled the downhill terrain we'd suffered, which meant there must be another route onto, and off, the plateau. We quickened our pace and soon caught up with a herd of ten cows and calves, each with a large metal bell around its neck. They regarded us with initial curiosity, then resumed their single-file trudge along the narrow track. We walked along at the rear of the clanking procession, frustrated by the slow pace of our bovine mountain guides, but afraid to overtake them in case we lost the path. We descended slowly, still unable to see our surroundings in the fog, and then began to follow a steeper uphill path, our laboured steps keeping time with those of the rear cow, and the almost hypnotic chime of their bells.

After an hour of climbing, a man-made shape appeared in the mist ahead and we recognised the mountain refuge where we'd almost shared our lunch with an eagle. It was now approaching 6pm. We had around an hour of light remaining, and a two hour walk back to the car. The safe choice would have been to bed down as best we could in the refuge, and light a fire to dry our clothes. The lure of a warm hotel bed, and more importantly, a few bottles of Trapella beer in front of a roaring log fire were too great to resist though. With an added spring in our step, we set out on the path back, which we managed to cover in half an hour less than on our outbound leg. We reached the car in darkness, and breathed a huge sigh of relief as we dumped our rucksack on the rear seat. It was at this point that I realised that the walking book was missing, lost somewhere on the mountain.

"Best place for it," was Kirsty's comment, and I agreed wholeheartedly, in a predictable example of a bad workman blaming his tools.

The Andorran mountain escapade was one of the few times that Kirsty's cool, calm and collected demeanour slipped. Another occasion, and another useful deployment of 'What's the worst that could happen?' was during a hair-raising sea crossing in the Philippines.

We'd taken our rental car by ferry from the island of Panay, south to Negros, and had reached the village of Malatapay. We intended to visit the marine reserve island of Apo, and negotiated a price with JR, a local mariner in his earlier forties. We'd be joined on the thirty minute crossing by April, a young American backpacker, who had arranged to spend a few days in a village homestay on the island. There was a gusty wind blowing as JR led us down the beach to where his fifteen year old son Arnel was steadying a small boat in the rolling surf. It was a double outrigger canoe, known locally as a bangka, fifteen feet in length and three in width, given additional balance by a bamboo pole float attached to either side of its thin hull, with an outboard motor at the rear.

We waded through the surf and clambered aboard as the little boat pitched and tossed with each incoming wave. Arnel clambered in alongside us, and JR manned the outboard motor, initially sailing parallel to the beach to try and miss the larger incoming waves. This was less than successful, and we were all soaked by the time we straightened up to follow a course towards the island.

Kirsty is an excellent swimmer who represented her county at the sport, and has partaken in long distance outdoor events such as the Great North Swim in Lake Windermere. I, on the other hand, managed to leave school without achieving a single swimming certificate, and taught myself to swim as an adult. I still couldn't swim any great distance, but always consoled myself with the thought that in terms of being able to save myself from drowning, I really only needed to be able to swim back to the side of a boat I'd fallen off, or a river bank I'd fallen in from.

That theory was now being firmly challenged in my mind, as we passed a headland that had provided some cover from the wind to enter the open sea between the two islands. Our small craft now crashed through increasingly large waves, while making some alarming creaking and cracking noises. I convinced myself that our skipper looked unconcerned, and the disconcerting noises the boat was making were normal. However, the fact that there seemed to be no life jackets aboard was a concern, to me at least. April was treating the increasingly rough crossing like a theme park ride. She whooped and shrieked with delight, as we were lifted by an oncoming wave, to plunge back into the depths of its trough, amidst plumes of frothy surf and the sound of the boat groaning in protest at the battering it was being subjected to. There was no whooping or shrieking from Kirsty, and I could tell from her grimacing face that, even as an accomplished distance swimmer, she was less than happy with the situation.

Unsurprisingly, the violent motion of the boat started to take its toll and before long, April's excitable squeals were replaced by the sound of retching, as she puked into a plastic supermarket bag, helpfully provided by Arnel. I was too worried to vomit. I'd picked the wrong time to consider 'What's the worst that could happen?' The answer was blatantly obvious. The small boat could spring a leak, or break up entirely during this rough crossing, and the only survivors would be the Wirral Freestyle Champion 1984, and a US tourist who floated to safety on an inflated plastic supermarket bag. I pushed the thought to the back of my mind and clung on for dear life as we ploughed headlong into the waves, rising around ten feet with our destination visible ahead, before crashing back down, the view reduced to one of churning water in all directions.

The crossing took around half an hour, and we must have looked a sorry state as we disembarked on the beach at Apo, all soaking wet and our eyes bright red from salt water. April handed Arnel her sick bag before she climbed gingerly from the boat and he tipped it into the sea and washed it out, presumably for the return journey.

The return journey! As we said goodbye to April, the realisation dawned that she would be staying on the island, whereas we would be travelling back later the same day. We'd agreed a return fare with JR. He would wait for us while we explored the island then take us back in the early evening. I decided to act upon my 'worst that could happen' assessment, and approached the red eyed skipper.

"Do you have life jackets?" I enquired. He looked puzzled and sought clarification from Arnel.

They conferred in Filipino for a few minutes, and the young man shook his head.

"No life jacket." He smiled proudly, as if carrying life jackets was an insult to the seafaring skills of his father.

I looked out across the choppy strait to the distant shore of Negros, and resolved not to get back on the boat until the worst thing that could happen, wasn't drowning due to a lack of basic safety equipment.

"No lifejacket, no go back. You must get lifejackets."

The older Filipino spoke, and his son translated the predictable answer.

"Need more money to rent life jacket. A thousand pesos."

It was modern day piracy at its best, but they held the trump cards, so I agreed to pay. We set off to explore the island, but were preoccupied by distant rolls of thunder and an increasingly darkening sky. It was no real surprise as we learnt about Apo's endangered sea turtle population from a marine researcher, to see Arnel appear at speed, looking concerned.

"Must come now." He urged. "Big storm is coming."

Just what we wanted to hear. His initial nervous smile gave way to an increasingly hurried passage through the village, until eventually we were jogging towards the beach, where his father was waiting with two locals. They were attempting to hold the boat steady amidst crashing breakers, like rodeo cowboys trying to calm an agitated, bucking stallion. The sky above Negros, five miles away, was an angry canvas of purple and black, occasionally illuminated by banks of sheet lightening. The previously aquamarine coloured sea was now a brooding, threatening shade of navy. It looked a long way to Malatapay.

Amidst the urgency to get us on board, it seemed an important fact had been overlooked.

"Life jackets!" I shouted to JR above the noise of the crashing surf.

He looked annoyed, but then obviously recalled the potential for additional revenue. A child bystander was despatched and quickly returned carrying two orange life vests. We clambered aboard and put them on immediately, as we made slow progress away from the beach.

It was no doubt going to be a rough and scary crossing, but my fear had abated. I'd now changed the answer of 'what's the worst that can happen?' I reckoned that it was now unlikely we could drown. When the boat broke up, Kirsty and I could rapidly evacuate, before JR and Arnel decided that life jackets were in fact a good idea, and attempted to reclaim them from us by force. We could then attempt to float back to land, or would maybe be rescued by villagers who had witnessed the calamity from the beach. The worst that could happen would be that the villagers would fail to spot the boat sinking, and we'd float around for a few days before being eaten by sharks.

"Very little chance of that though." I shouted to Kirsty above the noise of the sea. She looked unconvinced as she clung onto her wooden bench seat and was hosed down with a non-stop barrage of salt water. When an aircraft hits bad weather, your level of fear rises a notch when you sense trepidation on the faces of the flight crew. A hint of nervousness behind the calm exterior. The fixed smile slipping during a prolonged turbulence prompted drop, or an exchanged glance with a colleague betraying the feeling that all isn't well. And now we spotted that in JR and his boy.

The skipper stood grim faced at the rear of the boat, his eyes fire engine red, visibly cringing at the loud crashes and cracks which accompanied each plunged descent from the crest of a wave. Arnel sat at the pointed bow, regularly turning to meet his father's eyes, as if seeking reassurance. None of us spoke, and I pulled the cord of my life jacket tight, securing my own hi-vis comfort blanket. Halfway across the strait, we changed direction slightly, and suddenly huge waves were approaching from our starboard side. We now seemed dangerously misbalanced. The right outrigger float was disappearing beneath each wave, only to emerge and ascend to five feet above the water level. This had a worrying effect on JR, and he shouted to Arnel, who gesticulated frantically to get us to change our seating positions to help try and maintain the boat's balance.

It was a wild ride, as we motored towards a dark, forbidding sky amidst mountainous waves. Thunder rolled and lightning flared across the sky. I assumed it was raining, though it was impossible to tell from the watery midst of the maelstrom we were caught up in. There were occasions when the loud crash which accompanied our plunge from the apex of a particularly huge wave, seemed certain to herald the disintegration of the boat. Kirsty and I braced ourselves, ready to jump clear, and JR and Arnel winced at the potential loss of their vessel, and with it their livelihood. Then, just when we thought things couldn't get much worse, the steady 'put-put-put' of the outboard motor slowed suddenly and scarily. Then it stopped altogether. Arnel turned and we saw the fear in his eyes, as he shouted something incomprehensible to his father, who had begun a panic stricken yanking of the motor's starter cord, constructed from a piece of recycled washing line. Kirsty and I were seated opposite each other on either side of the thin hull, and the swell hitting the canoe broadsides, caused us to each take it in turns to rise high above the other, before swapping position in time with the waves. It was like riding a terrifying maritime see-saw whilst being hosed down with sea water.

Though we were both scared, my revised assessment of the worst thing that could happen had removed the potential for the abject terror this crossing would have resulted in, had we not been wearing life jackets. Had we made the journey without wearing the flotation aids, and survived it, there would have been a good chance that one of us would have died of a fear induced heart attack anyway.

After what seemed like an age, but was actually probably less than two minutes, JR managed to restart the motor just as it became obvious that Arnel's frantic baling was no match for the waves swamping us. With the water level reaching our calves, and a growing fear that the boat was about to be inundated, the motor sputtered into life and we lurched forward once more into the churning waves.

The return journey lasted nearly an hour. Another indicator of the level of peril a situation has actually presented, is the reaction of the 'professionals' when they know they've survived. JR laughed and shook his head, as his mates from the village splashed through the breakers to help haul us ashore. Arnel looked more shaken, and could only muster a faint smile as he was playfully cuffed about the head by an ancient, one-eyed fisherman. Hand gestures, relieved grins and slapped backs, left us in no doubt that our pilots viewed this as a rough crossing, and one they were glad to have survived. JR refused any additional payment as I handed our life vests back, in a gesture which I took to mean 'I guess you were right this time!'

Considering the worst possible outcome can be helpful in certain circumstances, less so in others. When a situation is in full flight, with no chance of calling a halt or changing the outcome, thinking of the worst fate that could befall you only adds to the terror. I experienced this on a trip to South America. We arrived in Buenos Aires on the hydrofoil from neighbouring Uruguay, and rented a car at the port. I'd read about the gauchos, the traditional Argentinian horsemen who are held in the same historic regard in their country as the American West's cowboys. We headed north to the Pampas, and the small town of San Antonio de Areco. The surrounding area is seen as the spiritual home of the gaucho, with a museum dedicated to the legendary horsemen, and ancient buildings and atmospheric cobbled streets, which have led to it being designated an area of historic interest by the Argentine government. I was half expecting a gaucho-styled theme park experience, but was pleasantly surprised by the feel of an authentic town going about its business. In particular, I loved drinking in the local bar, where all the male patrons wore the traditional outfit of colourful bombacha riding trousers, canvas alpargata shoes and an oversized 'boina' or beret, which they never seemed to remove.

One of the obvious attractions for a visitor to San Antonio is to take a gaucho trail ride. This is basically horse riding for non-riders, using trained horses following the same route every day, with no real riding skills required. I'm actually afraid of large horses, (a throwback to bad experiences with police horses at 1980's football games), but have enjoyed, or maybe endured, trail rides in a number of countries around the world. These have generally been pleasurable experiences, though I struggle to forget an occasion, in Texas, when my trusty steed became bored with the usual circuit, and took me up a rough, rocky hillside, before galloping hell-for-leather down the other side and jumping into a deep river, presumably to cool off. It seemed he'd forgotten he was carrying a terror-stricken tourist on his back!

Hoping for less of a white knuckle ride on this occasion, Kirsty and I were accompanied on our trail ride by Ignacio, an Argentinian horseman, and Tina and Brad, tourists from New York. All was going well as we plodded along through the countryside at a sedate pace. Ignacio spoke no English so was unable to tell us anything of note about the locality. We were therefore 'entertained' by Brad loudly educating us on his Real Estate company, his cars, the all expenses Caribbean sales conferences he regularly attended, and a childhood spent on his grandparents' farm upstate, where he rode daily, and became something of an equine expert.

It was a hot day, and our walking-paced amble clearly suited the horses, who dawdled to munch on hedgerows and scuffed their hooves on the gravel, as we made laboured progress along farm tracks and country lanes. Brad was getting frustrated, clearly wanting to demonstrate his horsemanship by achieving a faster pace from Angelo, his black gelding. His initial attempts at trotting were greeted with a discouraging shake of the head from Ignacio. My own horse, El Gordo, or the Fat One, lived up to his name with an excessively broad back, which caused my thighs to splay across his width a little more than was comfortable. I was therefore happy with the sedentary pace.

After an hour of plodding, we turned a corner into a long, dusty gravel lane, flanked by hedgerows, stretching a couple of miles into the distance. Like a teenager wanting to test a souped-up old banger on a quiet stretch of country road, the opportunity was too tempting for Brad. With a swift kick administered to Angelo's ribs and an old west style 'Giiiidyaap! Yeeeehaaaa!' he was away. Perhaps surprised by the unexpected kickstart, Angelo took off at an impressive speed, kicking up a cloud of dust behind him. For a split second we all paused in shock as Brad tore away. Then, all hell broke loose. El Gordo's ears flicked then sprang upright. He then seemed to recline slightly, and I wondered if he was going to sit down, to watch Brad and Angelo who were tearing off along the track. Unfortunately, he had other plans. The slight recoil was obviously to provide a springboard effect, and after taking his weight on his hind legs, he pinned back his ears, tossed his head, snorted violently and accelerated in pursuit of Angelo.

Ignacio watched in open mouthed horror as we tore forward. My screamed stream of profanities was quickly lost in a cloud of dust and a thunder of hooves, as El Gordo gladly took up the gauntlet thrown down by Angelo. I wasn't even holding the reins, and had been resting my hands on the pommel, the raised wooden 'knob' on El Gordo's ornamental seat. As we tore along the road, my mount and I quickly de-synchronised, and his upward motion coincided with my downward equivalent. The horse's broad back and my generous cargo shorts resulted in an excruciating explosion of pain in my testicles at every point of impact.

It was at this stage that I unwisely considered what was the worst thing which could now happen. On the outbound plane journey, I'd read a magazine article about the Superman actor Christopher Reeve, who was left paralysed from the neck down in a horse riding accident. I'd read of his brave fight to overcome his disability, and the terrible impact the accident had on his life. Now, as I careered at high speed along a dusty road in Argentina, on the back of a horse I had absolutely no control over, that worst case imagery, influenced by Reeve's plight, flooded my brain. I'd surely lose my grip on El Gordo's saddle, and my feet would slip from the stirrups to propel me at high speed onto the gravel. Worse, maybe one foot would remain lodged in place in the stirrup, and I'd be dragged along the bumpy lane, my head bouncing off the dusty surface. I was then haunted by thoughts of myself, trying in vain to control my high-tech wheelchair as I bumped around the ready-meal aisle in Asda. Having to sit in the beer garden of my local pub in winter, dusted in snow, with my chair unable to fit through the door. Nodding stoically to my friends in the stand at a Leeds game, as I'm wheeled to the disabled section on the touchline. A totally unhelpful use of 'what's the worst that can happen?' Or maybe it wasn't. Maybe it compelled me to hang on even more tightly, to cling to the pommel and bury my feet in the stirrups as we tore along the road. A mile back, Kirsty, Tina and Ignacio watched in silence before Kirsty, for some reason attempted to summarise the situation in pidgin English. "He doesn't like," she explained to Ignacio, as if he could flick a remote control switch and bring the terrifying ride to a halt.

Eventually I sensed El Gordo slowing, and dared to lift my head from its position behind his ears, to see that Brad had brought Angelo to a halt ahead. If he was surprised to see me arriving at speed behind him, he was probably taken aback even more by my reaction.

"You crazy bastard!!" I spluttered as I tried to catch my breath. "Why did you do that?"

"What's the problem? The horse was bored. I just wanted to let him stretch his legs." He was smirking, as I attempted to rearrange my damaged undercarriage.

"I couldn't stop the bloody thing. How do you make it stop?"

"Just pull back on his reins." That was the last I heard. It seemed my tone may have offended Brad, because he pulled Angelo's reins to turn him, then whipped his flank and whooped like an Apache Indian. Angelo had obviously enjoyed stretching his legs, as he took off again at literal breakneck speed, back in the direction we'd come from. El Gordo seemed to pause and consider his options, before deciding that this time, he wasn't giving Angelo as much of a head start. He tossed his head and snorted again, then took off, seemingly even faster than before. We hurtled along the road and amidst the thunder of hooves, I became aware of a high pitched whine, which I eventually located as coming from my own mouth. I gritted my teeth so hard as I bounced along that I couldn't breathe, and every jolt caused a jet of snot to spurt from my nostrils. It was then I remembered Brad's instruction to stop El Gordo.

I was a couple of hundred yards down the road from where Kirsty, Tina and Ignacio were sat, helplessly watching the terrible events unfold, when I decided to try and stop El Gordo. Kirsty was unaware that all I did was pull back on the reins. From her perspective, she only saw the horse dig his front hooves into the gravel and come to a sudden halt in a rising cloud of dust, then in the same motion, rise on his hind legs, whilst flailing his front hooves in front of his chest, as he tossed his head back and emitted a shrill whinny. I clung grimly on to his saddle, determined not to be thrown off at this late stage.

El Gordo calmed down when he saw the other horses, and trotted back to join the group, seemingly pleased with himself, as he threw his head from side to side and showered me with foamy saliva.

"Pretty impressive at the end there Matt," sneered Brad. "You looked just like the Lone Ranger."

"Wanker." I smiled, knowing he wouldn't have a clue what that meant.

Contemplating the worst possible outcome in the middle of a potential disaster which you have no control over, isn't an ideal situation. However, coming to terms with a potentially far reaching and deadly result after the event is even worse. The realisation that you came within a whisker of causing death and disaster was a harsh reality Kirsty and I had to come to terms with, in the unlikely setting of the Belizean island of Caye Caulker.

We'd spent a week in the Central American nation of Guatemala. After exploring the highland region around Lake Atitlan and Chichicastenango, we'd headed to the Mayan ruins of Tikal. Here we'd slipped a backhander to a couple of machine-gun toting guards, to be allowed into the temple complex before dawn, in order to watch the sunrise from the top of the pyramidic Temple Two. As the first rays of gold illuminated the eastern sky, the sounds of the awakening jungle grew into a crescendo of screeching, squawking, and twittering, culminating in the terrifying, prehistoric roar of a howler monkey in the canopy below us. Back at our guest house for breakfast, and needing some butter for my toast, I got into a multi-lingual muddle, and twisted the French 'beurre' into Spanish and somehow arrived at 'Burro.' I then strode into the kitchen and asked 'Tiene el burro? Quiero burro. ' The confused faces of the staff caused me to mime the action of spreading butter as I approached, and unsurprisingly they backed away with panicked eyes, fearful of the strange Englishman who had invaded their kitchen, wielding an invisible knife and shouting 'Do you have a donkey? I want a donkey! '

After Guatemala, we travelled by bus into Belize, and its gang warzone capital, Belize City. After a day spent exploring the clapperboard house streets around the port, and witnessing a gangster funeral, with a cortege of pimped-up cars driven by gun toting hoodlums, it was a relief to catch the high powered speedboat out to the islands, Caye Caulker and Caye Ambergris. Here, twenty miles offshore, it was a different world to the ghetto lifestyle of the mainland.

Caye Caulker was known as the barefoot island, as most residents chose to walk its sandy streets without the hinderance of footwear. Indeed, the island's motto is 'No shirt, no shoes, no problem.' With no real roads, traffic was limited to a few slow-moving golf carts, with even the island's small police force using a motorised buggy in the unlikely event of a crime being committed. There were a couple of small bars and restaurants, and a memorable nightclub sited in a wooden building with no floor. The sandy street extended right to the bar, and the dancefloor was a foot of thick powdery sand, making moonwalking all but impossible.

The northern tip of the island was the setting for a popular sunset viewing point – a simple bar, with a roof deck overlooking the ocean. An obvious spot for our first evening on Caye Caulker, it delivered a spectacular western skyline, resembling the palette of a landscape artist on an extreme acid trip. After a blood-orange sun had dipped below the horizon, streaks of red and purple bled into a dark amber background, which became a Caribbean photo cliché as I framed it behind the silhouette of a beach palm tree. An American couple sipping cocktails noticed me with my camera, and asked if I'd take a photo of them with the sunset. The man looked a few years older than his partner in the twilight, but cocktails in hand, in their loud holiday shirts and Bermuda shorts, they looked like that perfect couple in the holiday brochure, as I took their camera and positioned them to maximise the available light.

"Left a little. One step back. Perfect! " They grinned and sipped their drinks as I snapped away, with the shifting kaleidoscopic light show behind them. As any photographer will tell you, successfully capturing facial features without losing the colour of a sunset is a challenge, but, upon checking in the LCD display, I was pleased with the results.

"Okay, that's nice. Cuddle up! " I was now envisaging my shots blown up and framed, given pride of place in the couples' home, and the man put a protective arm around his partner.

"That's nice! Now a kiss! " I sensed hesitation, which I put down to typical American conservatism.

"I've got a fantastic shot lined up, go on, give her a kiss! " The man ducked his head nervously towards his partner, who grimaced and turned away.

I sensed a classic shot missed and cajoled the couple, "Come on, you're on holiday, let's have a kiss! "

Obviously fearful of what may happen next, the woman wriggled free of the man's clutch.

"For God's sake, you sick weirdo, he's my Dad! "

The morning after my failed attempt at instigating incest, we set off to see Caye Caulker. It's not hard to explore the whole five mile long, one mile wide island, in a single day, even a single morning, and Kirsty and I borrowed a couple of ancient, gearless cycles for a ride down to the mangrove swamps at the island's most southerly point. It was a hot, cloudless day, as we pedalled along wooden duckboards, through a dense foliage of aquatic reeds, alive with the hum of insects. After half an hour of sweaty exertion, we emerged from the mangroves onto an unexpected expanse of flat concrete, shimmering in the heat as it stretched away to the horizon.

We paused, and I scrabbled in our rucksack for the Lonely Planet. "This must be the abandoned airstrip I read about." I informed Kirsty confidently. Unfortunately, the bag contained a predictably large number of items which were completely useless on a cycle ride on a Caribbean island, but not the Belize Lonely Planet, which had been left in our room.

"Shame. I'd have liked to have read about it. I think it was abandoned in the early eighties." I wondered aloud if the control tower was still intact, and we set off along the runway to investigate. The ride on our primitive bikes was torture in the searing heat. The totally flat, dun coloured concrete pavement seemed to stretch for miles, and with no variation in the lush green foliage running on either side of us, it made for a mind numbingly repetitive ride. I had my head down and was around twenty feet ahead of Kirsty who was struggling gamely in my wake, when I noticed a change in the colour of the surface beneath my wheels. Occasional black stripes started to appear, which I soon realised were the tyre skid marks of the planes which used to land here. I enjoyed this link to the past, and began to visualise 1970's holidaymakers disembarking here in lurid flared trousers, large collared Hawaiian shirts and straw sun hats. As the black marks on the floor became more regular and pronounced, I looked up and spotted what I took to be a small control tower and terminal building in the distance. Puzzlingly, there was also an orange windsock hanging limply in the almost imperceptible breeze.

I was hot, tired and my brain had been temporarily numbed by a tedious ten minutes of pedalling. It therefore took several seconds for the question to form in my mind, of why a disused airstrip would still be flying a windsock. Failing to come up with an answer to that question, I revisited my recollection of reading about it in the Lonely Planet. I struggled to visualise where I was when I'd read that passage, until slowly, a recalled image formed in my mind. I was sat, perusing the book on a hotel balcony. It was dusk, and I was enjoying an early evening beer. I conjured up an image of the hotel. It was in Flores, Guatemala. Which meant that I was reading the Guatemala Lonely Planet, not the Belize edition.

In the split second that my mind joined the dots to arrive at a worrying conclusion, my attention was drawn to a noise. A distant droning buzz coming from somewhere behind us. I turned to witness an image which remains frozen in my memory. Kirsty, red faced and breathless, pedalling hard, facing downwards, eyes fixed on the runway. Descending from a clear blue sky over her right shoulder, the source of the noise, increasing in size by the second, as it sped towards us. Eyes wide with horror, I emitted a blood curdling cry. A single terrible word, and the last you want to hear whilst cycling along a functioning airport runway, which it was now obvious, we were.

"Pllaaaaaanne!!!"

Kirsty turned and for a split second we were both rooted to the spot as our brains struggled to compute what was happening. We rapidly established that our rusty cycles and perspiring, pedal-weary bodies were occupying a stretch of tarmac which would, in seconds, also occupy a fast moving fourteen seater, single propeller aircraft. Considering what was the worst thing that could happen at this stage was as futile as it was obvious. Our adrenaline kicked in, to propel our aching legs into action, and we quickly swerved onto the grass apron running alongside the runway. Once out of the plane's immediate path, we turned just in time to see its wheels kick up a cloud of dust upon touchdown, and I remember being amazed at how quickly it seemed to accelerate once upon the runway. In seconds, it was alongside us, close enough for us to see the angry face of the co-pilot staring incredulously at us, as it sped past. I could clearly see the passengers, and made eye contact with a fat, bearded man in a baseball cap, as he pointed us out to his wife.

The VERY worst thing that could happen, that being causing our own demise, and also the deaths of those on the plane, thankfully hadn't. In my mind, the next worst thing was our arrest for trespassing. I was pretty sure the incident would have to be logged officially as an aviation near-miss, in the same way that a bird-strike or a close encounter with an unidentified flying object would be. Therefore, the pilot was probably already alerting airport security, if there was such a thing on the island. I envisaged the Caye Caulker police force sticking a blue light on the roof of their golf buggy and chugging towards the airport at that very moment.

"Head for the mangroves!" I shouted, and Kirsty and I began pedalling back down the runway. I was casting nervous glances behind me, expecting to see a golf buggy bearing two burly officers struggling to catch up with us, when the chain came off my bike. There was no time to re-attach it, so I had no option but to continue our retreat on foot, running as fast as my shaking legs would carry me, whilst pushing my broken cycle. I was so hot I felt my head was going to explode, as I watched Kirsty disappear into the distant foliage, her 'every man for himself' reaction leaving me in no doubt who was getting the blame for the incident.

We'd cycled halfway along the runway, so our tortuous evacuation seemed to take for ever, but eventually I caught up with Kirsty who was furtively crouching in the undergrowth with her bike. We rode back to town in silence, as we both came to terms with how close we'd come to catastrophe, due to a simple case of guidebook confusion. We steered off the duckboard trail early, and pushed our bikes along the beach in an attempt to foil the law enforcement welcoming party we felt sure would be waiting for us in town. Back at the guest house, we stashed the borrowed bikes under a tarpaulin at the back of a garage, and hoped no one had noticed they'd been removed.

That night we skulked into the village, experiencing the difficulty of keeping a low profile in a place with only a handful of bars and restaurants, and visitor numbers that didn't quite reach treble figures. Thankfully, and surprisingly, our exploits didn't seem to be the talk of the island, and as far as we could see, seemed to have gone unnoticed. Sat outside a bar, (a different one to the previous night for obvious reasons,) we watched the usual spectacular sunset, and I began to relax. Inside I could hear an American tourist holding court at the bar, but couldn't make out his words, only that booming cadence peculiar to Americans, which seems to make their conversations carry so much further than those of other nationalities. Judging by the laughter in the bar, he was telling an amusing tale, accompanied by a flurry of waving arms and sound effects. I wasn't paying too much attention, until I heard him adopt a whining nasal growl, which was the unmistakable sound of a man impersonating an aircraft. Kirsty and I exchanged wide eyed glances, and I popped my head up, meerkat style, to peer through an open, shuttered window. The large bearded man was commanding the attention of two barmen and a crowd of six drinkers, as he dived and swooped in front of them, arms extended into make-believe wings, interspersing his impression of a plane with the excited narration of his story. I'd already recognised the Hawaiian shirt and baseball cap, and as he negotiated an inconveniently placed barstool to begin his final descent, he banked to the right and our eyes met. He stopped mid-sentence and did a double-take, but we were already gone, leaving our half drunk bottles of Belikin beer on the table as we made our hasty exit.

Yet another close call, and on this occasion, one which was actually more terrifying after the event, when we considered the worst thing that could very easily have happened. With hindsight, it was probably the second closest we came to a real disaster. The closest? That has to be Botswana.

11 WILD THING

I love Africa. Correction, I love wild Africa. I've visited around thirty African countries, and have learnt to enjoy their cities, but it's hard to love their horn honking, fume filled, plastic-bag choked, fake-guide duplicitousness. Their 'better take a taxi,' fast-hands-moneychanger, persistent beggar, big antelope edginess. The bush is a different place, with different dangers, and if you get it wrong, it's far more deadly than any African city.

The fast fall of darkness is when wild Africa comes to life. The sun turns blood red in its rapid descent, and the western sky is filled with a kaleidoscope of orange, crimson, purple and black. Birds fly to roost, beasts stir, and a faint hint of woodsmoke is carried on the first welcome breeze of evening. As the blackness becomes complete, the sounds of the night are carried from miles distant. A mother pacifying a child with a lullaby; the crack of an axe on wood; a village dog barking.

Then in the silence, the true sounds of wild Africa. Close by, the snort of a buffalo. Further, the crash of brush signifying elephants on the move. Then the chilling, guttural rumble of a lion's roar reminds you that you don't belong here. You're a visitor, and the rules of cities and civilisation no longer apply. The first time you hear the deep, rumbling growl of a lion in the suffocating blackness of an African night, some long forgotten, instinctive fear is set free, and you remember what it means to be human here, to be potential prey.

Spending time in the African bush in any guise is an incredible experience, but to be there alone, without a safari guide, under canvas and in one of the Continent's most untamed corners, is a life changing travel experience. For us, it was almost life ending.

Our first taste of wild Africa was in the relative civilisation of Etosha National Park in Namibia, a great place for an introduction to self-drive safari. The roads are generally an excellent mix of gravel and tarmac, and can usually be driven in any vehicle. Signage is good, so it's pretty hard to get lost, and wildlife sightings are helpfully written up with times and locations at the park visitor centre, so hunting out 'the big five' becomes less of the needle-in-a haystack task it can be in many locations.

The biggest danger in Etosha is to be lulled into the false sense that you're in a giant safari park. Though it can sometimes feel like a controlled environment, make no mistake that the animals here are wild, and often unpredictable. We had our first close call with an angry elephant at Etosha, when a belligerent adolescent took a dislike to our little VW Polo and mock-charged us away from his preferred water hole. That was our first experience of an elephant charge, but unfortunately by no means the last!

Etosha whetted our appetite for more African wildlife adventures and next we travelled to Tanzania, to see the great wildebeest migration of the Serengeti, and to experience one of Africa's, and indeed the world's, top wildlife spotting locations, the Ngorongoro crater. Unfortunately, restrictions on visitor permits meant that self-drive wasn't possible, so we had our first experience of a guided safari, and also of camping in the African bush. The first campsite we stayed in was unfenced, meaning animals were likely to pass through during the night.

"Not lions though?" I asked Noah, our guide.

"Oh yes, there are many lions here," he beamed.

"But, erm, couldn't they just rip open our tent and kill us?" I looked doubtfully at the thin canvas that would potentially be separating us from a pride of hungry lions.

"Lions never attack tents." He looked confident.

I wasn't. "Why though?"

"Nobody knows. They just don't." He gave me his best 'trust me' smile, and hurried away to collect firewood, which he'd explained we needed in order to stay outside our tents after dark.

"Once the fire goes out, the animals will come." Noah imparted another important lesson of wild Africa.

Before we retired for the night, we were also instructed that on no account should we visit the campsite's primitive drop toilet during the night.

"Lions, hyenas and baboons are attracted to salt in the toilet. They will visit at night to lick it. You don't want to surprise one in there."

We certainly didn't, so getting caught short in the night meant standing in the blackness outside your tent, willing yourself to hurry up, whilst you sensed scores of predatory eyes sizing you up from the bush.

Noah was a proficient guide, and was armed with a radio, tuned to a frequency used by other wildlife trackers where information was shared on animal sightings, and we were able to spot all the Big Five, including an elusive leopard that Noah insisted we sit and wait for a full hour to see emerge from its treetop daytime perch, as night fell.

Like me, he also enjoyed a campfire beer at the end of the day, and when our supplies ran out, he and I left Kirsty helping prepare a meal at the campsite, to go to a nearby safari lodge for replenishments. I was parched after a long hot day bumping along rutted tracks in our Land Rover, and couldn't resist cracking open a bottle of Tusker as we headed back, with darkness rapidly falling. A huge crimson sun had dipped too quickly below the horizon, and a furrowed browed Noah told me that driving after dark in the bush wasn't wise. I was just about to ask why when we rounded a corner at speed, and our headlights lit up the spindle legs of two adult giraffes teetering across the track a few feet ahead. Luckily Noah was alert enough to slam the brakes on, causing me to lose my bottle in the footwell, but avoiding what would have been a disastrous collision, for both ourselves and the animals. The first and only time a giraffe has spilt my beer!

If Noah was a diligent and knowledgeable safari guide, we have also been unfortunate enough to experience the lower quality end of the tracker spectrum. Possibly the worst safari guide I've had the misfortune to encounter, was an elderly man called Shadrach, who worked out of a lodge in Hwange National Park in Zimbabwe. The alert, watchful demeanour which is generally evident in proficient guides was non-existent in Shadrach. Most wildlife trackers constantly scan the bush whilst driving, then pull over suddenly to point out a distant cheetah, which our untrained eyes can't even see using binoculars. Shadrach bumbled along in his ancient Land Rover at a ridiculously slow pace, eyes fixed firmly on the pot holed track ahead, like an elderly gent on a Sunday jaunt to the garden centre. On more than one occasion we alerted him to the presence of wildlife by banging on the cab roof. Roles reversed from the norm, it was usually our guide who then screwed up his eyes as he scanned the horizon, vainly trying to locate what it was we were pointing at.

Hwange has one of the largest elephant herds in Africa, and with drought conditions affecting the area, and waterholes drying out, huge numbers of elephants were drawn to the few remaining sources of vital, life affirming fresh water. Many had already died of thirst, and huge pachydermous carcasses were a common sight along the dusty roadside. Dried into leather husks, they resembled macabre artworks, shrunken, twisted and unrecognisable as the majestic beasts we'd stopped to observe frolicking in the muddy water.

Amidst, the splashing, trumpeting mass, we spotted an ageing female stumbling in the shallows. Like a pensioner who'd accidentally strayed into the carnage of a Club 18-30 beach party, she warily eyed the rest of the herd as she attempted to drink, with slow, laboured motions. It seemed she'd had a long journey and could barely summon the strength to raise her trunk to drink. As we watched, she sank to her knees and keeled over in the shallows. Elephants will often submerge their heads whilst wallowing, but this was different. She struggled in vain to right herself, and we watched as her strength seemed to ebb away, until eventually she appeared to give up, and her head disappeared below the surface.

We pointed the sad scene out to Shadrach, who's expert view somewhat contradicted what was obvious to everyone else present.

"Yes, he is swimming. Looking for fish maybe." I wasn't convinced he could even see to the far side of the waterhole, as he squinted into the sun and waved his hand dismissively.

"Come, we must leave now. It will soon be dark." He set off ambling back towards the Land Rover, as a juvenile elephant nudged the still body of the old matriarch lying in the shallows, then trumpeted a call which I took to mean 'Dad, I think Gran's had an accident.'

By the last afternoon of our stay, Shadrach's lack of suitability for his role had become a standing joke, as we embarked on a sunset game drive. The open backed Land Rover contained Kirsty and I, plus Ben and Tamara, an Israeli couple, whose initial playful teasing of the old guide had progressed into full blown piss-taking hostility. Ben in particular, had moved from mild amusement at Shadrach's incompetence, to loud complaints at his driving style, shouted abuse at every missed animal sighting, and promises to seek a refund of the cost of the game drives. Most worrying for Shadrach was the fact that it was highly unlikely he'd be receiving any tips from these clients – most safari guides receive a small basic salary, with the majority of their income coming from gratuities from satisfied customers.

Fortunately, an uneventful hour into the drive, Shadrach's salvation seemed to materialise, like a gift from the safari guide's God. Rounding a bend in rough, scrubby brush, with scattered devilthorn bushes and mopane trees, even Shadrach's failing eyesight couldn't fail to spot a safari vehicle parked on the track ahead. A parked van is always a good indicator that there's something interesting close by, and, sensing a chance to salvage his tip, Shadrach accelerated to 5mph, and headed towards it.

Upon arrival, it was clear that the occupants weren't your bog-standard safari tourists. The professional khaki bush gear, enormous telephoto lenses and notebook filled satchels, told us that this was a group of serious zoologists who'd struck safari gold, by locating a pride of lions, who, unusually, weren't fast asleep. They were also a complete family group, comprising of a large male, a lioness and four cubs of around six months old. Their heavily bloodied fur told us they'd recently eaten – the cubs in particular were caked in gore, looking like they'd had a paint fight with crimson gloss.

The zoologists smiled and nodded silently to us as we pulled in behind them – the universal acknowledgement between vehicles when sharing a wildlife experience on a game drive. The lions were alert; the cubs play-fighting and chasing, the parents watchful but relaxed, displaying the quiet confidence of the apex predator. They watched us with an air of indifference as we observed them from a distance. Both vehicles had killed their engines and the only sounds were those of the bush – birdsong, cicadas, and the breeze rustling the leaves of the mopane trees which the lions were resting beneath.

Shadrack had seemingly been weighing up his options, and had realised that it would take something spectacular to get Ben back onside and salvage his tip. Alternatively, maybe he recognised that a life as the world's worst safari guide wasn't worth living, and he was attempting an appropriate method of suicide. All we knew was that the old man suddenly turned the ignition key, and the Land Rover's engine chugged into life. Our initial thought was that Shadrach had an eye on the time and wanted to get back to the lodge. It was therefore something of a shock when he pulled alongside the zoologists vehicle, our confused faces suddenly appearing between their zoom lenses and the animals. We shrugged, and smiled, wondering aloud what he was up to.

The lions were around twenty five feet from the edge of the track, and it was difficult to envisage how a better view could be achieved. Shadrach had it covered though, and to our horror, and the open-mouthed surprise of the zoologists, he executed phase two of his plan, as he pulled off the dirt road and began bouncing slowly over the rough ground towards the pride.

The ground was severely rutted, and the undercarriage of the Land Rover scraped on raised divots of earth as we lurched forward. The lions had sat impassively as we approached, but now, with our open sided vehicle around fifteen feet from them, they began to take an interest. The cubs had stopped playing, the lioness flashed her teeth and growled, and the big male stood, readying himself for action.

I remembered on our Tanzania safari, Noah telling me that lions have never been to known to attack safari vehicles, or tents. However, now that I was just feet away from a huge killing machine which could clear the low sides of our vehicle without even stretching, I began to think that there's a first time for everything. Kirsty had obviously considered the 'worst that could happen,' and was banging on the roof of the cab, urging Shadrach to reconsider his plan, amidst a stream of expletives. Ben had initially seemed pleased at Shadrach's initiative and had shouted encouragement as the off-road foray began, but now, with the lioness joining her mate in standing, and seemingly assessing our suitability as 'meals on wheels,' he too lost his nerve.

Shadrach took the hint and attempted to reverse. Unfortunately, in the excitement, he seemed to confuse reverse with fourth gear, and our vehicle sprang forward, causing the lions to jump in surprise, before stalling. Clearly flustered, Shadrach now couldn't get the Land Rover to start, and the engine sputtered its refusal three times, with the male lion now patrolling our vehicle's left side while sniffing the air, and emitting a menacing low growl. Searching for a potential weapon to repel 200kg of airborne lion, I reached in our rucksack and withdrew a pump action bottle of factor 30 sun lotion.

"I'll squirt it in his eyes." I informed Kirsty optimistically, as the male lion prowled alongside us, nostrils flaring as he caught the scent of fear in the air.

I looked toward the zoologist's van, still parked safely on the track, and every single occupant had their zoom lenses and smartphones trained on our vehicle, and the now circling lions, clearly envisaging a fortune from their viral YouTube hit 'Idiot Tourists Eaten by Lion Pride.'

It took around twenty minutes for Shadrach to reverse back out onto the track, and I can safely say that each minute seemed an eternity when feet away from a pride of lions, who seemed to be questioning their instinct not to attack those moving metal boxes filled with fresh human meat. With hindsight, perhaps if the pride hadn't already killed that afternoon, there would have been a good chance of me fulfilling that old workplace prediction that I'd meet a spectacular, big cat related end, instead of being run over by a bus!

Shadrach's own near-death experience came when we got back to the lodge. Normally placid and laidback, Kirsty seemed to be channelling the aggression of an angry lioness as we climbed from the Land Rover, and I seriously thought the guide's only gratuity was going to take the form of a black eye. Ben was not best pleased either, and the old man beat a hasty retreat, with no tips but no doubt thankful to be physically unharmed by either the wildlife or his clients!

Whilst lions tend to be front of mind in terms of threat to man in the African bush, other beasts can be equally as deadly. Deaths from attacks by hippos and cape buffalo are thought to outnumber the number of people mauled by lions. For Kirsty and I though, some of our most terrifying experiences have come from encounters with elephants. The adrenaline rush of sitting in a self-driven safari vehicle, on a narrow track, whilst a huge herd moves around you is something you never forget. The vulnerability you feel is heightened by the contradictory information available on what to do in such a situation. I've researched extensively online and asked numerous safari guides, but have received conflicting advice on whether to turn the engine off, or leave it idling, and rev it slightly if an elephant is approaching too closely. On the basis that a quick exit may be needed, I tend to adopt the latter strategy! When driving around elephants you also need to be able to quickly gauge what you're dealing with. A bull elephant, weighing over six tons, who could easily destroy a Land Rover, is a different proposition to a female of around half his weight. A family group with young calves is likely to contain new mothers, who are skittish and protective around their young, and may react unpredictably.

The absolute worst-case scenario though, is being confronted by a huge bull elephant in musth. Musth is the Sanskrit word for intoxication, and an elephant in musth, does have much in common with a belligerent human drunk, but is a thousand times more deadly! During the temporary state of musth, the elephant's testosterone levels surge six-fold, inducing a sexual frenzy which often results in terrifyingly destructive aggression, and attacks on vehicles and other animals. Bull elephants in musth have been known to gore adult rhinos and other elephants to death in unprovoked attacks, which is perhaps the wildlife equivalent of 'glassing' a stranger in a night club.

In addition to increased testosterone levels, the violent tendencies are thought to be related to pain in the beast's head, caused by a swelling of the temporal gland, which causes a pungent smelling secretion called temporin to pour from ducts behind the eyes. The elephant's penis can become permanently enlarged, causing it to trail on the ground, making the animal ejaculate and urinate constantly. The rear legs of a musth-bull are generally coated in a green-tinged cocktail of urine and semen, and he emits a constant low-pitched growl, known as the musth-rumble, as he sways along, encumbered by his sore head and painfully swollen genitals.

It was this terrifying sight we encountered on a small dirt track in South Africa, with only passing space for one vehicle, or one elephant. I paused as we approached, having spotted tree branches ahead swaying erratically, a tell-tale sign of elephants. Sure enough, upon stopping, we could hear the sound of crashing branches, and after a few minutes, our worst fears were realised as a large bull elephant emerged from the bush and began swaying slowly towards us. The track behind us was narrow and winding, and reversing would be very difficult, if not impossible.

Our only option was to wait. As he approached, around two hundred yards down the road, I noticed he was swinging his head from side to side, a sure sign of musth related discomfort. As he got closer, we spotted the staining on his front legs from the temporin, which was pouring from behind his eyes like sticky tears. We'd encountered bull elephants before, but not on such a narrow track, with so little space to manoeuvre. And we'd fortunately never met one that was in musth. All we could do was sit and wait, praying that he passed us without attempting to attack our vehicle, or mate with it, which would have equally dire consequences.

Waiting helplessly whilst watching the approach of this huge animal, fifteen feet tall and at six tons, more than double the weight of our Toyota Hilux, with the power to easily destroy the 4x4, made us appreciate that for all man's cultural and technological advances, there, in the African bush, the forces of nature were still very much in the ascendency.

We felt very insignificant, and helpless, as he lumbered towards us, and we caught the first sickly sweet scent of temporin, and felt the resonance of his low growl above the sound of our idling engine. My foot rested on the gas pedal, my planned tactic being that if he attacked, it would hopefully be when he drew alongside us, allowing me to accelerate away in a forward direction. With no hope of a speedy retreat in reverse without ending up literally in the bush, I could only pray he wouldn't launch a head-on assault.

The seconds as he approached us felt like a lifetime. He knew we were there, in his path, but showed no sign of aggression. If anything, he seemed to be weighing up his options for passing us. Maybe the throbbing pain in his head, feeling like an annoying toothache, made a frontal charge seem unappealing. Whatever the reason, to our enormous relief, when around twenty five feet from our vehicle, he suddenly turned off the track, and began tearing at the roadside foliage with his powerful trunk. I depressed the accelerator gently and we crept forward, then when I was certain he was fully occupied in stripping the lower branches of a leadwood tree, and there was no chance of him catching us in a rapid turn and pursuit, I put my foot down and we sped away in a cloud of dust, our hearts still thumping, part in fear, but also in awe of the raw power of nature witnessed at close quarters.

Elephants can pose a very real danger, and that was brought home to us when we visited Majete Wildlife Reserve, in South Western Malawi. We were self-driving in the ill-fated vehicle with defective brakes, which was now also proudly bearing the scratched stickman porn on its paintwork. Majete is widely seen as an African conservation success story. After its large mammal population was wiped out entirely by poaching by the late 1990's, the Malawi government embarked on extensive species re-introduction and anti-poaching programmes, and at the time of our visit, there were over twelve thousand animals living within its three hundred square mile boundary, including black rhino, lion and over four hundred elephants.

We stayed in a lodge close to the park entrance and arrived at 6.30am, recognising dawn as one of the optimum times to spot wildlife on the move, before the sun gained the heat of mid-morning. The visitor centre was typically haphazard. We were the first visitors of the day, and had to rouse an olive-uniformed guard from his slumber to open the gates for us. I asked for tips on where to see animals, and his advice lacked detail but proved to be accurate.

"Many elephants! Everywhere!" he beamed, waving his anti-poaching assault rifle like an excited schoolboy.

We set off and very soon came across a large herd, mainly comprising of mothers with infants of varying ages. They were moving through the bush on both sides of the road ahead of us, heading in our direction. Noting the presence of young babies, I adopted a cautious approach, and stopped the vehicle, allowing the elephants to approach us, rather than vice versa. We sat with the engine idling for around fifteen minutes while the herd passed around us at very close quarters. At one stage, Kirsty could have reached out of her window and touched a young female as she lumbered past. The elephants seemed edgy and wary, and the arrival of a safari jeep driven by a local guide and carrying a European couple, seemed to induce more nervousness. For the first time, I sensed what I could only describe as irritation at our presence, and it was a relief when the herd had passed us.

Around an hour later we came across another large group of females and their young, on a stretch of sand road running parallel to a river. The elephants were grazing around twenty feet from the edge of the track ahead of us, and initially seemed untroubled by our arrival. I was careful to approach slowly, to ensure that they'd seen us, and we wouldn't be surprising them. I made sure I didn't rev the engine and drove at a steady pace towards them. In other words, I did everything right. It was therefore a shock as we drew closer, to see a large female turn to look in our direction, toss her huge head and trumpet loudly, before charging towards us. In a mock charge, the elephant will flap its ears and raise its head, in order to appear as threatening as possible. On this occasion, the ears were pinned to the side of the head, which was lowered towards the ground. All indicators that this was no bluff calling exercise - this was one very pissed-off elephant.

She was about thirty feet away from us but was unfortunately in the direction we were heading towards. Driving forward would actually be taking us closer to the fast charging beast. However, my reversal speed would obviously be slower, and it was unlikely I'd be able to maintain the 20mph needed to outrun a charging tusker for long enough to escape. I had to make a split second decision, and gambled on being able to accelerate forward quickly enough to evade being rammed from the side. I put my foot down and we hurtled forward, bouncing out of ruts in the road surface which slowed us initially and made it appear that the elephant was going to win this dangerous race. With a final stab of the accelerator, and with the rear end of the vehicle fish-tailing in the dust, we sped forward to pass around ten feet ahead of the tusks of the enraged, trumpeting animal. I glanced in the rear-view mirror and saw that she hadn't given up. We bounced along the road with the elephant in hot pursuit for around two hundred yards, until she disappeared into the red dust cloud churned up by our wheels.

The rest of the day followed a similar pattern of close encounters with nervous, unpredictable elephants behaving more aggressively than in any of our previous encounters with them. My usual rules of driving near elephants went out of the window, as it became impossible to gauge how the animals were going to react to our presence. The culmination of what had become a fraught, and at times, scary drive, was an encounter with a huge bull elephant who was on the rampage in a dry riverbed in the late afternoon. We needed to negotiate the steep banks to cross the gully, and as we approached, couldn't see the animal, only large branches being torn from trees in a display which seemed more likely driven by the violent urges of musth than hunger. We edged forward, but without actually entering the water course it was impossible to see exactly how far away the elephant was, or which direction he was facing. The fact that we also couldn't assess the terrain on the river bed meant we had no idea what speed we could achieve while passing the animal. Proceeding would effectively be a game of Russian Roulette, safari style! Once descended, we may not be able to easily ascend the far bank, leaving us trapped in a ditch with an angry, testosterone fuelled bull elephant.

We considered what was the worst that could happen. Then we turned around and drove back the way we'd come – an additional ten miles of dusty, bumpy, dirt-track driving. It was getting dark when we finally reached the entrance gate, and this time we had to rouse the same guard from his late afternoon nap. My confidence in driving near elephants had been shaken by the day's events, and I needed to understand whether their behaviour was typical. The guard's response to my question was somewhat unexpected.

"Yes sir. Our elephants are THE most aggresseeeve in the whole of Africa." He beamed a brilliant white toothed smile, like a proud father boasting of a child's top mark in a maths test.

"Erm, sorry, what do you mean?" He took my confusion as a rebuttal of his claim, so added some additional information to prove his point.

"Yes, highly aggresseeeve. They attack tourist from...erm, where is the place...maybe Canada. No, New Zealand." He rubbed the grey stubble on his chin as he struggled to recall this all-important detail.

"Maybe Japan? No, he was a white man...Australia? No, not Australia. I forget the name..." He furrowed his brow as he attempted to summon the name of the far-off mystery land.

Kirsty and I were less concerned with the supposed victim's nationality than the detail of what had happened.

"When was this?"

"What day is today?"

"Monday."

The furrowed brow returned and a quick backwards count using his fingers provided us with an answer.

"I think Thursday sir."

"Last Thursday?? What happened? Is he okay?" After the day we'd just had, this news was disturbing, particularly as no one had thought to inform us before we set off on our drive.

The guard looked a little sheepish now, the pride in his 'most aggressive' elephants tempered by a nervousness that he was perhaps sharing too much info. He muttered something under his breath and turned away.

"Sorry, I didn't catch that. Is the tourist okay?"

"He is dead sir." His eyes looked to the floor and an embarrassed smile played on his lips. "Yes, dead. It's very sad sir." This time the news was imparted in the manner of a parent telling a six-year-old that their rabbit had died.

Even in a country like Malawi, with primitive communications and authorities who are potentially both willing and able to suppress inconvenient facts, it seemed implausible that such an incident would go unreported. Also, that tourists would still be allowed to self-drive amongst potentially dangerous elephants less than a week after a fatal attack. We therefore viewed the information with scepticism as we left the reserve and headed back to our lodge, where a quick Google search on the steam-powered, dial-up Wifi confirmed our suspicions – no elephant attack had been reported.

A month later, I was sat in a meeting in an air conditioned, glass walled office in London. The pine-look desk in front of me was replete with Pret-a-Manger sandwiches and burgundy Costa Coffee take-out cups. A colleague in modern 'Telco-casual' office attire of jeans and an open necked blue shirt, was taking us through a Powerpoint slidedeck on budget gap closure, conflicting KPI's and customer-led sales incentives. Around half the twelve people in the room were surreptitiously flicking their phone screens, as if checking for an important email, but were more likely on Twitter or Facebook. As was often the case, my mind was seven thousand miles away. This time I was back on the dusty, rutted roads of Malawi. Reliving the tense moments when we were surrounded by a large herd of skittish elephants. Revisiting my decision to drive forward, rather than reverse when faced with the charging female. Pondering on what would have happened had we chosen to risk crossing the riverbed with the rogue bull elephant. The behaviour of the animals still puzzled and troubled me. I picked up my phone and googled 'Elephant attack Majete.'

The screen flashed into life around fifty times faster than it had when I'd last searched those words at our Malawaian lodge, and the story emerged via three Scandinavian news agencies.

'An experienced Norwegian safari leader has died following an elephant attack during a safari in Majete Reserve, Malawi. Sigurd Halvorsen,71, a native of Haugesund, had led hundreds of safaris in Africa and was also a keen nature photographer – an interest that tragically led to his death. The critical injuries he sustained were from an incident that occurred in mid-November, after which the man was treated at a hospital in South Africa, but unfortunately died of his injuries.'

A chill ran down my spine as I read how the vehicle containing Halvorsen and six tourists was overturned by a charging elephant. They scattered as the animal continued to attack the vehicle and once in the open, the dead man was pursued, before being trampled and gored, sustaining grave injuries. Further online investigation suggested that the Majete elephants may have learnt their aggressive behaviour from a 'rogue herd' of over eighty animals which was relocated from Mangochi in Southern Malawi in 2009. This group seemed, over time, to have lost their fear of humans, bringing them into conflict with locals, resulting in the deaths of over twenty farmers and countless elephants since 2004. The hope in relocating some of the troublesome animals, was that the placid nature of Majete's incumbent herd would rub off on their Mangochi cousins. Instead, it seems the reverse may have happened, and the southern herd's aggression had infected the previously benign Majete families. After years of conflict with humans, perhaps this shouldn't be a surprise. As everyone knows, elephants never forget.

"I think you are either very brave, or very crazy...maybe a little of both?" The Frenchman looked me up and down, a puzzled half smile playing about his lips, between drags of his cigarette. I nodded, a great feeling of relief washing over me. In terms of the very, very worst that could happen, the appearance of the three 4-wheel drive safari vehicles on this remote track in Botswana's Chobe National Park, had prevented what was fast escalating into a life-threatening episode. On this occasion the worst that could happen, could very easily have been mine and Kirsty's deaths.

It was therefore difficult to argue with the Frenchman's summary of our situation. His party had found us stranded, on a rarely used, deep sand track, in one of the most remote and hostile environments on earth. We had no distress flares, satellite phone or GPS tracker. There was no cellular coverage and no one knew where we were. We had food and water to last maybe five days, but it could easily be a month before another vehicle drove this track, maybe longer. We had no gun. Hiking cross country to seek help would likely result in attack by one of the numerous lion prides who called this desert region their home. Of all our 'what's the worst that could happen?' situations, this was easily the most serious. Before our rescuers arrived, this one looked likely to be our last.

Our adventure had begun when I'd read about Chobe National Park, a 50,000 square kilometre expanse of sandy flatlands, populated by few humans and many wild animals. It is rightly viewed as one of the wildest, most untamed areas of Africa, and probably the world. I desperately wanted to undertake a self-drive safari in Chobe, but the cost of renting a self-contained 4x4, with rooftop-tent and cooking facilities in Botswana's capital Gaborone, or the northern gateway town of Maun, was hugely prohibitive. As usual, I looked at cheaper ways to do a two week trip, and found a company in neighbouring Zambia who would rent me a fully equipped Ford Ranger for around half the equivalent cost in Botswana. We'd cross the Zambezi River using the Kazungula vehicle ferry, and enter Botswana at the border town of Kasane, then follow the river from which Chobe takes its name, until we entered the wilderness, where we'd spend a week camping in our self-contained vehicle.

I'd made it clear in my emails that my plan was to go to Chobe, but only one employee of the Zambian rental company had ever been there. With hindsight, it's unlikely anyone in the town of Livingstone had any idea how tough the conditions were across the border. The staff spent time showing us how to erect the rooftop tent and work the cooking facilities in the flatbed of the Ford Ranger. They also showed me the winch, to be used to extract the vehicle should it become stuck in a river, deep sand or mud. Unfortunately, showing me consisted of pointing at it. They obviously didn't feel it necessary to show me how to actually use it.

We had expected tough driving conditions when we'd planned the trip. How tough it actually was, took us by surprise though. It was the dry season, and the ill-defined tracks were made up of deep, fine sand. It was like driving on swirling dunes, and handling of the vehicle bore no similarity to driving on tarmac or gravel. This wasn't helped by the fact that I'd stupidly forgotten to deflate the tyres, and their lack of traction made driving feel like trying to control a speedboat on a choppy sea. For the most part I was trying to follow the faint tyre grooves of other vehicles in the sand, but occasionally these had been obscured by the harsh desert wind, which called for a slow-down to snail's pace as we tried to pick out the best route, avoiding deep sand which could strand us.

Eventually we arrived at our first campsite at Ihaha, a dusty spot next to the Chobe River, and I began to collect wood for a fire. Although we had a gas-powered hob on the Ford Ranger for cooking, I remembered advice from Noah on our Tanzania safari, that a night time fire was necessary to keep predators at bay. What he'd failed to tell me, and was especially relevant now, was that hippos are attracted to light, and a riverside fire may draw the attention of the animal widely reckoned to be the most likely to kill humans in Africa. Perhaps fortunately, I'd failed to gauge how quickly the dry mopane wood burnt, and not long after we'd eaten, our supply of fuel was exhausted, and we were forced to retire to the relative safety of our tent on the cab roof.

We'd read an online forum which warned of bandit attacks on lone vehicles, and we were the only ones at Ihaha that night. Also, Kirsty had pointed out that a lion could easily climb onto the bonnet of the Ford Ranger, thereby positioning itself just inches from our sleeping faces. Having read that banging pots and pans can scare lions off, and identifying a big kitchen knife as the best bandit deterrent, we retreated to the tent with most of the contents of our vehicle's cutlery drawer secreted in our sleeping bags.

Lying in our tent, we listened to the sounds of the bush. Hippos snorting in the river a couple of hundred yards away, the hoot-hoot cry of a hyena, and the distant bronchial cough-growl-cough-growl of a lion, all meant that a sound night's sleep was unlikely. I felt that I hadn't even nodded off when I was awoken by the sound of thunder. A deep rumbling which seemed to increase steadily, until realisation dawned that it was indeed getting closer. I sat up and peeled back the tent's fly screen. We peered wide eyed into the milky, moonlit night, shocked to see an approaching blur of flashing black and white. Dozens of zebra, spooked and running for their lives, dashed in panic around our vehicle, and at once we understood why a group of the animals is referred to as a 'dazzle.' It was clear that the Chobe lions were hunting.

In the morning, we set off to drive to our next camp and were almost immediately forced to change route and backtrack. A family group of ten elephants were striding down the narrow sand road towards us. Two big adults flapped their ears to show us that they definitely had the right of way, as we performed a hurried U-Turn to clear the way for them to pass. The 125 mile drive from Ihaha to our next camp at Savuti took nearly six hours. Six hours of bone jarring driving on some of the most challenging tracks I've encountered anywhere in the world. We saw few other vehicles, and signage was non-existent. On a couple of occasions, we picked the wrong route and became temporarily stuck, and it was hard to prevent our minds straying to thoughts of the unfortunate Bullens.

In September 2011, Mr. and Mrs. Bullen, a South African couple, were travelling in the same area of Chobe, and became stranded in deep sand. After two days, and with no sign of rescue, Mr Bullen set off walking to find help. His wife was found in the vehicle three days later, down to her last half litre of water, and probably a day away from death. Mr Bullen has never been found, his body presumed to have been devoured by the predators which killed him. The risk of attack from animals is ever present in Chobe. Therefore, leaving the vehicle even for a few moments to remove stones or branches from the track, required absolute vigilance, with Kirsty posted as a lookout on the cab roof.

Despite the tough driving conditions, once we arrived at a camp site and erected our tent, gathered wood and lit the vital night-time fire, then got the 'brai' fired up and a couple of steaks sizzling, we knew it was worth it. After the first night's wood shortage, foraging for firewood became something of an obsession for me. However, ever mindful of the danger posed by Chobe's resident wildlife, I was constantly watchful when gathering my sticks. With adrenaline pumping and every sense heightened, I knew that behind every collapsed tree trunk, bush thicket or termite mound, there could be a pride of snoozing, hungry lions who would view me as an easy meal. Creeping along, heart thumping, cringing at the crack of every snapped twig and with an armful of mopane branches, I'd never felt so scared, or so alive.

Then in the evening, sitting by the fire, with no other humans for miles around, with a couple of cold Castle Beers in hand, gazing at the amazing celestial canopy spread above us was an unforgettable feeling. And the difficulty in reaching those isolated and wild places made that feeling even better.

A couple of days into our adventure we were exploring an area of grassland running parallel to a small, fast flowing river. Two cool-dude Italians in shades, driving a new Land Rover waved us down and said they'd been told of a leopard in the low branches of a tree, near the corpse of a baby elephant. We confirmed the location of the unfortunate infant, and set off with them to try and locate the leopard, which is one of the most elusive of safari 'spots.' (Pardon the pun!) After driving for around twenty minutes, the track we were following disappeared into the river and emerged in the form of steeply rutted, sandy tracks on the far bank. The Italians exited their Land Rover and assessed the crossing, before taking the decision to proceed. They plunged cautiously into the water, which immediately submerged their van's bonnet. I watched as they struggled across, and lurched up the steep incline at the other side, from where they called and waved, encouraging me to follow. I wasn't sure. The water looked deep, and Kirsty was advising caution, but as any man will tell you, when two other blokes have just completed a driving challenge and are throwing down the gauntlet to you, there's only one course of action.

Kirsty's last words as we plunged down the bank were 'Oh no.'

As she uttered the words, a huge bow wave came over the front of our vehicle and hit the windscreen. I ploughed forward, with 4-wheel-drive engaged, and our bonnet fully submerged beneath the fast-flowing water. It was at this point that I looked toward the far bank and noticed that the Italian's Land Rover had a snorkel – a device used to elevate the air intake above the water line, therefore preventing moisture from entering the engine. As it dawned on me that our Ford Ranger unfortunately didn't share this feature, I felt the front of the vehicle begin to rise in the current, and drift in the direction of the river's flow. I panicked and did the worst thing possible and accelerated. I just wanted to get onto dry land as quickly as possible, via the shortest route to the far bank. With the water lapping around the bottom of our windscreen, we reached the far side, and again I pressed hard on the accelerator. With engine screaming, we emerged from the water and hit the steep slope at speed. There was a huge bang and our wheels span as we struggled to clear the incline.

The Italians laughed and shouted 'Bravo!' as I got out of the cab to inspect the damage. The Ranger was wheezing, choking and spluttering like an asthmatic cross-channel swimmer. Alarmingly, the bull bars at the front of the vehicle were no longer aligned with the bumper, they now stuck out horizontally at a ninety-degree angle. Closer inspection revealed that their connection brackets had been forced up through the engine compartment as we'd hit the bank, but by some fluke had seemingly failed to cause any serious damage.

The Italians sped off in search of the leopard, but our van was clearly suffering the effects of its immersion and, after spluttering and lurching along behind them for twenty minutes, we were forced to abandon the hunt and turn back. I was hoping to find a bridge or even a ford, but after an hour of searching, we came to the conclusion that there was only way back across the river - the same treacherous point we'd crossed it earlier.

We arrived back at the crossing point to find two 4x4's containing an assortment of red faced South African men of varying ages, swilling beer from cans, who seemed to be some sort of hunting focused bachelor party. One of their vehicles had become stranded in the river, and four overweight, shaven headed men in too-tight, too-short shorts were drinking cans of Castle, while the contents of their wallets dried on the bank. Luckily, they had a winch, and unlike me, knew how to use it, so had been able to recover their van.

"What happened to your bull bars?" asked a middle-aged Afrikaaner with a spectacular ginger moustache, looking confused at their unconventional angle. I explained our previous encounter with the river and my nervousness about the return crossing. There followed a heated argument between the men on the best strategy for re-crossing the water, which seemed likely to end in violence, as they all loudly put forward their conflicting theories. There was general agreement though, that their winch line should be attached before we entered the water, to avoid anyone having to wade into the potentially croc-infested river to attach it, if, as seemed likely, we became stuck.

My main concern as we entered the river for a second time was that the engine would pack up completely, and we'd float away downstream, so at least the attached winch cable made that 'worst thing' less likely to happen. Amidst a clamour of shouted drunken advice and much waving of arms from our South African friends, I managed this time to retain my composure, in order to maintain a steady pace as we crossed. Again, large waves bounced off our windscreen, and at one point I almost stalled as we descended into a large pot-hole in the rocky river bed, but we eventually emerged on the far bank to the cheers of the South Africans. I unhooked the winch, and we stuttered and spluttered back to camp, our new bull bar arrangement causing some quizzical looks from the few other campers present as we returned at dusk.

The following morning, we were awake at first light, roof-tent packed and ready to go. We wanted to see lions hunting, and dawn is the best time to catch these daytime snoozers in a more lively frame of mind. There's really no such thing as a main road in Chobe, but the track which leads from Savuti Camp to the airstrip is probably the closest you get, in that it's deep sand, but usually has two or three sets of vague tyre tracks to follow. We'd bounced along this route a few times, and had seen great herds of elephants, untold numbers of giraffes and cape buffalo, and so many members of the antelope family that they no longer warranted a second glance, but we'd seen no lions in the area.

We therefore decided that our best bet was a detour on a minor track, which appeared as a thin dotted line on our map, though we had already discovered that due to the shifting sands and ill-defined roads, the map seemed to bear little resemblance to real life. It helpfully had GPS coordinates for various points, though that was of no use to us as we had no GPS device. With a total lack of signage and one small track looking very much like another, we had no real way of knowing whether the trail we were following, actually was the dotted line on our map. After driving for over an hour, we'd seen no other vehicles, or lions, and even in Chobe's rough, wild and isolated terrain, the route was proving incredibly tough going. The challenges of driving in deep, powdery sand were compounded by the undulating ground, and gentle inclines which would have been almost undetectable on a gravel road, became tricky obstacles which our vehicle struggled to scale.

It was while ascending one of these small slopes that our slow progress was brought to a grinding halt by a large bang, as our front axle made contact with a boulder concealed six inches below the sandy surface of the track. My attempts at reversing back from the obstacle only succeeded in burying our wheels even deeper. We were embedded to such a level that when I attempted to exit the cab to take stock of the situation, I struggled to open the door. The sand reached halfway up our wheels, and was above the door sills. We were well and truly buried and I cursed myself for not demanding a full lesson in use of the van's winch.

An hour later, I was coated in a fine sheen of sweat and dust, having failed to make any progress at all in shovelling us clear of the deep sandy trough in which we were trapped. Kirsty sat on the cab roof, scanning the scrubby brush for the lions we now desperately hoped not to see, and it began to dawn on me that there was no easy way out of this.

We'd bitten off more than we could chew, and this time it could result in the most serious of consequences. The morning heat was increasing, we were on an isolated, seldom driven track, miles from any camp or lodge, and had no way of knowing when, or if, another vehicle would come this way. I'd spotted thorn bushes a few hundred yards back down the track, so was already formulating a plan to get a fire going, to generate some smoke signals which would hopefully be spotted from Savuti Camp, or by one of the light aircraft using the nearby landing strip. We had enough food and water to last maybe a week at the most, but seven days stuck in the bush in searing heat, surrounded by deadly predators, wasn't a prospect either of us even wanted to contemplate. We both silently considered what the worst was that could happen, then dispelled the terrible thought without voicing it. The unfortunate fate of the Bullen's suddenly seemed all too real.

Our immediate surroundings were low dunes flecked with scrubby foliage to the right, and a boulder strewn hillock, two hundred yards to the left. The latter was a perfect daytime resting spot for lions, and Kirsty voiced concern at my suggestion that I forage for brushwood to light a fire. We'd turned the engine off to conserve fuel. Our fridge ran from a gas bottle, but would also function via the vehicle battery, so, now very much in survival mode, we began to work out the optimum use of the resources available to us. That meant no engine, so no air-con, until the heat on the roof became intolerable and we allowed ourselves a five minute AC-Cool-down in the cab.

Sitting back on the cab roof in the heat, vainly scanning the horizon for signs of potential rescue, Kirsty and I were lost in our own thoughts. Neither of us spoke. I silently cursed my stupidity in trying to beat the system in order to cut costs. I berated myself at a lack of research on just how tough it was to self-drive in Chobe, as a lone vehicle and lacking in the necessary technological back up and bush skills training. I reflected on what it was that drove me to seek out adventure in wild places like Botswana. Was it my safe, comfortable, corporate air-conditioned-office lifestyle? My centrally heated suburban home, with Uber/Amazon instant gratification and 'always-on' connectivity, a life without danger or risk that had brought me here? Or was it that deep-seated latent urge to explore well off the beaten track, that I'd first felt as a child, which had finally done for me?

Any feelings of self-pity at my own likely demise were lost in the wave of guilt I felt at bringing Kirsty here. We had lengthy discussions when planning trips. Details of where to go, and how, was a joint responsibility. But the logistics of this trip were down to me. This savvy-travelling, cost cutting, self-driver had found a way to achieve what should have been a bank-busting safari, on a budget. I'd traversed national boundaries and exploited regional currency variations to halve the cost of the adventure. And now I'd killed us.

We sat in silence, a strange calm having descended. That often quoted workplace prediction of my likely cause of death echoed in my head, and I almost smiled, reconciling myself to the knowledge that I'd always choose being eaten by a lion to be being taken out by the number 96 bus to Headingley anyway.

Perhaps we'd both drifted into a fitful, cab-roof sleep when we sensed the slight, almost undetectable shift in the sounds of the bush. Something new and alien above the click and buzz of insects, and the hiss of breeze blown sand. Something unnatural, mechanical. We both sat up, as the now unmistakable sound of a motor, growing louder. We scanned the clear blue sky and quickly discounted an aircraft. The sound was land-borne, and was approaching from behind the rocky hillock.

If we'd been praying on the cab roof, then God couldn't have responded in a more spectacular manner. Not one vehicle, but three. A convoy of French and Swiss travellers who we recognised as those who'd regarded our unconventional bull-bar arrangement with amusement the previous evening. Our relief must have been evident, and we struggled to maintain our reserve. English people don't do hugs and back slaps after all!

They were experienced 4-wheel-drivers and regular visitors to

Africa. After hearing we had no GPS, Sat-Phone or distress beacon, Valentin gave me his 'brave or crazy' judgement, but later admitted that on their first visit to Botswana they had experienced a similar fate to us. They had been trapped in their vehicle in a deep, crocodile infested river, up to their chests in water, for four hours until someone luckily found and rescued them. They vowed at that point never to visit again without a back-up vehicle equipped with a winch. After fifteen minutes of towing and digging we were finally freed from our sandy tomb, and our saviours more or less insisted that we join their convoy - replete with winches and tow ropes, a GPS, in-cab radio transmitters, plus a party member who was a qualified zoologist and wild animal behavioural expert.

Driving in a four vehicle convoy was a game-changer in terms of where we could go, and what we could see. Having back-up vehicles allowed all of us to take risks that would be suicidal for a single van. We crossed deep rivers and flooded plains, explored tracks which seemed almost undriveable and felt untouched by humans. We shared a typically French picnic lunch of cheese and wine under a towering baobob tree, until we were forced to hastily retreat to our vehicles when a large bull elephant suddenly arrived to gatecrash the party. We watched an enormous elephant herd splashing in a river, at a distance Kirsty and I would never have dared to consider, until Stephanie, the zoologist, detected a subtle change in the matriarch's mood, which sent us all scurrying away to safety. We saw lions hunting in the distance, and snoozing by our front wheels. We picked a slow course between a hundred-strong buffalo herd, and were befriended by a pack of curious hyena cubs, who approached the strange human visitors while sniffing the air, bobbing their heads and squeaking like pet shop puppies.

It was a great day which I'll never forget, though it was physically and mentally exhausting. Back at Savuti Camp, night fell quickly, and I headed to the primitive, and now pitch-black shower block. Flicking on my torch to try to locate the tap, I noticed dozens of spiders, the size of my hand, suspended in multiple webs just above my head. I was too hot to care, and stood beneath the welcome chill of the cold shower in the total darkness, with my eight-legged companions, reflecting on how close we'd come to disaster that day.

I returned to our camping pitch, and knowing Kirsty has slight arachnophobic tendencies, warned her about the inhabitants of the showerblock roof. She'd had her own unexpected wildlife encounter while I was gone though. After getting the brai grill fired up, she'd returned to the Ford Ranger to retrieve the night's meat from the fridge, only to come face to face with a huge elephant emerging from behind the vehicle. With no time to retreat, she was involuntarily frozen to the spot, as the huge beast lumbered out of the darkness, gave her a quick 'once-over' from round ten feet away, then continued on its way into the night. A typically heart-stopping end to a day neither of us are ever likely to forget.

Wild Africa is an amazing place, and a self-drive safari, apart from being a fraction of the cost of an accompanied tour, is a real test of your resources and sense of adventure. I have some great memories and a host of tales from Chobe and the other safari trips we've experienced over the years. However, Botswana taught me an important lesson – that the right level of research and preparation is absolutely vital. We were lucky and got away with it. As Mr and Mrs Bullen unfortunately discovered, not everyone does.

12 ALL CREATURES GREAT AND SMALL

Seeking out and interacting with wildlife in its natural habitat can be a fantastic travel experience, but if you lack the inclination to spend time in the bush, there are plenty of other opportunities to experience the natural world, in often unexpected, and sometimes unwelcome locations!

In Africa in particular, with urban areas increasingly encroaching on wild spaces, a surprising range of wildlife can be encountered within towns and cities, maybe none so surprising as the beast we bumped into on a night out in South Africa. We were visiting KwaZulu-Natal province, and had spent the day self-driving in iSimangaliso Wetland and the Hluhluwe iMfolozi Game Reserve. The latter is home to one of Africa's largest populations of both black and white rhino, and we felt privileged to observe these highly endangered animals in the wild, and at close quarters. It was a sobering thought to watch three black rhino wallowing in the cool mud of a waterhole, and consider that the species is likely to be extinct in twenty years if nothing is done to quell the Far East's senseless craving for their horns.

In the late afternoon, we came across two young, male white rhinos on an expanse of grassy veldt, running parallel to the track we were driving. They seemed agitated by our arrival and began behaving like typical teenage lads – posturing and trying to appear threatening; charging left and right, snorting loudly, tossing their ungainly heads and stamping the ground. Their bravado worked with Kirsty, and she urged me to drive on, but I'd noticed that the rhinos were on a small elevated grass shelf, and would have to negotiate a steep slope to get anywhere near us. I therefore cruelly refused to budge, as the two-ton beasts rampaged around, a hundred yards away, their behaviour seeming to rub off on Kirsty, who was becoming increasingly concerned.

I eventually realised that my little prank wasn't going down well, even after I pointed out that the rhinos would be unable to reach our vehicle quickly without a set of step-ladders, and we drove on, in silence, as is usually the case when Kirsty doesn't appreciate one of my 'jokes.' To further heighten the tension, on our drive back to the small, Elephant Coast town of St Lucia, we drove into a mini-hurricane.

I've driven through some violent storms on my travels, but nothing like this. The late afternoon sky became as dark as night, and a gale-force wind whipped up from nowhere. Rain, then hailstones the size of marbles bounced off our windscreen, to such an extent that I was still unable to see through it, even after slowing to 10mph. It was like being in a car wash, with an electrical storm of unbelievable ferocity raging around us as we crawled along at walking pace. The sheet lightning was almost constant for a ten minute period as we travelled through the eye of the storm, and the continual flash of lightning strikes on the road ahead was like driving across a nightclub dancefloor with a strobe light on constant repeat.

We eventually limped into St. Lucia and found a town mopping up after the storm. All power was out, and glum faced shopkeepers and householders were hauling sodden produce and furniture onto the pavements to dry, with the town's drainage system having failed to cope with the sudden influx of rainfall. We had a quick shower and headed out as night fell, our torches illuminating the footpaths, with news received that electricity was unlikely to be restored until morning.

The town is situated on a wide estuary flowing into the Indian Ocean, and the bars and restaurants on its small main street are backed by water. With approaching car headlights dazzling us as they loomed out of the darkness, we felt quite disorientated as we stumbled along the path leading to the town centre, guided by the flickering beams of our small torches. We could see brightly coloured, flashing lights in the distance and hear music playing above the buzz of generators, so headed in that direction, with no obvious point of reference in the otherwise dark streets. Kirsty was walking on my right, and her tight grip on my arm told me she was still on edge following the earlier rhino encounter. The extent of her nervousness became apparent a couple of seconds later, as she seemed to levitate a foot in the air, whilst taking five sizeable chunks of flesh out of my arm with her nails, and emitting a blood curdling yell.

"ITTTSSSAAARHIIIINNNNO!!!!"

I was barged out of the way as she fled across the road, leaving me peering into the gloom, laughing whilst trying to spot the cow which I could hear crashing through the undergrowth by the side of the path. Seconds later I was following Kirsty, at an even greater speed. Probing the foliage with my torch, I'd spotted two red eyes staring back at me. In the split second it took me to wonder why the cow's eyes were so far apart, and also why it's skin appeared to be made of grey leather, I managed to deduce that Kirsty's rhino was in fact an adult hippo, and true to form, it seemed to be attracted to the light of my torch as it emerged at speed from the bushes and charged towards me.

A hippo can run at 20mph and this one would have needed to be at top speed to catch me, as I hared across the road with the animal lumbering after me. I leapt a small fence onto the patio area of a bar where a number of drinkers were shouting encouragement to me, or perhaps more likely, to my pursuer. Safely in the bar's beer garden with drinks in hand, we spent an enjoyable half hour watching the hippo as it ambled along the town's dimly-lit main strip. Cars swerved as the huge beast appeared suddenly in their headlight beam, and more than one early evening boozer leapt a fence or ducked into a doorway, as they realised the approaching animal wasn't a drink induced hallucination.

"Rhino?" I teased Kirsty. "Cow?" She replied. We called it a draw.

Bumping into wildlife in the unexpected setting of a town centre is one thing, but having it visit you in your hotel room can be testing at times. However, it can also be highly satisfying when the initial response of hotel staff is a nonchalant 'So what?' shrug, which turns into horror when they appreciate the extent to which the local fauna has invaded your room!

This was the case when Kirsty and I were staying on the Thai island of Ko Samet, in a bamboo, thatched roof, beachfront bungalow. We were puzzled on the second morning when I stood on a small cat turd as I made my way to the shower. We hadn't noticed any cats, but had left the windows open during the night, so it was possible that we'd been visited by a local feline who'd left us this unwanted gift to mark its visit. I flicked the deposit out of the door and thought nothing more of it. Returning from an afternoon's motorbike exploration however, we were more perturbed to find another small shit pellet nestling in the centre of the pillow on our bed. This felt like a deliberate act. The placement on the pillow felt symbolic – the inherent threat being that the next excremental assault could be delivered upon our sleeping heads, and we resolved to close all the windows that night.

It was therefore, with a rising feeling of victimisation, not to say revulsion, that we woke in the humid light of dawn, to recoil at finding two fresh faecal deposits lying on the sheets of the bed. Clearly, whatever was emptying its bowels on us was doing so from the beams of the thatched roof - we were literally being shat upon from a great height.

Cleaners were summoned, faeces examined and heads scratched, as the presence of any cats around the guest house was denied. We accepted the staff's apologies, but I informed the manager that we would be forced to sleep in our crash helmets, visors lowered, and photos of our unusual sleeping attire would be added to Trip Advisor, in the event of a further incident that night.

At around 5pm I was lying on the bed reading, when I sensed a slight movement above me. I glanced towards the roof, and my eyes strained to focus on the shadowy recesses of the thatch. A further flicker of movement attracted my gaze to a large wooden beam which ran the length of the bungalow. I scanned it from left to right and saw nothing. Dark and gnarled, the beam was hewn from a single tree trunk, its shape irregular, especially around a foot to the right of where I was lying, where a large knot in the wood caused a tumorous bulge which I hadn't previously spotted. A large, sloping tumorous bulge, which was now moving along the beam as I watched. I leapt to my feet, shouting to Kirsty, who was in the shower. The faecal phantom had revealed himself!

Moments later I was in reception. The young desk clerk smiled a resigned smile. Another European tourist complaining about lizards in his bungalow.

"Ya Sar, is just gecko. Is okay," he trilled with the sing-song Thai intonation that can be endearing when spoken by a child or cute teenage girl, but bloody irritating when being delivered by a twenty five year old man with an ill-disguised, forced grin.

I shook my head and smiled back. "This is no gecko pal, I think you need to have a look."

It took me a few minutes to convince him, but eventually he accompanied me to the bungalow where Kirsty had now locked herself in the bathroom. The young chap swaggered in, no doubt expecting to catch a gecko in a cup. Instead, he found himself screwing up his eyes, following my pointed direction. His terror-stricken cry of surprise was hugely satisfying as he spotted the monitor lizard. Five feet long, with a split, flickering tongue and a tail which hung from the end of the beam, it resembled an adolescent crocodile.

After shaking his head and muttering some undecipherable Thai curses, the clerk fled and returned soon after with an older man, who seemed to be a gardener and was obviously an expert on monitor lizards, as he had brought specialist equipment in the form of a sweeping brush. With the young clerk holding a chair balanced precariously on the bed, on which the old man wobbled and teetered, he set about his task with enthusiasm, but little hope of success. Thrusting the brush towards the lizard and shouting 'Hey you! Hey! Hey!' unsurprisingly only caused it to retreat further into the roof, where we could see its head and flickering tongue taunting us.

"Okay now Sar, lizard gone," the desk clerk assured us. We were unconvinced and slept that night with the sheets over our heads. As we lay in the darkness, I commented that I was surprised a monitor lizard could climb into a thatched roof and balance on a thin beam, as they always seemed clumsy, cumbersome reptiles. I immediately wished I hadn't had said that, as an aerial shit strike suddenly became more appealing than the potential for a five stone lizard landing on us in the night. We got up and put on the crash helmets.

An even more pleasurable shattering of the laidback insouciance of a hotel employee, happened on the East African Island of Madagascar. We were in the rugged east of the island, exploring the Pangalanes Canal, a 375 mile long, man-made channel connecting a series of lakes and lagoons which run parallel to the Indian Ocean coast, linking the towns of Tamatave and Farafangana. We'd arrived by boat, enjoying the area's unique scenery - traditional Betsimisaraka villages, decorated with the huge horns of sacrificial zebu cattle; local fishermen on floating mobile homes – bamboo rafts supporting a small raffia hut; and crowded local ferries, the passengers pointing excitedly, waving and cheering at the sight of our pink faces.

We were staying at a rustic lodge near the third largest of the lakes, Lake Ampitabe, which could safely be classed as 'off the beaten track.' Our boat journey was followed by a bone jarring five mile 4x4 drive which took over an hour! We could literally have walked it as fast, and I did wonder why the lodge didn't invest in packhorses to collect guests from the boat, rather than a battered Land Rover.

The owners were a young, bohemian French couple, living out their fantasy of a Robinson Crusoe type existence far from civilisation. Gaston was about thirty, dark, swarthy and slenderly muscular. He was unshaven, tanned and bare of chest and foot, as he showed us to our thatched roof bungalow. The room had unshuttered, unglazed windows looking towards the lake, an outdoor cold water shower and a mosquito net covering the bed.

"You are totally in ze nature 'ere. Zer are insects and repteels which will come in ze room, but zey cause you no 'arm. We don't 'ave chemical fly spray, we respect ze nature ere." Gaston was looking at me suspiciously, correctly assuming I was the sort of character who would unleash a 50% Deet repellent at aggressive insects at the first opportunity. I nodded my agreement unconvincingly.

After an afternoon's exploration we returned to the bungalow and Kirsty bagged the first shower. I scratched as I removed my t-shirt, feeling the tickle of insects on my skin. I shook off the shirt and a couple of large black ants fell to the floor and scurried away. I next detected a tell-tale crawling in my hair and retrieved a similar six-legged intruder from there. At this point I happened to look at the roof of the mosquito net, and through the white gauze, spotted indistinct dark shapes which seemed to be moving. Using a bamboo chair as a makeshift step ladder, I elevated myself to a level where I could see the top of the net, which contained a couple of hundred ants, hurriedly marching in all directions around the net's surface. My powers of deduction told me that the roof was the likely source of our unwanted visitors, and I peered into the shadows of the thatch. I struggled to see clearly so reached for my torch and shone it into the straw of the roof.

Kirsty heard my cry of 'Jesus Christ,' and emerged from the shower, to join me in gazing upwards in horror as the beam of my torch scanned the thatch. The roof was made up of three large panels, and one of them, the one above our bed, was a moving, creeping, crawling mass of black insect bodies. The ant colony must have numbered in the millions, and they were now sharing our bungalow. As we stood, open mouthed, staring at the ceiling, dozens of ants were crawling on each of us, though thankfully weren't biting, yet.

Gaston was being Gallic and handsome, gazing at himself in a wall mounted mirror, and performing some manly task when I arrived at reception. I didn't know the French word for ants, so simply advised him that there were 'beaucoup de insects' in our room. Gaston sighed and regarded me with ill-disguised contempt.

"Yes, I told you zer would be insects in ze room. You are in ze nature." He shrugged and ran a hand through his ruggedly unkempt hair.

"No, I mean LOTS of insects. You really need to come."

After a couple of minutes of negotiation, in which Gaston tutted, shrugged, rolled his eyes and gazed at his perfect abs in the mirror, he shouted to his wife in French, that "this English tosser has got some flies in his room, so I'm going to have a walk up, shrug nonchalantly and tell him it's not my problem." That was the impression I got anyway.

Only that's not what he did. Gaston slouched into the bungalow with the air of a teenager being marched to his bedroom for an enforced cleaning exercise, and followed my pointed finger to the ceiling. His mouth fell open, and his eyes widened. Then the most satisfying transformation from aloof, cool-dude natureboy, to shit-scared, jibbering wreck took place before my eyes.

I couldn't make out what Gaston was shouting as he took off at speed towards the main building, and was disappointed not to hear my favourite school French expression of 'Zut Alors!' The word 'Termeetes' seemed to feature heavily though. What, at the time, I didn't appreciate was that an infestation by a large ant or termite colony such as this, could wreak devastation on the lodge. Termites in particular, could totally devour our hut in a matter of weeks, and carpenter ants would cause similar structural damage.

Minutes later, Gaston was back, accompanied by a resident ant expert, you've guessed it, the gardener again! The wiry old man of around seventy five, was rapidly despatched onto the roof, which he began to dismantle by ripping up the thatch. Kirsty had by now done the sensible thing and positioned herself on our room's porch, with a cold THB beer.

Gaston was babbling 'Nous cherchons la reine!' as palm fronds were tossed down from the roof, landing at our feet, and I eventually worked out that we needed to find the colony's Queen. Only the Queen ant lays eggs, so the act of insect regicide is necessary to prevent the continuation of the colony. With a lifespan of around twenty five years, the longest of any insect, the Queen ant is a high production egg machine, whose offspring could cause devastation for years to come, so the hunt for her was on!

Assuming she wouldn't be wearing a crown, I asked how we would spot the Queen, and Gaston held his thumb and forefinger about an inch apart, indicating that she would be what, in Yorkshire, we'd call 'a big lass.' The search continued, with Gaston and I sifting through palm branches alive with ants, looking for 'La Reine.' Once a palm frond had been searched, Gaston employed a hi-tech system to rid it of insects. He ignited the contents of an anti-perspirant aerosol with a lighter to create a makeshift flamethrower, then incinerated the fast moving ants. 'We respect ze nature' eh, Gaston?' I thought.

Although Gaston and I were covered in crawling insects as we searched the palm fronds being tossed from the roof, we remained free of bites. It was therefore something of a surprise to suddenly see the gardener, silhouetted against the rising moon, begin to cry out in pain and flail his arms wildly, to such an extent that it seemed he was about to tumble off the roof. Gaston and I exchanged puzzled glances, until, a couple of seconds later, we also came under attack. The tickly itch of insects on my skin and hair was suddenly replaced by the sensation of being jabbed repeatedly with sharp pins. Alerted by our squeals of pain, Kirsty peered from the porch to witness Gaston and I performing a bizarre dance in the moonlight, hopping from foot to foot around the flaming foliage, slapping our heads and bodies, while swearing in French and English. We were soon joined by the gardener who flew down the ladder like a fireman on a pole, before disappearing into the darkness, howling in pain, having borne the brunt of the ants' attack.

Later that night, sat outside our new room, the previous one now roofless and full of ants, I scratched my bites and reflected on what had happened. The soldier ants who launched the attack on us, clearly only did so after a command from their Queen, who was presumably around thirty feet away in the roof. I wondered aloud whether they were alerted by sound, smell or some sort of unexplained, natural extra sensory perception. Whatever it was, it worked. We failed to find 'La Reine' that night and the next day we left Gaston and the gardener igniting the roof thatch with homemade flamethrowers, their respect for nature temporarily sacrificed in favour of economic survival. I gave them a wave as we rattled past in the Land Rover, resisting the urge to shout 'Long live the Queen!'

Whilst travelling, I've shared my living space with a variety of insects and reptiles, and even the odd mammal. In Ghana we stayed in a guest house with a semi tame, mona monkey, which featured in a memorable scene as I exited our room to find Kirsty reclining on a sun lounger, her eyes closed and a serene smile on her face, as her hair was fastidiously groomed and styled by the resident ape. I half expected her to tell me she'd booked him to Shellac her nails later!

I welcome geckos into my room, as I love their nocturnal sing-song call, but most importantly they also help to control my personal nemesis, cockroaches. I can tolerate large spiders hanging from the roof, frogs in the shower, and even dive-bombing bats around the lights, but I hate roaches with a passion.

On an evening out in the Malaysian capital, Kuala Lumpur, Kirsty and I were searching for a restaurant where we could eat outdoors. We'd just flown in from the chill of an English February, and air-conditioned coolness held no appeal. We wanted to feel the unfamiliar humidity of a tropical evening as we ate. Unfortunately, we'd headed away from the popular entertainment area around Changkat Bukit Bintang, to an area of local restaurants. And in Kuala Lumpur, restaurant-visiting locals see no reason to sit outside to eat, like rural peasants.

Just when it looked like our alfresco dining plan had been thwarted, we spotted an Indian restaurant with pavement chairs and tables. But no customers, which is not usually a good sign. With no other options, we approached and were greeted by a smiling waiter, who seemed happy to have someone to serve. His smile soon disappeared though, when I indicated that we wanted to sit outside.

A minor argument ensued where he tried his hardest to sell us the benefits of eating inside the brightly lit, empty, air conditioned dining room, but we insisted on taking a pavement table. He frowned, confused why we'd want to sit outside, and brought the menus.

By the time our Onion Bhaji starters arrived, it had become apparent why he wanted us to sit indoors. To say there was a cockroach infestation on the street outside the restaurant is an understatement. I was wearing my trusty Timberland open-toed sandals, and quickly became aware of a repeated tickling sensation, which I tried to ignore. Eventually I peered under the table, to see the pavement alive with fat, orangey brown cockroaches, which were scurrying around at high speed, as if on tiny wheels, with some bolder ones investigating my feet and threatening to explore further north up the leg of my shorts.

Having adamantly insisted on sitting outside, our pride now wouldn't allow us to back down and shuffle in to the restaurant. So we sat, twitching and jerking our legs, occasionally slapping our shins, and trying to ignore what was going on beneath the table. The final straw was reached shortly after our main course arrived. Attempting to tear off a chunk of naan bread, I caught a glimpse of movement to my right, and time seemed to stand still as an uninvited guest attempted to join our table.

A large, greasy, black rat was already in mid-air and heading towards the naan bread when I spotted it. In a split second, I somehow leapt from my seat, brandishing my curry stained knife like a samurai sword, and flung the plate of naan towards the flying rodent whilst screaming 'RRRRRAAAAAAAAAATTT.' In that same moment, the rodent somehow managed to twist and change direction in mid-air, in order to abort his spectacular table-crashing attempt.

Any thoughts of maintaining our pride were quickly abandoned, as Kirsty and I scooped up our plates, flicked a couple of cockroaches off our legs and hurried inside, to be met by the smug faced waiter. Eating outside is one of the great pleasures of travelling in warm climates, but you do always need to consider the possibility of unwanted guests trying to join you for dinner!

Animal related activities feature highly on the tourist agendas of many countries. Spotting whales, riding camels, washing elephants in rivers, and swimming with dolphins, turtles and stingrays, are all billed as 'once in a lifetime' experiences which can be fun for a couple of hours, though the treatment of the animals is a concern in some countries. Also, the whole thing can feel somewhat contrived and tacky - the photos of Kirsty and I, cajoled into dressing like Lawrence of Arabia, and lurching across the Tunisian desert on a pair of bad tempered camels, are unlikely to feature on my office screensaver anytime soon.

One animal encounter we didn't want to miss though, was tracking mountain gorillas in the wild. As usual, the stipulation for our trip was that it needed to fit into a two-week timeframe, allow us the freedom to set our own agenda, and, importantly for an activity which can cost thousands of dollars, it had to be do-able at a reasonable cost. I quickly established that the cost of tracking permits in the East African nation of Rwanda were roughly double the cost of those in neighbouring Uganda, where the intriguingly named Bwindi Impenetrable Forest National Park sold off-season permits for $500 per person – still hugely expensive, but we saw this as a true once-in-a-lifetime opportunity, with the world population of mountain gorillas standing at less than a thousand, and hovering perilously close to extinction.

To offset the cost, I identified a cheap Ugandan car rental firm in the capital Kampala, who would deliver a car to me in Rwanda for an additional $100, thereby providing the option of a one-way rental, which fit nicely into a two week trip. We flew into the Rwandan capital, Kigali and spent a couple of days exploring the city. Our first stop was the Genocide Memorial museum, which houses the remains of a quarter of a million people killed in the Tutsi/Hutu conflict of the early nineties, and explains the events which led to the onset of the bloody civil war in the country.

Wandering the clean, orderly and friendly streets of Kigali, which had the feel of a small country town rather than a capital city, we struggled to comprehend how the population now lived and worked alongside neighbours who may have represented a hated, murderous enemy only twenty years earlier. The Government had formulated a programme of 'reconciliation and forgiveness,' in the form of village courts, known as Gacaca, where victim's families came face to face with those who had murdered and raped, and destroyed homes in a vicious campaign of ethnic cleansing, which left over a million dead in a nation of less than seven million.

The premise of Gacaca was that the perpetrators confessed to their role in the genocide and begged forgiveness from the families of their victims. It seemed difficult to believe, but our time in the country suggested that, somehow, it was working, as we sensed no obvious tension in Kigali or other towns we visited. In fact, Rwanda felt like one of the safest countries I've visited in Africa, with the people displaying a real pride in their community. Driving through the hill country towards the Ugandan border, we saw cheerful, stooped pensioners picking up litter and sweeping leaves on country roads, and kids filling in holes in the tarmac with sand, in return for coins tossed from car windows.

After an eventful rainy season journey, negotiating washed out roads, landslides, tough negotiating old local chiefs, and crafty bus drivers, we finally arrived in the mist shrouded village of Ruhija. Situated within the Bwindi Forest, close to the border with Democratic Republic of Congo, Ruhija sits at two thousand metres above sea level, and consequently enjoys the damp, chilly climate we were well used to in northern England. Wandering the quiet, muddy streets, it seemed we were the only foreigners in town, and we soon attracted the attention of the villagers, including the local primary school teacher who press-ganged us into an impromptu English lesson delivered to the whole ragged, barefoot class. As usual the lesson basically entailed me drawing animals on the blackboard, and getting the kids to recite their English name, while I attempted to recreate the noise of the said animal. I've performed dozens of these lessons in African schools and can safely say that no one draws a better chalk pig than me, though my donkey impression maybe needs some work, and often leads to distressed expressions on young faces, and even occasional tears.

We were up at dawn the following morning, kitted out in our walking gear, and anticipating a tough day of high altitude jungle trekking. At the time, there were fifteen families of habituated gorillas in Uganda which it was possible to track, with a total population of around four hundred animals. The gorilla groups are assimilated to tolerate humans, via a process which takes at least two years, and once habituated, the gorillas become used to the daily presence of tourists and generally display an aloof disinterest in their visitors. However, to protect these most endangered of mammals, stipulations around the issue of permits are strict. Each gorilla family can accept a single tracking group per day, for a maximum of an hour, with each group consisting of four paying guests plus researchers and local trackers. Any illness has to be declared, with even a runny nose likely to mean you are excluded from the trek, with no refund issued. Getting a permit felt akin to securing an audience with the pope!

Kirsty and I were joined by two Germans as we climbed into the back of a Land Rover, along with four local tracking guides, who were armed with semi-automatic rifles as protection against poachers from the neighbouring Democratic Republic of Congo. The well-armed DRC militias view the gorillas as a source of bush meat and body parts which can be used for Ju-Ju – magical charms worn to ward off evil, or to create witch doctor medicine. Our trackers were in radio contact with colleagues who were already in the forest, locating where the apes had slept the previous night and following their trail, to try and steer us in the right direction, and reduce the likely distance we'd need to walk in the difficult terrain.

Our adrenaline was pumping as the Land Rover bounced through red soil mud puddles in the chill morning mist. Despite our hefty investment in the permits, there was no guarantee we'd actually locate any gorillas. We'd read numerous forum posts from travellers whose 'once-in-a-lifetime' trek had turned into a six hour slog through knee deep mud in torrential rain, with not so much as a fleeting glimpse of a chimpanzee as a reward.

After driving for half an hour, our driver stopped, and we disembarked. We were already damp from the steady mountain drizzle by the time we'd tightened our boots, sorted out our backpacks and each been issued with a stout walking stick by our guides. It was time to set off. Led by the chief guide, a serious looking man with large, white, horse-like teeth, we plunged into the green abyss of the forest. Less than ten minutes later, we strode back out, without breaking sweat! The radio had crackled into life almost as soon as we'd set off, with news that a large gorilla group was nearby, so after a couple of hundred yards, our jungle trek was terminated and we were ushered back to the Land Rover.

The engine chugged into life and we bounced along the track for another mile before drawing to a halt again. There seemed to be an added urgency now, as again we followed the guides into the forest. I'd wondered why they told us to leave our walking staffs on this occasion, and all became clear within a few minutes. A raised hand slowed our pace, and silenced our excited whispers, as we crept forward. Scrambling down a steep incline I spotted a young blonde woman in khaki fatigues squatting by a tree trunk. Beside her was a man with a notepad, and two armed guides. The man and woman were German researchers, and they gave us that 'safari jackpot' satisfied half-smile, and we followed their nodded direction towards the foliage on our right.

A twenty strong gorilla group, appeared, scattered amongst the dense bush. This was the Kyaguliro gorilla family, comprising of a harem of eight females and their offspring of various ages, a couple of 'teenage' blackback gorillas, and lying nonchalantly in the midst of his family,a giant silverback, named Rukina. Thirty years old, and widely accepted as being one of the most impressive gorillas in existence, he monitored our approach with a casual indifference, resting his huge head on one hand whilst sucking on a long grass stem, looking like a lazy farmhand, albeit one weighing 200kg.

The gorillas were so close, I barely needed the long zoom lens on my camera, and soon the only sound in the forest was the constant click of the shutter, the crashing of branches as young apes play-fought and explored in the branches around us, and the whining buzz of a million insects attracted to the heat and odour of the gorillas.

It was a truly amazing experience, and a huge privilege to spend time at such close quarters with these endangered animals in the wild, and amazing that we'd located them just minutes from the road. Fortunately, there was to be no six-hour muddy slog for our group!

The lack of interest the gorillas showed in us, almost made us forget that these were wild animals. Habituated to humans, but still unpredictable and dangerous. This fact was brought home to us as one of the young blackbacks decided to go walkabout. We hadn't noticed him make his way around behind us, hidden within the foliage and he suddenly appeared, alongside the female researcher. A blackback is a sexually mature male of around eight to twelve years old, subordinate to the silverback, until he is old enough to challenge him to take leadership of the group, or to set up a family of his own. Not as large and powerful as his father, but an intimidating presence none the less, he emerged from the bush and gave the young woman a long, hard stare. She immediately dropped her head to face the ground, and turned slightly away, in deference to the gorilla who seemed to be challenging her. I watched the guides tense, and flick the safety catches from their rifles. It was clear the woman was terrified, both of a potential attack, but also as the gunning down of one of her research subjects would presumably be seen as a serious blackmark on her

PhD thesis!

The stand-off continued for a number of minutes, away to my left. I'd moved clear of the rest of the group to take some close-ups of Rukina, and he seemed to be playing up to the camera, fixing the lens with a steady, confident stare, whilst nibbling leaves from a twig, swatting at an annoying gorilla toddler, and gurning with curled lips, to achieve a fair impersonation of seventies comedy legend Les Dawson. I clicked away, taking no notice of the potential feud developing between the young blackback and the researcher, until I became aware of movement in front of me.

I was standing on a small ridge, alongside a thick clump of ferns, on the far side of which I could now sense movement. I stooped to peer through the bush, and my gaze was met by two large brown eyes staring back at me. The blackback had clearly grown frustrated at the lack of response his threatening pose had earned from the researcher, and had decided to check out the human who was rudely disturbing his dad's morning nap. The swarm of flies which now enveloped me, told me he was only around half a metre away on the other side of the bush. I could hear him breathing and my nostrils were suddenly filled with his strong, earthy, wet-beast scent as he began to probe the bush around the level of my waist with an inquisitive hand. I imagined he was debating which part of my body would detach most easily when he launched his attack. Peering over the bush, I saw that the rest of our group were now monitoring the developing situation. The researchers and trackers looked terrified at what could be about to occur, the Germans were wide eyed and open mouthed...only Kirsty seemed to be taking it in her stride. She'd whipped out her iPhone, flicked it onto video mode and, to my eyes, seemed to be mentally willing the young gorilla on.

The spectacularly toothed tracker had stealthily approached from the rear, and now appeared over my shoulder, rifle at the ready.

"Don't move." he hissed in my ear. There was little chance of that. I was rooted to the spot with fear.

He peered through the bush at the blackback. "He is smelling you now." He whispered. He won't be the only one in a few minutes, I thought, as my legs shook uncontrollably.

Time seemed to stand still, as the blackback sized me up from the other side of the bush. The goofy toothed tracker and I, stood still and silent; Rukina gave his son a look which said 'what are you up to now kid?'; Meanwhile, Kirsty kept focusing her phone on me and I half expected her to shout 'bloody get on with it then!' to the gorilla, as her chance of You Tube fame receded.

After what seemed like an age, a crunching of foliage indicated that the blackback was making his move. The tracker gripped my shoulder, perhaps in fear, or more likely to stop me bolting. Slowly, a black hand with a leather-glove palm, pulled back the bush and a huge head appeared a foot away from my chest. If I'd extended my hand, I would have patted his nose. I'd pulled up my hood to protect me from the cloud of flies which accompanied my new acquaintance, and as he observed me with a thoughtful, slightly tilted head , my hood suddenly felt somehow inappropriate, almost impolite, and I tugged it off, so he could get a proper look at me. Under the watchful eye of the young gorilla's father and a nervous tracker with a gun and prominent teeth, we eyeballed each other for maybe thirty seconds. He no longer seemed threatening, but curious. A teenager playing at being a man. He wrenched a handful of leaves from the bush, turned and ambled away, taking his thousand-strong fly swarm with him.

Six months after our visit, the great silverback, Rukina, was killed by a freak lightning strike, and civil war split the Kyaguliro family, as rival males fought to become the dominant silverback. Upon hearing the news, I wondered whether my blackback friend had felt confident enough to mount his own leadership challenge. If I returned to Bwindi in ten years, maybe he would be the new kingpin, surrounded by his harem of wives and countless offspring.

Or maybe none of them would be there? It's easy to imagine a fragile population of just four hundred animals being wiped out by disease, poaching or some natural disaster. The more I considered it, I realised the chance of me ever seeing gorillas in the wild again, at such close quarters was slim. This really had been a once in a lifetime experience.

13 THEY CALL IT CHARACTER BUILDING

Travel is all about taking the rough with the smooth. For every once-in-a-lifetime, memorable moment, there'll be another that you really want to forget, but which will haunt you for the rest of your days. For each idyllic, white-sand beach sunset, there'll be a day of cold, damp drizzle in an uninspiring town. And every moment it feels great to be alive and out exploring the world, will be countered by one when you're so ill, you can't move from your room, and are sure the grim reaper is about to deliver your room service.

Illness is a fact of life when travelling in the developing world. Most instances of travel related sickness can be alleviated by over the counter remedies, but every so often, you're stricken by symptoms which render you incapable of even moving from your sweat soaked bed. I experienced one such occasion in, where else, but India!

We were in the city of Varanasi, its position on the sacred River Ganges establishing it as one of the world's holiest sites for Hindus. Viewed as a highly auspicious place to die, devout followers of the religion believe that taking their last breath in the ancient city will help them achieve moksha, the escape from the endless, tiresome cycle of reincarnation. Consequently, the stepped stone ghats alongside the river's sewage filled waters, are flanked by crumbling buildings housing hospices and old folk's homes. Here, ageing, wealthy Indians spend their final days, eagerly anticipating the moment they will expire in the sacred city, to be absolved of the sins accrued in all previous lives. There are even hotels offering 'death beds,' with discounts for those expected to live less than fifteen days. I assume those customers are encouraged to write their Trip Advisor reviews immediately after checking in.

Varanasi is one of the most unsettling and unusual cities I've ever visited, and walking the narrow streets alongside the Ganges can feel like a descent into a hellish medieval lunatic asylum. Sadhus, the ascetic Hindu holy men, wrapped in blankets or sometimes naked and coated in ash, wander the mud and cobble lanes and may stop you to discuss English cricket in cultured tones, or gibber incoherently with manic, fevered eyes. Horrifically mutilated beggars tug at your clothes, begging for alms. Shifty, furtive fixers hiss and offer illicit beer concealed in a tea pot, intoxicants being banned in the area close to Mother Ganges. Sacred cows squeeze past slow-moving cycle-rickshaws in the narrow alleyways. Then suddenly, the usual honking, chattering buzz of backstreet India is shattered by a fast approaching jangle of bells, shouts and chanting as a funeral cortege approaches. A group of twenty men, wild eyed in grief and ecstasy, lurch and jog towards you, bearing the shroud-wrapped corpse of a family member, destined for the burning ghats.

If the backstreets of Varanasi are a culture shock, Manikarnika Ghat, the cremation ghat, can feel like the most foreign place in the world to western eyes. Huge funeral pyres burn day and night - a twenty four hour, three-hundred-and-sixty-five day a year production line of transition from this world to Nirvana. Spending an hour here is to witness a non-stop stream of corteges arriving and depositing the recently departed onto a pre-prepared bonfire of sandalwood. The chief male mourner, usually a husband or eldest son, clad in white robes and head freshly shaved by an attendant priest, lights the pyre, and the body is quickly consumed by the flames, the ashes from which are then deposited into the sacred waters.

Fire cleanses the earthly body of its sins, and wealthier citizens are able to invest in a larger pyre, therefore guaranteeing that they will enter the river in the form of dusty ash. The less affluent may need to opt for a smaller fire, and only partial burning, with their charred half-corpse joining those of the sin-free, children and priests, in bobbing downstream amidst the heavily polluted Ganges' other detritus.

The smoke-choked burning ghats, a fiery riverside vision of

hell, backed by atmospheric, crumbling, centuries old buildings, are a photographer's dream. However, overt camera use at a funeral would obviously be unacceptably intrusive, so I sought out a suitable vantage point on the first floor of a derelict building. From an open window, I was able to surreptitiously capture the unique scenes unfolding below me, without being observed. Or so, I thought. After around twenty minutes, I was joined by Arup, an eighteen year old wearing a matching combo of green slacks and anorak, and enormous, polished black, clown-shoe brogues. He explained that the body being ignited on the closest pyre was that of his uncle, Harish, who had died suddenly from a mysterious fever a couple of days earlier. Arup seemed quite cheerful as we observed his father apply a flaming torch to the sandalwood, expressing more interest in my camera than the funeral ceremony he was supposed to be attending.

As the flames took hold, acrid black smoke began to pour from the pyre, and just before it was consumed by the flames, uncle Harish's corpse delivered an unexpected farewell wave, as his arms extended rigidly in a jerky upwards motion which brought to mind Tommy Coopers trademark hand shuffle. I resisted the urge to say 'just like that' to Arup.

A sudden breeze caught the billowing black smoke rising above the flames, and in seconds, Arup and I were coughing and spluttering as it filled the room through the unglazed window frame. Visibility was reduced to arms-length, and we both began choking, as we struggled to find the doorway leading to the staircase. My eyes were stinging, and I shuddered to think what the bitter taste in my throat was caused by, as we felt our way along the walls in order to escape. Outside, Arup and I grinned at our soot blackened features, and I did wonder whether uncle Harish had taken his revenge for my thoughts of Tommy Cooper, at the glorious moment his earthly form finally escaped the cycle of Samsara, or constant reincarnation.

At dawn the next day, Kirsty and I were in the middle of the Ganges, in an ancient boat, which was being rowed by an equally ancient boatman. Watching the sunrise above the river is a

Varanasi 'must do', with the added attraction of observing the inhabitants of the city perform their morning ablutions – bathing, cleaning teeth, washing babies and clothes, and no doubt attending to their toilet requirements, whilst submerged in the filthy waters. Our boatman also had a keen eye for another of the Ganges unique attractions, which he pointed out in a near constant single word commentary. 'Body' he would announce with a gentle smile, as another partially burnt corpse floated past us.

I'd began to feel unwell whilst on the river, and by the time we disembarked, I was sweating profusely and shivering like the proverbial defecating dog. I had a thumping headache and my stomach felt like a washing machine on a fast spin cycle. The sight of a skeletal man with an extended, leprosy eroded stump, almost caused me to make an unexpected liquid donation into his begging cup.

Our cycle rickshaw driver could clearly see I was in discomfort, and obviously fearful of the damage a sudden bodily evacuation would inflict upon his carriage, pedalled to our hotel at speed, his muscular stick legs pumping away on the pedals. I staggered through reception, slumped in the lift, and Kirsty somehow dragged me to our room, where I collapsed on the bed.

Within seconds, I propelled myself upright, and lurched from the bed towards the bathroom. Before I'd taken two steps, I emitted a deafening, growling retch from deep within my chest and a jet of bright orange vomit sprayed from my mouth and hit the wall with a splash. I attempted to raise my hand to stem the flow, but the force with which I was expelling the puke only bounced it back to spatter my face. I wheeled around and caught sight of Kirsty, sitting on the bed, wearing a horrified expression. Seconds later she was taking evasive action, as a stronger, follow-up stream of sick squirted from my mouth as if directed from a powerful garden hose. Thankfully missing the bed, this jet of vomit sprayed across the wall, the bedside table and lamp and finally the mirror and toilet door, in an amazing, brightly coloured arc. By the time I slumped, exhausted, back on the bed, the room looked like it had been decorated by Jackson Pollock after a couple of days on the Scotch. I lay there panting, exhausted by the violent convulsions which had gripped my body, as Kirsty embarked upon a thankless clean-up exercise.

Our time in Varanasi unfortunately coincided with the assassination of a local gangster/politician, whose supporters had reacted violently, and on the previous evening, sporadic rioting had broken out in parts of the city. Heavily armed police were now on the streets, curfews had been imposed and a ban on alcohol, the dreaded, so-called 'dry day' which can often last a week, was in force. Kirsty's attempts to leave the hotel to undertake some solo exploration in my absence, were met by a strict refusal from hotel security. She was confined to the hotel's garden with a book, whilst I rode out my fever in our room, and chanting mobs burned effigies in the streets outside.

The nearby sounds of mob violence punctuated my fitful sleep, and fed my disturbed mind with images which fuelled a series of terrifyingly bizarre nightmares. I dreamt that the gangster politician and his men, dressed as Mexican bandits, wearing ponchos, sombreros and bandoliers, were trying to tug my bed sheets from me to take to the laundry. 'Ton lit est sale! 'Your bed is dirty,' they hissed in French, for some inexplicable reason. Then when I woke, gasping in a pool of sweat, they were still there, in the corner of the room, smoking and sniggering, as Ben Kingsley, dressed predictably as Ghandi, told them jokes through a crackly microphone, in the style of Bernard Manning.

Punctuated by frequent dashes to the bathroom, I drifted in and out of consciousness throughout the day. In rare, lucid, waking moments, I tortured myself with thoughts of the disease I'd obviously contracted by inhaling a burning, diseased corpse the previous day. Had I succumbed to the same fever that had suddenly taken uncle Harish, just like that? At some point, my fevered tossing and turning caused the sweat-soaked sheets to wrap around me, and in my dreams they became a shroud. I opened my eyes just in time to see the aged boatman at the head of my bed, pointing a group of bell ringing mourners towards me with his usual cheery catchphrase, 'Body!'

In the late afternoon, the quiet of the room was shattered as an overkeen mourner rang his bell right next to my ear. I sat bolt upright, expecting that to end the nightmare, but the noise continued. A shrill, single-note bell, which hurt my ears and caused my heart to beat hard. I scrambled in the darkness and located a puke-sticky bedside telephone, which I struggled to hold in my clammy, shaking hand.

"Hello." I croaked. The shouty, sing-song Indian voice on the line shocked me awake.

"Hello. Hello. Mr Matthew....can you hear me?"

"Yes...who is this?" I rasped.

"Hello Mr Matthew, it is Mr Nita. Can you hear me sir?" My mind raced. Mr Nita? The name was familiar. I cast my mind back to the planning stage of our two week trip, and settled on a series of email exchanges with a travel agent who was arranging our flight tickets to Nepal. His office was in the south of Varanasi, and I clearly recalled an agreement that the tickets would be delivered to our hotel. In the absence of any other candidates, my befuddled mind decided that this was who I was now speaking to. What I failed to recall was a more recent conversation with a travel agent based in the foyer of our hotel, who was arranging some train tickets for us. His name was Mr Nita.

"I can hear you Mr Nita, but the line is not good."

"I..HAVE..YOUR..TICKETS," He shouted, and the line crackled. "You can come and collect them now."

I had guessed this may happen, so had made doubly sure the tickets would be delivered to us, and I wouldn't have to take a lengthy detour through Varanasi's traffic and cow clogged streets to collect them. The requirement was now doubly important in a city under partial curfew. I was furious, and flicked on the light and dragged myself from the bed, somehow thinking this would add weight to my argument.

"No!" I shouted.

There was a pause. "I'm sorry Mr Matthew, what was that?"

"I said no." I repeated loudly. "There is no way I'm coming to collect those tickets."

There was another longer pause as Mr Nita considered this unexpected response.

"Erm, Mr Matthew, your tickets are here in the office, you just need to..."

"You listen to me..." I bellowed, stalling slightly as I caught sight of myself in the sick-flecked, full length mirror. Kirsty had hosed me down in the shower, but I still bore some tell-tale orange stains, and there was scattered, regurgitated food debris in my hair. My body looked concave, and glistened with a sheen of perspiration in the dim light. I looked grey, like the corpse of a drowning victim hauled from the toxic Ganges.

"...there is no way I'm coming to your office to collect the tickets. You must bring them here. Do you understand?"

"But Mr Matthew, I'm alone in the office. I can't leave..."

"That's your problem Mr Nita. Even if I wanted to, I couldn't collect the tickets. It's far too dangerous." This caused another lengthy pause as Mr Nita processed my objection.

"Danger? There is no danger Mr. Matthew." For some reason, the potential for me to be lynched by a rioting mob seemed to have amused him, which incensed me even more.

"I'm not risking my life to come and collect the tickets Mr. Nita. You have to bring them here, as arranged, or I won't be paying you!" I barked, then slammed the phone down and crashed onto the sweat-soaked mattress. I closed my eyes, and my head pounded from the exertion of berating the travel agent.

Three minutes later, there was a tentative tap-tap-tap on the door.

"For God's sake, what now?" I muttered as I staggered to my feet. Picking up a towel to hastily cover my underpants, I wrenched open the door to see a small, middle aged Indian man recoil as he looked me up and down. He seemed vaguely familiar.

"Yes?" I was still in barking mode. From his jacket pocket the man produced a white envelope which he pushed tentatively towards me.

"Your tickets Mr Matthew," he whispered nervously.

My mouth fell open as I struggled to comprehend what had just happened. It now seemed that my fever had either robbed me of the ability to measure the passage of time, or I'd blacked out for an hour immediately after the phone call.

"How did you do that?" My eyes narrowed and I stared hard at the now shaking travel agent.

"Ah...do what Mr Matthew?"

"How did you get here so quickly?...Or were you really here the whole time....? Just what is your game Mr Nita?"

"No game sir, no...." Mr Nita was in reverse gear as I jabbed my finger in his direction, dark conspiracy theories filling my fevered imagination.

"So how are you here already? Your office is miles away." I was staggering along the corridor as the little man frantically back-pedalled .

Mr Nita's shouted response of 'I used the elevator,' should have alerted me to the fact that I had the wrong travel agent, but at that point, I realised I'd dropped the towel and was pursuing my quarry in my underpants, as a terrible feeling of nausea overcame me.

"Tickets!" I shouted, and Mr Nita tossed the envelope in my direction. As I bent to retrieve the package, I was overwhelmed by violent stomach cramps and roared in pain. Unsure which end I was about to explode from, I half crawled, half staggered back to the sanctuary of the bathroom, as a wide-eyed Mr Nita watched in fascinated horror from the end of the corridor.

After spending a frustrating day and evening under house arrest, Kirsty returned to the room around 8pm and shook me awake. I felt groggy but my fever had passed. I started to tell her some of the bizarre dreams that had plagued me, including one where I chased a small Indian man down a long corridor in my underpants. When I looked up, she was looking quizzically at an envelope she'd retrieved from the table. I cut the story short, rested my head on the pillow and said a silent apology to the restless ghost of uncle Harish, taken by a fever, just like that!

Luckily for me, I was stricken by the curse of uncle Harish whilst I had access to a hotel room. Being ill in transit is a different kind of hell altogether, and one that Kirsty has unfortunately had to contend with on more than one occasion. One of her most uncomfortable experiences occurred on a trip to Namibia, where she was afflicted with acute stomach problems whilst we were travelling through the desert region populated by the Nama people. This colourful tribe wear an archaic style of dress introduced by missionaries in the 1800's, and speak in a language of clicks, so asking for directions was like having a conversation with Skippy the bush kangaroo. It had been an interesting afternoon's drive.

Our journey had been punctuated by a number of enforced toilet stops, and by late afternoon, with sunset approaching, Kirsty was again clutching her midriff as we rumbled along a narrow, sandy track which we hoped would lead to the bush lodge where we planned to stay that night. The track was flanked by high thorn hedges, limiting our field of vision to the route ahead and giving us no clue as to the whereabouts of the hotel. Kirsty was groaning in discomfort, and as I glanced across towards her, my attention was drawn to a flash of colour in the hedgerow. I subconsciously moved my foot towards the brake, which most probably averted disaster, as a huge Kudu antelope suddenly appeared in mid-air in front of us, having vaulted the hedge. An adult Kudu can weigh over 250kg, and a direct hit would have wiped out both our VW Polo and the animal, so my instinctive jab on the brake was literally a life-saver. The shocked deer landed inches from our front bumper, and wild-eyed with fear, immediately took off again, leaping the hedge on the opposite side of the track to disappear into the bush.

Kirsty and I gulped, breathed a huge sigh of relief and as we drove on, I was about to speculate on the worst thing that could have happened in the incident. For Kirsty though, another 'worst case' was looming large, indicated by a deep intestinal rumbling, not helped by our near miss.

"Pull over. Now!" She yelled, and I started to say that I thought the hotel couldn't be too far.

"NOW!!" She emphasised the urgency of the situation, and I slammed on the brakes. Kirsty was out of the car and running into the undergrowth before we'd even drawn to a halt. She returned, ashen faced, a few minutes later, having been forced to relieve herself beside a large termite mound, situated next to a small lake in a forest clearing, close to the track. We drove on in silence, and soon the road curved to the left, and we arrived at the hotel less than five minutes after Kirsty's emergency evacuation.

The lodge was in a remote, wild area and we carried torches as we made our way to the restaurant that evening, with Kirsty feeling better, and having being warned that animals were likely to be at large in the hotel grounds after dark. We were greeted at the restaurant by a waiter dressed in khaki, who explained that his food service role also incorporated an element of wildlife spotting, with the dining area overlooking a waterhole frequented by native animals. The restaurant was already busy, but we were shown to a table in a prime position, which the waiter told us he'd 'saved just for you.' I was sure he winked at Kirsty, but thought nothing of it as we were seated, and he started to explain what we may see from our vantage point.

"Gemsbok, kudu, eland, and if you're lucky, maybe even black rhino and elephant could all visit," he smiled. Then, stooping towards Kirsty, he leaned in to point out a feature at the far side of the waterhole.

"You see the termite mound over there?" He had a mischievous glint in his eye, as Kirsty peered in the direction of his pointed finger.

"In the late afternoon, it's possible to see some VERY interesting sights around there." It took a moment for Kirsty to recognise the termite mound and the 'small lake' she'd visited an hour earlier.

"What can I get you to drink?" grinned the waiter. "A cold beer? It's very warm tonight isn't it?" He smirked as Kirsty's face turned crimson. She clutched her stomach again and I thought she was going to bolt for the door, but the sight of a full restaurant of diners who all seemed to be smiling and nodding knowingly in her direction rooted her to the spot.

A couple of gemsbok antelopes and a single large Kudu lapped at the muddy pool of the waterhole that night, but nothing spectacular enough to get the diners reaching for their cameras. Kirsty was left hoping her earlier visit had also escaped the attention of any long-lens snappers!

Other than taking the usual hygiene precautions, there's not too much you can do to avoid illness when travelling. Self-inflicted misadventures can be harder to tolerate though. I've stayed in a few grotty hotel rooms, but the fact that a two week schedule requires some careful planning, usually means that pre-trip research delivers a passable standard of room in most cases. The exception is in locations where there is no choice of accommodation - A hotel which is the only option in town, with no competition, so no requirement to maintain decent standards of service. It's literally their way or the highway.

One such instance we had the misfortune to experience, was on the island of Borneo. We'd driven north from the capital, Kota

Kinabalu, to the village of Kota Belud, hoping to attend the weekly 'Tamu' or Sunday market, and see the renowned Bajau horsemen, known as the Cowboys of the East.

We arrived late on a Saturday afternoon, and it quickly became apparent that something was afoot in the village. The streets were deserted. Most of the shops had shutters drawn, and those showing any signs of life were in the process of stacking produce in preparation for closing. I stopped our car and approached a gaggle of traders who were loading crates of spikey rambutan fruit onto the back of a pick-up truck, driven by a boy of about thirteen, and asked what was going on.

"Holiday! Holiday!" grinned an acned teenager wearing a straw hat, and displaying an unappetising set of Roquefort cheese teeth.

Having discovered that Trip Advisor's top hotel recommendation in town was closed for renovation, and that there was only one other option, Orange Lodge, with no reviews and no stars, we set out to find it, hoping they'd have a nice bar and restaurant which would remain open over the holiday weekend.

We spotted the bar as soon as we parked the car. It was iron and rusting, and served to secure a paint spattered shutter under a cracked neon sign which flickered and flashed 'O ANG ODG.' The building was a two-storey concrete box, bordered by a dusty main road, and what seemed to be the local rubbish dump. A scab encrusted, ginger dog tore noisily into a hessian bag filled with entrails as I rapped on the shutters, half hoping the hotel was actually closed.

Unfortunately, after a short wait in which I assessed the possibility of sleeping in our Toyota Echo, the shutters rattled open and a small, middle aged woman greeted me. She'd either been applying red emulsion with no paint brush, or undertaking some gruesome butchery task, and hurriedly wiped her red stained hands on her cardigan as she waved me inside, giving her crimson palms a final wipe on a cat slumbering on the reception desk, as she retrieved a set of keys.

"Have room. Sixty Ringgit. Nice room, best room." She smiled reassuringly, as a large bluebottle settled on her forehead.

Normally, I'd ask to see the room, but with no other options in town, and a twenty five mile drive over a mountain range in the dark to the next settlement, Nabalu, it was clear that beggars couldn't be choosers. I said I'd take it, handed over the cash, which equated to about fifteen dollars, and summoned Kirsty from the car. And as we lugged our rucksacks up a narrow, sweat-sticky staircase to the room, it seemed we'd literally stumbled upon the beggar, in the form of a dishevelled old man sleeping on a plastic chair at the top of the stairs.

Prodded awake by a jab from the receptionist's red fist on his temple and a tirade of shouted abuse, he lurched to his feet, and upon seeing two European guests checking in, reacted as may be expected had we been dressed as St George and Lady Godiva. His eyes widened and his mouth fell open, allowing a thin stream of drool access to his chin. He exuded a toxic air of the local moonshine - langkau rice spirit. Obviously cognisant of the rule that first impressions are important, the manageress decided he wasn't portraying her establishment in the best light and proceeded to shove and kick him down the steps.

After delivering a final, impressive forearm smash to the back of the old man's skull, she returned and flashed us a friendly grin, before leading us down the corridor towards our room. A strip light flickered, and our feet stuck to the lino as we stepped over an impressive range of construction related equipment which was stacked outside each room. Toolboxes of varying sizes, hard hats and clay coated work boots, interspersed with an occasional vermin box trap, had replaced the usual hotel corridor litter of discarded room service trays. It was clear the Orange Lodge served as a dormitory for that most discerning of traveller, the transient Bornean construction worker.

The manageress led us to a maroon painted door at the end of the corridor and opened it with a flourish. It seemed that a previous guest had attempted to open it with his steel capped workboot, as the lower wooden panel was cracked and splintered, but patched up with grey masking tape. A cloud of flies sprang to life and buzzed with excitement as we entered the room, and our diminutive guide proudly showed off the room's features. A rusting fridge stood forlornly unplugged under a similarly plug free television of late eighties vintage.

"Not working." Our guide stated the bleeding obvious with another winning smile.

A rusting metal garden chair was propped alongside a chipped formica dressing table, which boasted a mirror festooned with grubby, peeling stickers of Malay pop stars of the nineties. The little woman dragged the chair over to the window, and used it as a makeshift step ladder to access a lethal looking air conditioning unit. A couple of index finger jabs into a mysterious hole which may have once housed a power switch, brought the machinery to juddering, clattering life. I actually had to look out of the window to make sure someone wasn't hitting the exterior of the fan with a metal bar, such was the din it created.

"Working!" snaggly teeth flashed in triumph, as the cool air filled the room, and I could almost taste the legionella bacteria.

Our tour continued with a demonstration of a working cold tap in the bathroom, though the proliferation of exposed wiring leading to the showerhead clearly seemed a risk too far, and this area of the facilities was summarised with a waved hand and 'Shower. Water. Working!' One of the resident labourers had been mixing concrete in the toilet bowl. At least I hoped that's what it was, as I baulked at a closer examination.

The room key was pushed into my hand with another proud smile, and Kirsty and I were left to survey our surroundings. It was now clear that Kota Belud was a one horse town, and, peering through the insect encrusted window pane, I was pretty sure I could see the horse. What I'd first assumed to be a billowing dust devil on the far side of the rubbish dump, now manifested itself as a swarm of fat bluebottles, circling the bloated corpse of a recently deceased beast. One of the cowboys of the east was clearly in the market for some new transport.

"Let's go and have a look around town," I suggested, and we hastily departed, receiving a cheery wave from our friend on reception as we left. Ten minutes later we were back. The entire town was closed, apart from a couple of small local shops which were busily packing away their produce. No bars, no restaurants, no other hotels. We'd glumly considered the pot noodle shelf in one of the stores, but then remembered we had no kettle in the room. Our Saturday night looked likely to consist of crisps and beer in our dungeon of a room, and if we were lucky, an opportunity to play with some of our fellow guests' power tools.

A grotty hotel room in an amazing location is tolerable. As is fantastic accommodation in a mediocre town. An awful room in a closed-down town is hard to bear though. So we made our decision. We'd do a reverse runner. Instead of sneaking off without paying for a room we'd slept in, we would escape without using a room which we'd already paid for!

Kirsty distracted the receptionist by asking directions to the market, and while the little woman was engaged in pointing out the street to a seemingly non-comprehending Kirsty, I grabbed the bags and sneaked out of a back door. After receiving her directions, Kirsty slipped out after me, and we set off for a long drive over the mountains on a pitch black road.

Before leaving town however, we stopped for provisions at the last remaining open shop. Kirsty stayed in the car as I dashed over the quiet road and into the store. Emerging a few minutes later with a carrier bag containing snacks and drinks, the sky suddenly darkened above me. I looked up to see a huge flock of green-tinted starlings, numbering several hundred, swooping above me amidst a high pitched chatter of squeaking. I stood and watched, as the murmuration swooped and whirled around a copse of small fruit trees beside the shop. More birds were arriving by the second and filling the sky as I watched. Unfortunately, it quickly became clear that the fruit the birds were eating was having an unfortunate impact on their digestive systems. As I looked upwards, the first bomb of guano scored a direct hit just above my right eyebrow. I turned to head for the safety of the car, but it was too late. A collective intestinal disorder had taken hold of the flock, and within a couple of seconds, I was under an intense bombardment of bird shit, as I ran towards the car, trying unsuccessfully to shield myself with my carrier bag. I flung open the car door and breathlessly leapt in. Kirsty looked at me in shock and disgust. She hadn't seen the aerial assault, and was now dumbfounded as to how I'd returned from a five minute detour to a shop looking like a plasterers radio, caked from head to foot in bright white bird droppings. Kirsty attempted to wet-wipe me clean as we set off, and we reflected that Kota Belud's parting gift seemed a highly appropriate summary of our visit to the village.

In terms of self-inflicted discomfort, a badly chosen hotel room could be seen as a stroke of bad luck. Choosing to subject yourself to a sexual assault in the name of experiential tourism is much harder to take. Unfortunately, our opportunity to experience the delights of Ayurvedic massage turned into a puzzling incident, which left me wondering whether my masseuse was just giving me maximum value for money, or had taken a shine to me!

We were in the Indian State of Kerala, and were travelling via the usual method of transport in the region, a converted rice barge. These floating hotel rooms can be rented by the hour, day or week, and represent great value, as are covering both transport and accommodation. We'd therefore rented a barge, with skipper and one-man crew for two days. Lazily chugging along Kerala's inland waterways is a great way to chill-out after days spent in frenetic Indian cities, and on the country's lethal highways.

Every village seems to offer Ayurvedic massage, which treats mind and spirit, as well as the body, and is used instead of mainstream medicine in many rural areas. It seems to be a 'must-do' for visitors to Kerala, and our skipper, Chandran, sealed the deal by telling us of a village he knew, on a seldom visited canal, where the masseuses were the 'best in Kerala' and the cost was half that charged in the tourist areas.

The word 'village' seemed a little generous to the scrubby collection of bamboo huts we approached along a narrow stretch of waterway, carpeted in lilies and flanked by high reeds on both banks. All seemed deserted, but a blast on the boat's horn from Chandran resulted in the appearance of an old man in a grubby dhoti loin cloth. As we docked, the skipper shouted to the villager in the local Malayalam dialect that he'd delivered a couple more victims. The old man waved and conveyed the message towards the huts that it was time to get out the engine oil...

Plagued by a bad back, I love a massage when travelling. Whether it's an impromptu beach rubdown by a calloused-handed old woman with no training beyond wrestling livestock, or a 200 Bhat special from a magic fingered Thai expert in an airconditioned Bangkok salon, there's nothing like a good massage to relieve aches and pains.

"This looks....interesting." Kirsty commented as we were ushered towards two tiny bamboo and thatch huts. Clearly there would be no air-con today.

Upon entering my allotted hut, I was struggling to see in the dark, but made out a massage bench, onto which a teenaged boy was folding a soiled grey sheet. He looked about sixteen, dark of skin, wire thin, but with well-defined muscles. He was stripped down and ready for action, wearing the same style grubby dhoti as his grandad.

"Please." He gestured to the bed.

I stripped to my undies, as had been the norm in my prior experience of massages. Unfortunately, it was to become clear that this was no normal massage.

"No. All." Said the boy, shaking his head and gesturing towards my boxers, which I tugged off, then lay on my back, feeling very naked. He got to work immediately, slopping a thick coat of oil onto every part of my body. And I mean EVERY part. I felt like a seabird after Deepwater Horizon.

Exactly what happened next is hard to describe, but is probably best recounted from Kirsty's viewpoint. Similarly stripped naked in the neighbouring hut, and lathered in oil by a hook nosed, sharp fingered crone, she was perfectly placed to eavesdrop on the increasingly bizarre running commentary from my hut.

"Ooooh, yes, right there. That's got it. Ouch. Ouch.Ouch. Mmmm...not sure about that. Wooahh! No, No, don't touch....Ah! Ooooh. I don't think you need to....Woaaahh! Don't pull that...Aaaaargh! That stings. Jesus Christ. Be gentle. Oh God. Don't squeeeeze...OUCH!! I'm not sure I want....Oh dear."

"Turn please."

"On my front?"

"Yes"

"Can't be any worse. Okay, that's better. Oooh yes. Right there, that's got it. Hmmm...not sure about....woaaahh! No. No. Relax? That's easy for you to.....Oh God. No, not there. Jeeeeesus! What's that?? Well take it out. You're not meant to...Aaaaaargh. I feel like a bloody glove puppet. Stop please...I don't like this. Please. I'll pay more. Just stop."

Kirsty's attempts to control her hysterical laughter at my plight had reduced the trauma of her own internal examination, and she emerged giggling after half an hour, to find me sat on a bench staring at the ground, shaking my head. We'd been told that the 'special' Ayurvedic oil must be left in place for four hours after the massage, so I sat in a slick of gunk, swatting at wasps and shooing away a malnourished kitten which was licking my toes.

"I can't believe I paid someone to do that to me." I observed sadly, as Kirsty wiped at the Castrol GTX which was dripping out of her hair and down her forehead. The villagers smiled and waved as we got back on the boat. My masseuse was holding a cheap camera phone, and I hoped I'd imagined him winking at me as we climbed aboard. The last thing I needed was to relive the experience in a You Tube clip entitled 'Ayurvedic Massage Orgy Part 2- The Human Glove Puppet.'

Thankfully, barring the occasional instance when the office lavatories became more familiar than usual in the days following a trip, we rarely experienced any lasting impacts upon returning home from our adventures. The exception to that was a trip to West Africa, when I limped from the plane with a leg the size of a large ham, pulsing and festering with the sort of infection which Africa is so good at inflicting.

We had arrived in the Ghanaian town of Cape Coast, a hundred miles south west of the capital, Accra, and immediately sensed a hostile atmosphere upon entering the town. Cruising through the streets in our rental car, trying to locate our hotel, resulted, as is normal, in stares from the locals. Generally, our smiles and waves are returned, and we may even collect a tail of chasing children, yelling 'Mzungu, money!' On this occasion though, our smiles were met by frosty glares. Groups of youths stared and gesticulated and shouted incomprehensible insults. Maybe we just drove down the wrong street at the wrong time, encountering a particularly unfriendly set of locals. Or maybe the town's slaving history, with its Swedish built 17th century fort, weighs heavily on its inhabitants, and what they may view as triumphalist, colonial history tourism isn't welcome.

We found the hotel, a cheap affair on a hill, its dowdy demeanour brightened somewhat by the breeze-carried song of a gospel choir practising nearby. We set out to explore, a little more cautiously than usual, but apart from some aggressive begging, from a man in a Michigan State University Rowing Team cap near the fishing harbour, we were left alone. The desk clerk at our hotel was at pains to emphasise that on no account should we walk the streets after dark though.

"Take a taxi, even for a small distance." he warned.

Predictably, with an eye on repeat business, that advice was echoed by the driver of the cab which took us to a small bar on some bluffs overlooking the crashing waves of the Atlantic. The place was quiet for a Saturday night, but we had a nice meal and a few beers, and Kirsty was happy to spend the rest of the evening here. Unfortunately, I had other ideas. On the taxi journey to the bar, I'd spotted flashing neon a couple of hundred yards away, and my enquiry to the barman confirmed it be the Mango Bar, which he described as a 'disco chop bar,' popular with young locals and which hosted live music on a Saturday. My sort of African bar.

Kirsty was unsure, especially when I said that as it was so close, we wouldn't need a taxi. She was even more unsure as realisation dawned upon setting out to walk towards the thumping 'Hiplife' music and flashing lights, that the 'couple of hundred yards' was as-the-seagull-flies, and there was no direct path between the two bars. The barman pointed us up the road, and told us to look out for a path on the left which would take us to the pub.

"Not too far." He assured us. Kirsty's question of whether it was safe, was met with a smile and a shrug. Not very reassuring. However, emboldened by a few bottles of Guinness Foreign Export super strength stout, I saw no point in waiting for a taxi, for a journey we could complete on foot in five minutes. We set out up a slight incline along the deserted road, aiming for a street lamp on the corner, at the top of the hill.

We were about thirty feet away when we saw the gang. Ten youths, mid to late teens, sitting on the wall beneath the street light. Turning around would have invited trouble. There was only one tried and tested method to deal with this potentially dangerous situation.

"Kirsty...Big Antelope!" I bellowed, getting immediately into my role as the biggest, baddest beast in Cape Coast.

The kids had spotted us and monitored our approach. I strode out in front, scowling, with chest expanded and fists clenched. I glanced at Kirsty and had to struggle to stay in character. Her big antelope demeanour was more befitting of a bad tempered primary school teacher with a painful case of haemorrhoids, which was at least likely to confuse a gang of West African street criminals.

As we drew level with the youths, I turned to face them and met the stare of a plump youth in a woollen Chicago Bulls hat. I raised my eyebrows and tilted my head in a slight upwards motion, which I hoped he interpreted as 'Whassup homie?' rather than an invitation to join us for a night at the disco. Or to rob us.

I sensed the youths continuing to watch as we passed, so I delivered the 'coup-de-grace' of the big antelope strategy, with a spectacular hawking and emission of phlegm onto the road surface. The impact of this was lessened somewhat by the pile-plagued school ma'am ticking me off.

"I wish you wouldn't do that." Kirsty scolded, shaking her head.

Once past the potential mugging hazard, all we needed was to find the path leading to the bar, which we could now see across a dark patch of wasteland. We carried on along the road without seeing any turn-off, and soon the sounds of thumping music were receding and the lights were behind us. It was clear we'd missed the path.

An elderly man in a pork-pie hat approached, pushing a dead goat in a wheelbarrow, so we asked where the elusive route was.

"Back that way, by the corner." He pointed back to where the gang were slouching, watching us. I didn't fancy walking back past them. I had no phlegm left for one thing. Walking ahead on the dark road also seemed to be asking for trouble, so reaching the bar was our only option. I asked if there was another way.

"There is a path over the field," the goat-pusher pointed over the dark wasteland. "But it's hard to follow in the dark."

Five minutes later, we'd proved him right by losing the faint track, and were now blundering along in the dark, guided only by the distant lights and music of the bar.

"Big Antelopes Kirsty!" I shouted, as I strode ahead. Then I disappeared.

The hole was liquid filled and sharp edged. Both these facts became immediately apparent as I plunged into it with a splash. My right leg was submerged up to thigh level, but total immersion was prevented by my left shin smashing onto the edge of the hole. The pain was excruciating, and I could tell I'd done some serious damage. Kirsty helped haul me out, and I staggered towards the light of the bar to assess the injury.

I was wearing jeans, which had been magically transformed into two-tone, brown and red, one leg of each colour. The brown was from the stinking contents of the sewer which soaked my right leg. The red was from the blood which was pumping out of my left shin. I'd never before witnessed the phenomenon of blood spurting from my body in time with the pulsing of my heart, but that was the sight which greeted me as I rolled up my trouser leg.

The bar employed a one-armed doorman, who looked puzzled as we approached. He seemed about to say something, but decided against it, and restricted himself to sniffing disapprovingly as I limped past. Once inside, we headed to the bar. I needed a drink. The pub was a semi-outdoor set-up, with drinks served from a concrete counter facing an unoccupied courtyard dancefloor. A handful of couples and groups of single young men sat on stools around high tables, nodding along to a banging Reggie Rockstone track.

The arrival of two white faces hadn't gone unnoticed and as I slumped at the bar, I was aware of a hovering presence at my left shoulder.

"Hello my friend. My name is Solomon. I am a businessman of this town." He pronounced this as 'Beeeznessmaan.'

"Hello Solomon." I grimaced, bracing myself for the usual hard-sell of get-rich-quick nonsense. However, before I could try to rebuff him, my potential Beeezness partner's nose began to twitch.

"My goodness, what is that smell?" Solomon was clearly as repulsed by the stench of raw sewage as Kirsty, who had positioned herself fifteen feet away.

"That's human shit Solomon." I smiled and took a swig of my beer. "My leg is soaked in it you see. And my other leg is drenched in blood." I pointed to my jeans, which were dripping a fetid pool of foul smelling liquid into a pool around my feet.

"Oh Goodness me. Ah...that is terrible my friend." Solomon was backing away.

"What did you want to talk to me about?" I shouted, as he reversed hastily, shouting 'It's not important my friend.'

I finished my drink and ordered another round, communicating with a distant Kirsty using hand signals. I enjoyed utilising my new 'Beeeznessman repellant' to full effect over the next hour, repulsing a non-stop stream of would-be partners with my foul aroma of African sewer.

Eventually, having calculated that I'd probably lost more than a pint of blood, we decided to head back to the hotel, and I squelched out of the bar and into a taxi, my trainers alternately splurging blood and excrement with each step.

After swilling away the filth from my legs back in our room, Kirsty and I assessed the damage. I had a hole in my shin, roughly the diameter of a ten pence piece, and the depth of a couple of pound coins. Directing the jet of the shower into the wound momentarily cleared the blood and allowed a glimpse of glistening white. Whether bone or cartilage, I was unsure, but Kirsty was encouraging me to go to hospital.

Saturday night in a small-town African emergency department, with potentially dubious levels of hygiene, was less than appealing though, and I was confident that I had the means and know-how to counter any infection.

"Pass me the hand sanitiser." I calmly instructed Kirsty with the confident air of a surgeon about to perform heart surgery.

"You're not...you can't." Maybe it was morbid fascination that caused her to hand it over, and seconds later the whole hotel was aware that she had. I'd braced myself for some pain, but the impact of squirting neat alcohol into a gaping wound is hard to describe. Needless to say, the visceral, animal-like howl I emitted was probably heard above the music back in the bar. I lay shaking and whimpering on the bathroom floor as we waited for the night manager to appear with the police, but no one came. It seemed that banshee howls were par-for-the-course on a Cape Coast Saturday night.

After experiencing misfortune such as my sewer plunge, a sensible person would recognise that the planets are misaligned, that bump in the road you hit was actually a black cat, or their guardian angel is having a night at the bingo. Call it a day, and go to bed. Unfortunately, I'm not that person.

With Kirsty mopping up the bathroom bloodbath, I decided to set about erecting our trusty mosquito net. With my wound wrapped in thick swabs of toilet roll, held in place by a tightened flightsock, I positioned a chair on the bed, in order to attach the net to a hook I'd spotted already handily screwed into the ceiling.

A metal balcony chair on a soft mattress is never the most stable platform, and my throbbing leg made balance even more difficult as I teetered on the bed. Mosquito net in hand, I reached upwards as my legs wobbled on the chair. I would best describe the noise I heard next as a loud, dull thud, at very close quarters, and a sudden impact on my raised arm knocked me backwards onto the bed. As the chair crashed to the floor, I struggled to comprehend what had just happened. Then, looking involuntarily upwards, a sickening, split second realisation dawned, as I saw a large, three bladed ceiling fan rotating at speed above me.

I've read numerous accounts of accidental limb amputations,

where the victim is unaware of their fate, until they spot their own favourite workboots revolving in the blades of a combine harvester. Or attempt to make a 999 call and find they no longer have a hand. And I knew now, that's what had happened to me.

Attracted by the noise, Kirsty poked her head round the bathroom door and stared quizzically, as she saw me laying on the bed, not daring to check the damage.

"Have I still got two arms?" Is a question I'd thankfully never asked before, nor had cause to since.

Luckily, it seemed that either the fan blade wasn't sharp, or maybe I only partly inserted my limb into the rotation, and the physical damage was limited to a long bloody stripe across my forearm. Kirsty forced me into bed at that point, deciding that we couldn't risk a third-time-unlucky incident.

And for future reference, I can confirm that hand sanitiser is not an effective substitute for an Accident and Emergency department. I awoke the next day to find that my leg and foot had bloated to around three times their normal size, as infection, not surprisingly, took hold. We were travelling home in a few days, so I persisted with my painful DIY hand-sanitiser treatment, and limped back into work with a leg like Popeye's arm. Not surprisingly my colleagues reacted with their usual mix of 'why on earth do you go to these places' bemusement, and 'another tall travel tale' amusement. It took two weeks of strong NHS antibiotics to get the infection under control, and to this day I have a large circular scar on my shin, to remind me of my character building evening on the West African coast.

14 POLICE AND THIEVES

In addition to physical discomfort and illness, another main concern for travellers venturing far off the beaten track is likely to be safety. How high is the risk of falling victim to a crime, and if the worst happens, what will the experience of dealing with the local police force be like? In some countries, the dividing line between police and thieves is blurred into ambiguity. In others, the supposed law enforcers are viewed as an even bigger threat than the actual criminals.

To date, I've been fortunate in managing to avoid any serious criminal acts. A teenage mugging in Benidorm, and an all too common phone snatch in Barcelona. A car radio stolen in Sarajevo, and the previously mentioned Ukrainian passport incident, leave me feeling that I've done pretty well, considering some of the places I've travelled to.

I research thoroughly before any trip to a new destination, using the Foreign Office's travel advice website, which provides up to date info on potential threats in every country in the world. If the Foreign Office say don't go, I take that seriously. However, word on the street from forums and other travellers often needs to be taken with a large pinch of salt, as was the case when Kirsty and I traversed the old pirate island of Hispanola in the Caribbean.

An island with a split personality, Western Hispanola, better known as the Dominican Republic, has been colonised by package tourists from the US and Europe, with strips of all-inclusive resorts bordering the white sand beaches of Punta Cana and Samana. Saying you want to visit the eastern side of Hispanola however, is guaranteed to cast a dark cloud over your travel company rep's welcome cocktail party, for that half of the island is Haiti. The country was deemed the poorest in the western hemisphere even before it's capital, Port-au-Prince, was reduced to rubble in the devastating earthquake of 2010. Since then, Haiti is generally viewed as the Third World transplanted into the Caribbean. Dirty, diseased and dangerous. Kirsty and I decided to see for ourselves.

We rented a car in the Dominican Republic, and after a couple of days at the beach, headed west to see the little visited, mountainous interior of the island. We then parked our car in the city of Santiago, and caught a bus across the border, intending to visit Haiti's northern coast, around Cap Haitien, and the mountain top citadel of Sans Souci, which can be reached only by donkey.

We crossed one of the most chaotic borders I've ever witnessed, with the surreal sight of hundreds of traders carrying rusting wheelbarrows above their heads, attempting to squeeze through a narrow passageway to reach a sprawling no-mans-land market between the two nation's borders. Bloodied vendors crawled from the melee clutching bruised ribs, as others pushed forward to take their place in the heaving mass of thin black legs, topped by rusting iron shells. It looked like a vicious territory battle between warring factions of some mutant species of armoured terrapins.

Having eventually cleared the border, the difference between the Dominican Republic and Haiti was stark. The smooth asphalt of the wealthier half of the island was replaced by the potholes and dust of the developing world. It was like turning a corner in your rented Fiat next to the harbour in Puerto Banus, and suddenly finding yourself trundling down Mogadishu High Street.

As we bumped along past crumbling shacks and skinny cows, my attention was drawn to the only other obvious non-locals on our bus, a couple of fifty-something American men. I'd engaged them in conversation at the bus station, curious as to what was taking them to Haiti. A somewhat garbled and unconvincing explanation helped form my opinion.

"Sex tourists." I confidently (and correctly) informed Kirsty.

And now they seemed to be carrying out a mid-journey wardrobe change. Logoed polo shirts were removed to reveal plain cotton t-shirts beneath, and brand name training shoes were stuffed into holdalls to be replaced by cheap plastic sandals. One of the sexual adventurists spotted my puzzled expression and leant over to explain.

"We've been strongly advised," he whispered furtively, casting wary glances towards our fellow passengers, "that non-locals will be spotted the minute they get off the bus. As soon as we're outside the bus station, they'll steal our clothes and shoes. Especially our shoes." He looked toward my trusty Timberland sandals, recently refurbished by a Mumbai street cobbler, with a worried expression.

I thanked him for his concern, but decided that as I wasn't about to exit the bus station in the style of David Carradine's barefoot wanderer, Kwai Chan Caine, there was little I could do to repel the infamous footwear fiends of Cap Haitien.

Upon arrival at the bus station, the two Americans skulked out of a side door, clutching supermarket carrier bags containing their clothes. We walked out of the front door without attracting any unwanted attention beyond the usual clamour of taxi touts and money changers. I surveyed the footwear of the locals, and decided that the majority would probably decline my sandals, with their mysterious and unshiftable odour of rabbits anyway. The next day, we spent an enjoyable afternoon wandering the crumbling French colonial streets, with gingerbread houses and rusting, New Orleans style balconies, and exploring the chaotic Marche de Fer, or Iron Market, which sells everything from toiletries to Voodoo paraphernalia. In a square near the city's Notre Dame cathedral, we spotted the Americans sat outside a bar, swigging bottles of Prestige Beer, surrounded by a bevy of giggling, plump 'bouzens.' I noticed the plastic sandals had been replaced by hideous white Nike's.

"Having a good time?" I shouted.

"Wow! What a town! What a country! Phil loves it so much he's gonna buy a place here!" Another bullshit travel crime myth bites

274

the dust, I thought, as we were accosted by a group of smiling, plaid-clad schoolgirls chasing a photo, rather than our shoes.

Another case of a town being unfairly blighted by its online reputation, occurred in the perhaps unlikely setting of the Caribbean island of St.Lucia. As usual, we'd given the high end resorts a miss, and opted for a simple room in Soufriere, on the island's west coast. Proximity to two mountainous volcanic masses, known as The Pitons, which ascend precipitously from the sea close to the small town, placed Soufriere within the orbit of well-heeled tourists and cruise ship passengers. However, it seemed they didn't like what they experienced, having been disgorged from their tour buses. Trip Advisor led us to believe that the town was dirty, ugly and was besieged by legions of aggressive beggars. More than one post on the review site mentioned being pursued back to the safety of the bus by an army of well organised, potentially violent pan-handlers.

Within a day, we'd discovered the reality. The multitudes of beggars mentioned online, were actually two old crackheads, John and Jeff, who stealthily covered the town's dusty streets with such ruthless efficiency, that they achieved the effect of a vagrancy hall of mirrors, often seeming to be in more than one place at the same time!

Their encyclopaedic knowledge of the back alleys and cut-throughs in the old settlement of clapboard houses, allowed them to reappear, cup in hand, in front of a tourist who had rebuffed them in a different street only minutes earlier. And so, the legend was born, of hordes of pushy beggars, who all seemed strangely similar in appearance.

I quickly realised we were dealing with the same serial offenders, and decided to introduce them to my own special method of begging rebuttal. A beggar will have a readily rehearsed response to your rejection of his demands for cash, in order to prolong the negotiation. The aim of the begging game is to maintain the discussion for as long as possible, until the victim's defences are eventually worn down, and the easiest option is to toss a coin into the cup. Therefore, the best response is one that the beggar could never foresee, or have any pre-planned response for. The more incongruous and unexpected, the better.

I first encountered John outside Eroline's market in the centre of town. Kirsty was indulging her passion for exotic, overseas grocery stores, and I was sitting on a bench outside, watching an old man attempt to wrestle a reluctant live cockerel into a plastic shopping bag.

I smelt John before I saw him shuffling towards me. His baggy denim dungarees, red and white chequered shirt and red baseball cap, could have given him the appearance of a jocular children's entertainer, but the heavy staining, particularly around the crotch area of his jeans, would have resulted in instant dismissal from the set of Play School. He sported an enormous pair of white dead-mans-trainers, secured around his too-small feet using yellow string, and his imploring, crack-addled face placed him somewhere between the ages of fifty five and eighty five.

"I'm hungry, please help me." John gripped his stomach to emphasise his point, but we'd already been warned that the local beggars' hunger tended to be more focused on Class A's than calories. John's beer breath also seemed to confirm this.

I stood up, and John's face lifted as he sensed acknowledgement of his request. It seemed I may be a potential soft touch.

"My garden wall is four feet high." I looked John in the eye as I delivered this message. John paused for a couple of seconds, opened his mouth as if to speak, then closed it again and awkwardly shifted his gaze sidewards.

"Four feet high." I raised my hand slowly, to regain John's attention, until I reached the appropriate forty eight inch level.

"A four foot wall. Do you understand?" I stared hard into John's bloodshot eyes, and he looked confused, embarrassed and a little scared.

"No sir. I do not." He mumbled.

"Well, there we are then." I smiled contentedly and regained my position on the bench. John paused for a couple of seconds, his mouth trying to form words which just wouldn't appear. He then stumbled away, looking over his shoulder a couple of times, seemingly to try and work out what had just happened.

During the next twenty four hours, we were approached by John, or his partner in crime, Jeff, at least ten times. On each occasion, I responded with an ever more baffling and unexpected response.

"Is a tomato a fruit or a vegetable John? "

"Erm...I don't know that sir, could you spare some..."

"I have to hurry you John, please give me an answer."

"Oh...fruit...no vegetable."

"Incorrect John!" I gave him a big smile as a consolation prize, and John shuffled off down the road, muttering and shaking his head.

We stayed in Soufriere for three days and by the second day, John and Jeff could identify me from a long distance, and did all they could to avoid me. I even resorted to playing them at their own game – I'd see John spot me, then take evasive action and duck into a side street. I'd jog along a parallel road to emerge and greet him, shambling out of the alleyway.

"John! Who was the second man to pretend to land on the moon? Because it never really happened did it John?...John, come back!"

I'm sure John and Jeff were never as happy to see the back of a European visitor as the day I left their town. Fittingly, as we were leaving, we stopped at the town's only set of traffic lights. John appeared suddenly from the pavement, having clearly spotted the opportunity presented by a rental car, with Jeff hovering on the pavement in anticipation. I waited until he was a couple of feet away before winding down the window and greeting him in the manner he'd come to expect.

"John, did you know it's physically impossible for a human to lick their own elbow." I almost felt like giving the old junkies some cash as they turned tail upon spotting me, and scampered down towards the port, where they'd be sure to find some less annoying victims.

There's a saying in South Africa that they can never solve the crime problem, as the middle classes would have nothing left to talk about. I love South Africa. I like the people, the scenery, and the fact that a favourable exchange rate generally makes a two-week trip highly affordable. However, you can never truly relax. You always need to keep your wits about you and be aware of your circumstances. Millions of South Africans live in townships, which can vary from shanty towns of unofficial dwellings using stolen electricity, to smart streets with neat gardens, a functioning police force and civic amenities such as litter collection. Some people view guided township tours as 'poverty tourism,' but I see them as an opportunity to experience the lives of a sizeable proportion of the South African population.

We were in Johannesburg, a year before the 2008 World Cup, when the authorities cracked down hard on crime, and reclaimed a number of previous 'no-go' areas. We'd joined a mini-bus tour to Soweto, to see Vilakazi Street, the address of two Nobel prize winners in Nelson Mandela and Desmond Tutu; learn about the Soweto Uprising of 1976; and spend time with local people in their homes.

We were driven by an elderly, bespectacled local called Clive who was a proud 'Jozy' resident, and who railed against his hometown's reputation as a dangerous warzone. He was particularly irked by the proliferation of razor wire, search lights, high walls and gates with '24 hour armed response' signs, which seemed to adorn every home we passed en-route to Soweto. Clive's theory was that it was all needless, and that most of the city was totally safe. However, when one home in a street installed additional security measures, it immediately made their neighbours feel vulnerable. So those neighbours installed even better security. Then their neighbours did likewise. And the cycle continued, in an uncontrollable upward spiral of home security, fuelled by a crime obsessed media, and companies making a fast buck from selling all manner of products to make the jumpy residents feel slightly safer.

"Look at it all. Wire. Alarms. Guards. Like a bleddy prison camp!" Clive flicked his hand angrily at the creeping anti-crime contagion he saw as a blight on the city.

There were eight of us in the minibus, including a studious looking Spaniard with a pony tail, who unwisely took Clive to task on his assertion that Jo'burg was no more dangerous than most European Cities. Quoting an alarming murder rate of fifty two slayings per day in the Gauteng region, he managed to antagonise Clive to the point where the old man angrily cut him off, mid sentence.

"Those stets relate to gang activity in the townships! They skew the numbers...most of the city is NOT dangerous."

Then, to prove his point, he decided to embark on a bizarre, back-to-front argument strategy, by deviating from the usual route, to show us an area of town which he informed us WAS highly dangerous.

"You think this place is dangerous? I'll show you where IS bleddy dangerous. We're going to Hillbrow." And with that he hung a sharp left off the main road, and sped down a side street, still muttering angrily under his breath.

Kirsty and I looked at each other. As usual, we'd done the research, and knew that Hillbrow wasn't the sort of place to conduct a guided tour. With law and order a distant memory, businesses, residents and even the police had long since retreated, leaving Hillbrow with a reputation as the ultimate 'no-go' area.

After driving for twenty minutes through non-descript suburbs, the high-walled houses were slowly replaced by rust stained apartment blocks and abandoned shop units, their shutters adorned with spray-paint tags, the local gang equivalent of canine scent marking. Pedestrians were scarce, and vehicles gunned their engines at red lights, their drivers nervously scanning the street for car-jackers.

It was early afternoon, and the deserted streets fuelled my hope that most serious gangsters were largely nocturnal and wouldn't be awake yet. Disconcertingly, Clive had slowed down and was peering through his bottle-bottom specs, trying to make out the street signs.

"Ach. It's all changed round here. I used to know my way by the shops. They're all gone now." It was clearly his way of telling us he was lost. We crawled along debris strewn streets, complete with hunched winos surrounding bonfires in bins, and I commented that if this was a film set, you'd tell the designer that he'd gone overboard on the urban misery. Our slow driving pace suggested we were about to commit a drive-by shooting, and I scanned the windows of the semi-abandoned flats above, expecting to see a look-out on his phone.

Up to that point, Clive may have felt that his flawed 'whataboutism' strategy had failed, as the area was undoubtably deprived, but we'd seen no evidence of imminent danger. That changed as we turned right at a non-functioning traffic signal. If the movie set-designer had over-egged the pudding on the previous streets, he'd ratcheted this one up a notch, to the level of sacking-offence, ridiculous cliché.

Burned out cars, check. Fires in bins, check. Boarded up shops, check. Winos, plenty. Tooled-up, drug dealing gang members wearing balaclavas and bandanas, obviously.

It was scene straight out of The Wire, but surprisingly Clive failed to react, and continued to crawl along the long street, as the groups of scowling, skulking youths warily monitored our approach.

"Will these guys be armed?" asked the Spaniard, and Clive reacted with undisguised glee.

"Armed? You better believe it," he crowed. "These boys will have better hardware than the police. That's why they don't dare come here."

"Shit, this is really bad." I stated the obvious, as Clive revelled in what he saw as a confirmation that the majority of Jo'burg wasn't really dangerous, simply due to it being safer than this hell-on-earth.

"This place is REALLY dangerous!" He coughed out the 'R' of really as if he had a furball in his throat, and smiled to himself in the rear-view mirror. Job done.

Only it wasn't, quite. Our van had tinted rear windows, so the edgy youths, watching us crawl towards them could only see an elderly, bespectacled black man at the steering wheel. It would be a clever 'Trojan Horse' ploy, for a rival gang to employ an old man to roll slowly onto their turf, then open the back doors and unleash a deadly hail of fire from a hidden assassination squad. On the street, heads bobbed nervously, warnings were shouted, hands reached ominously inside jackets. In the van, all was silent. I reached over and pushed down the lock button on the sliding door. As I did so, I caught the eye of a German gap-year student. He looked close to tears.

Halfway along the street, we drew level with a group of five youths in puffa anoraks, standing beside a burning bin. Johannesburg's high altitude makes it chilly in winter, but one youth obviously felt the cold more than his gangmates, as he was sporting an enormous fur hat, very similar to one I'd once 'borrowed' from a shepherd on a drunken night in the mountains of Armenia.

The young man screwed up his eyes as we passed, trying in vain to see what, or who, was in the rear of the van. He was undeniably photogenic, and unfortunately, the temptation to record him in all his glory was too much for one of our number. One of the Dutch girls on the back seat decided to risk a sneaky photo, but unfortunately forgot that the tinted glass would trigger her camera's flash.

All hell broke loose. The gangster's fur hat was nearly dislodged from his head, as he recoiled at the flash exploding a couple of feet from his face. The Dutch girls screamed. I caught a glimpse of Clive's panic-widened eyes in the rear-view mirror, in the split second before he accelerated.

"Everyone down! Get on the floor!" he screamed. We had no choice. The sudden acceleration propelled us all from our seats, and we crouched below window level, hoping the gang's 'better hardware' wouldn't pierce the obviously non-armoured shell of our converted Ford Transit.

Clive's previous steady pace belied an obvious past life as a getaway driver, and with his own head lowered to just above the steering wheel, we raced along the street. I heard no gunshots, but the noise could easily have been drowned out by the screams from the bus. My own included.

We ran a red light, rounded a corner on two wheels, then became airborne as we cleared a small hill to emerge back on the main road.

"You see, ladies and gentlemen. THAT place is dangerous, not this." Clive nodded happily and we carried on to Soweto, which did indeed seem like a Cotswolds village in comparison to the mean streets of Hillbrow.

South Africa has long suffered with its reputation as a dangerous criminal hotspot, but in my experience, a traveller is much more likely to be robbed in the countries on the Continent's west coast. West Africa, is for me, the 'Daddy' of highway robbery. And the main culprits are the police.

It's widely accepted that Nigeria is the worst country in the region for petty roadside police corruption. I've never driven there, but based on my roadtrip through the country, I reckon Ghana must run it a pretty close second. Police roadblocks and vehicle checks are frequent, but unlike other West African nations where roadside shakedowns are often conducted amidst an undercurrent of barely concealed menace, such as that by my mitten-wearing friend in Togo, Ghanaian police extortion tends, more often than not, to be a case of Keystone Cops, Gone Bad.

In the numerous 'stop and search' incidents we experienced, the officers tended to be rather well-upholstered, with rolls of fat bursting forth from their smart beige uniforms, their plea of 'I'm hungry, my friend,' more likely to mean they were interrupted during their mid-morning snack of chichinga kebabs, than were facing imminent starvation.

And it was graft with a grin. Waved to a halt, you'd observe the bulky mass of officer approaching, giving your vehicle the once-over, looking for any infraction that would result in an immediate cash-only fine. Then a large, shiny, podgy face would appear at the window, usually with a beaming and hopeful smile, to launch into their sales pitch.

"What is your country my friend? Ah, England. A beautiful land, sir. A wealthy country. Not like Ghana sir. No....we are so poor sir. We are so, so hungry." All delivered with an air of flesh trembling jollity and elaborate African handshakes. The generic scene setting – You're rich, I'm poor, was a preamble to the closing pitch which could vary from the poignant to the ridiculous.

"Daddy, do you have a gift for your son?" grinned a young constable with far too many pearly white teeth for his mouth.

"I don't have a son."

"Daddy, I am your son. Your loving African boy!" This unsurprisingly resulted in my wallet remaining in my pocket. As did 'I have malaria. You have nice hair. My father's head is terribly swollen with mumps. My refrigerator is broken. I love your Tony

Blair, and I need to buy fifty goats so I can marry my fiancé.'

I prided myself on not coughing up a single cedi in two weeks of driving those lawless lawmen's lanes, averaging around five roadblocks a day. I would return the officer's smile, and often get out of the car to engage in evermore elaborate handshakes, backslapping, shared cups of tea and on one occasion, an impromptu roadside jive with an eighteen stone lady constable. We always parted on good terms. I'm sure in most cases, by the time we drove on, they'd forgotten whether they'd managed to extract any cash from me or not.

Then, with a few days remaining of our roadtrip, I met my nemesis. The drill began as usual. A pole extended across a dusty road, next to a single storey concrete shack. A Ghanaian flag flopped limply atop a makeshift bamboo flagpole. A row of light brown uniforms lounged on a bench in the shade, and one of their number rose enthusiastically as we approached, and waved us to a halt.

Late forties, business-as-usual borderline obese, with a tiny 'Hitler' moustache and a sweat-shine, fleshy head which was two sizes too big for his skull. Consequently, loose jowls drooped beneath piggy eyes, squinting under a peaked cap.

I waited for the tap on the window which would herald the arrival of a smiling fat face and comical, half-hearted extortion attempt, but none came. Instead, through the rear-view mirror, I could see the unsmiling officer bending to rub at a smudge of dirt on a rear brake light. I decided to meet the challenge head on, and exited the car.

"Good afternoon, I'm Matthew." I beamed and extended my hand, in anticipation of the usual complex finger shuffle and click greeting. His piggy glare flicked towards me momentarily, then he continued the detailed examination of my car. Obviously disappointed at finding nothing unlawful on the exterior, he turned his attention to the boot, and barked an order to remove our bags. Once placed in the dust, he began an examination of the spare tyre and tool kit.

Kirsty had now joined me on the roadside, and we monitored the search in concerned silence.

"This one is a bit too efficient for my liking." I mumbled a little too loudly, and he cast me a disapproving glance while opening the rear door. He then struggled to heave his considerable bulk onto the backseat. The whole process was being watched by his six colleagues, sat in an unsmiling line around twenty feet away. I began to wonder whether he was being assessed in some way, and half expected to see them raise a row of ice-skating style score cards to rate his performance. Eventually, the appearance of his fat arse, slowly emerging from the back seat, told us the check was over.

"Licence. Passport." He extended a pudgy open palm.

"Is there a problem officer?" I could tell by his self-satisfied demeanour that there was.

"Oh yes." He was writing down details from my driving licence in a well-thumbed notebook. I noticed that he clenched the pen in his fat fist without using his thumb, like a toddler.

"What is the problem officer?" He was obviously holding out for dramatic effect and he ignored me, while carrying on dabbing away at his notebook. If I'd had a wax crayon I'd have handed him it.

Eventually, it was time for the big reveal.

"Mr Matthew, we have a serious problem." He announced with a flourish. "Your vehicle has no fire extinguisher."

It was my turn to pause and consider my next move.

"I can see that's a problem officer. However, it's not my problem. This is not my car you see. It's a rental car, so the problem is for the rental company."

His eyes flickered and he licked his lips. The battle of wits had begun, and it wasn't one I intended to lose. Nor did he, and he cast a glance towards his colleagues, who were closely monitoring the exchange, and he decided to wheel out the big guns.

"You are driving the car, sir. Therefore, you are the offender in this case. This is very serious. You will be fined and failure to pay immediately, will result in an appearance before the magistrate tomorrow morning." Before he'd had time to bask in the glory of playing his trump card, I responded with one of my own.

"Fine." I replied and crossed my arms.

"What?" his tiny eyes blinked nervously amidst thick folds of flesh.

"I said that's fine. It's not my car so I'm not guilty. I'll go to court tomorrow and tell the judge that." This was unexpected, and caused his lips to twitch and his nostrils to flare.

"I don't think you understand..." He was smiling, but I could sense this wasn't how he'd expected the exchange to go. "You will be confined to a jail cell tonight, and transported to the court tomorrow."

"Very well officer. I haven't booked a hotel for tonight. Let's go." Kirsty was looking at me in horror, but I knew he had no intention of locking me up on a trumped-up charge. He knew it too, and was beginning to panic.

"Sir, the jail house is no place for an English gentleman such as yourself. You will experience extreme discomfort there." He cupped his groin and grimaced in an obvious attempt to convey the type of discomfort I could expect to experience. I extended my arms in a 'cuff me' gesture.

At this point, the game was over. I'd called his bluff and he had nowhere to go. He'd struggle to explain to his boss why he was jailing a European tourist over a missing fire extinguisher, so that wasn't an option. I wouldn't pay his fine. And his friends were now beginning to smirk and snigger, as they speculated on how the extortion attempt was progressing. The score cards bearing a number six were looking unlikely. Stalemate. Which was no good for either of us. I needed to give him a way-out. A face-saving outcome which would mean neither of us won, but importantly neither lost either.

"To be honest, officer. I have a problem, which means I can't pay my fine. It's a little embarrassing." I grimaced and lowered my voice, drawing him into my confidence. "The truth is, I have no cash. I've been robbed."

"Robbed? This is terrible sir. Where did this robbery occur?" He'd snapped at the bait like a fat catfish.

"I changed the last of money at a hotel in Elmina. It turns out the Cedi notes they gave me were fake. Worthless. I have nothing left." I hung my head in mock shame. Kirsty played her part by shaking her head sadly and kicking at the car tyre in frustration.

"This is a most awful occurrence sir. You are a visitor to our country. I am ashamed that you have been subjected to such an evil confidence trick. I will launch an investigation immediately. What is the name of the hotel?"

I made up a name, and he daubed it forcefully onto his pad. His colleagues were now animatedly discussing what was going on.

"I will bring these crooks to justice sir! You can be certain of that."

"Thank you so much officer. I know I can rely on you." Now was the time for smiles and extravagant handshakes, before he strode purposefully back to his colleagues to inform them that he hadn't robbed us, as some bastard had beaten him to it. As we drove away, Kirsty pointed out that our roadside poker game had taken half an hour, time we could have saved by paying a 'fine' of about a pound.

"Not the point." I said. "You should never give them anything.

Unless you have a gun pointing at your head." Little did I know how prophetic that statement was to prove a couple of years down the line.

Handing over cash to corrupt cops is always a last resort for me. I'd much rather barter my way out of highway robbery situations, and I stock up on likely 'gifts,' before embarking on a journey in areas where I feel we're likely to be shaken down by police, army or an un-uniformed hybrid of neither. Such was the case when Kirsty and I took a cheap package tour to the West African nation of Gambia. We spent a couple of nights in Kololi, a strange resort filled with aging European sex tourists looking for some seedy action with the locals. Only in this case, unlike in the fleshpots of South East Asia, (and Haiti!), the punters were 90% female. The strip of sleazy bars running down to the beach were a great people-watching spot. German pensioners with white hair and skin the colour and texture of cheap leather, shared cocktails with teenage rasta beach-bums. On a palm fringed dance floor, two bingo pals from Macclesfield with tight grey-perm, holiday hair-do's, thrust their flabby backsides towards the grinding pelvises of a duo of muscular young bucks. It was hard to stop your mind straying towards unsavoury images of what would happen later in their sweaty concrete beach bungalows.

Two days of African resort life were enough for us and we packed a bag, and left the hotel. We intended to sneak off unannounced, but were spotted by Angela, the tour rep, a buxom thirty year old squeezed into an orange uniform which perfectly matched her skin colour.

"Off exploring, you two?" she trilled. "Don't go to the market on your own, it's dangerous. We have a trip though with free barbecue included...."

When we'd made the reservation, it was with the intention of travelling to the Casamance region of neighbouring Senegal, but in the period since then, an inconvenient civil war had resulted in the region being placed firmly on the FCO 'Don't go. At all' list. We therefore had a rethink and headed north towards central Senegal and the wetlands around the town of Toubakouta.

We caught the local ferry from the capital, Banjul, across the Gambia river to the town of Barra, where we took a bush taxi to the Senegal border at Karang. A typical dusty, fly-blown frontier town, we attracted some curious stares as we lugged our backpacks through throngs of money changers and donkey-cart taxi operators, all touting for business in a curious dialect derived from the languages of English speaking Gambia and Francophone Senegal. It was clear that few independent travellers passed through here.

We located the bush-taxi stop and piled onto the backseat of a banana yellow 1990's Mercedes. A teenage boy in school uniform was seated alongside the driver and we assumed we were in for a long wait. The general rule of thumb with bush taxis, or taxi-brousse as they're known in French speaking African nations, is that they only leave when it's physically impossible to fit any more passengers into the vehicle. We've travelled long distances in taxis which resemble a student rag week stunt, or world record attempt at squeezing most bodies in a car.

It was therefore a pleasant surprise when our driver crunched the vehicle into gear and we set off, with just three passengers in a vehicle which most often carried ten. We'd been travelling for about twenty minutes, when our driver slowed and noisily sucked his teeth. The boy murmured something, and they both visibly winced as they stared through the shimmering heat down the road ahead. Road block.

Kirsty and I sighed. We'd half expected this and had stocked up accordingly before leaving Banjul. Cigarettes and some cheap local spirit were stashed in our daypacks alongside water and snacks for the journey. The hope being that we could head off any search party with this obvious prize booty, before they began investigating the more interesting, and valuable, contents of our backpacks.

Our driver approached the barrier slowly and muttered 'Gambia Police.' This was strange, as we were in Senegal, and I was concerned they were operating 'off the grid' and were therefore even less likely to adhere to any lawful boundaries than usual. Their uniforms also seemed less than official, with a mixture of ill-fitting blue police overalls, khaki and camouflage and the usual European football shirts. I began to wonder whether they were a gang of opportunists who'd burgled a dry-cleaners.

Our driver stopped the car, and as usual, the eyes of the first 'officer' lit up when he spotted two white faces on the backseat. He shouted excitedly, and we caught our first sight of the main man.

A roadblock always has a main man. Generally older and better dressed than his teenage foot shoulders, he generally reclines on his own special throne in the shade. Sometimes, he may even have added luxuries such as a beach sun lounger and perhaps even a standing fan, trailing an electrical lead from a wooden shack. The role of the main man is not to take part in the search. He merely directs proceedings whilst exuding a cool air of authority and menace.

Alerted by the shout from his young acolyte, our main man rose slowly to his feet as we were helped from the car by firm grips on our upper arms. Our bags were already being extracted from the boot, and eager fingers tugged at the zips.

The main man looked at us and grinned. He had two gold teeth and aviator shades. His apparel consisted of a crisp royal blue shirt and matching slacks, patent leather 'winkle-picker' shoes and a beret. He looked like Samuel L Jackson on his way to the Oscars.

"Passports please." He flashed us a sinister smile.

Kirsty stepped forward with the documents, but he pointed her towards a skinny youth in a Paris St German shirt. *The main man doesn't do admin.*

"We are a special police unit working to prevent smuggling in this area." He boomed. "Are you perhaps smugglers?" He cast an accusing sideways glance towards our driver, who looked at the floor.

"We will examine your luggage and find out." He flicked a finger to indicate that our bags be brought closer to his throne. *The main man only observes searches for contraband from a position of comfort.*

It's never a nice feeling to see someone poking and prodding at your possessions. It's bad enough when it's a grim-faced airport official fingering your smalls in front of a line of frustrated tourists. But seeing your well-packed rucksack's contents tossed asunder on a dusty African road, by gun toting teenagers, who may or may not be police officers, is a different level of intrusion altogether.

As usual, my plastic supermarket carrier bag of electrical accessories elicited the most interest, and a squinting youth in a ripped camouflage t-shirt took great delight in emptying the contents into the gutter, where he and a boy with a withered arm picked at them quizzically.

"What is this?"

"Charger for camera battery." A screwed-up nose indicated his lack of interest or understanding, and it was tossed back into the dirt.

"What is this?"

"It's a battery pack for a mobile phone." I decided it was now time to unveil the delights hidden in our day packs.

"Cigarette anyone?" Either they were non-smokers or cigarettes were so cheap in the country, they weren't worth stealing.

"No cigarette. What is this?" The boy held up a tangle of USB cables and charging leads in his deformed hand, while his mate assessed it with mismatched eyes. I couldn't even begin to explain the composition of the technical spaghetti.

"Whisky? We have whisky, would you like some?" One red eyed teenager seemed about to step forward, before the boy with the withered arm barked out a rebuke.

"No whisky, we don't want your whisky. We are searching for contraband." He glanced over to the main man who nodded his approval from his throne. *The main man doesn't approve of drinking on duty. Unless it's him doing the drinking, of course.*

Kirsty was trying to dissuade a man with a tall afro from sniffing her make-up, and I winced as another member of the group stuck his nose into my bag of dirty underwear. I looked in our daypack for inspiration and spotted a packet of Hobnobs which I'd bought on a whim at the market in Banjul.

"Chocolate biscuit?" I thought I'd throw it out there, with nothing to lose, and it drew a predictable response.

"We don't want your biscuit!" The squinting youth hissed as he glared at me, and also at Kirsty who was standing ten feet to my right. Clearly angered by my repeated attempts to deflect him from his search, he stuck the barrel of his ancient rifle into my bag and began flicking items of clothing to and fro, resulting in the contents of my bag being spread across a fifteen foot radius of the dusty track. I could hear Kirsty trying in vain to explain that her heated hair-straightening tongs were not some sort of hi-tech weaponry, and I glanced over to the taxi driver, who was looking on glumly as the contents of his wallet were spread across the car bonnet. The young boy was sat cross legged on the floor, close to tears. This had all the potential to be a roadblock 'worst thing that could happen.'

Suddenly, a deep resonant boom caused all present to pause, and turn towards its source.

"I will have a beees-keeet." The main man had spoken.

"I'm sorry?" I whimpered.

"I said I would like to sample one of your chocolate beees-keeets." He flashed a nine-carat smile from his throne.

All search activity ceased as I stepped forward, clutching the packet of Hobnobs in a shaking hand, and gingerly proffered the open packet towards the main man. With a strangely dainty and somewhat feminine motion, he dipped into the box and retrieved his golden, choc-topped prize between thumb and index finger, and raised it slowly to his gold-studded mouth.

The whole roadside assembly - Kirsty and I, the ragtag search militia, and a nervous, sweating taxi driver and his passenger looked on in fascination as the main man nibbled tentatively at the Hobnob, like a nervous rabbit sampling an illicit allotment lettuce. His jaw rolled and his eyes closed, like a gourmand sampling an exotic cheese. The silence added to the suspense, until eventually, his Adam's apple twitched, he licked his lips and opened his eyes.

"Mmmm-mmmmm.....This chocolate beees-keeet is delicious!" He slapped his thighs and bounded from his throne. "Perhaps this is THE most delicious beees-keeet I have tasted in my life!" He grabbed the packet from me and turned to his men, the satisfied grin momentarily replaced by a stern demeanour.

"All of you...take a beees-keeet!" He thrust the open box towards them, and a stampede of skinny youths jumped to attention. *When the main man tells you to eat a biscuit, you eat a biscuit.*

Each and every one of us was included in the distribution of the obviously delicious confectionary, with the bemused taxi driver and his young passenger nervously dipping into the packet, under the barked direction of the main man.

"Come, hurry, take a beees-keeet." He snapped, as he continued to gnaw on his initial Hobnob, whilst already fingering a sticky second.

With all thoughts of a search for imaginary contraband long forgotten, twelve sweating men, plus Kirsty and a confused schoolboy, all stood by the dusty roadside under a sweltering African sun, munching on our fast melting biscuits, nodding and smiling at each other, and marvelling at the power of the Hobnob.

Whilst I generally resist attempts at extortion by the authorities while travelling, it's important to be able to recognise when a situation has become genuinely dangerous, and handing over some cash is a small price to pay to avoid an outcome which could be life changing, or even life ending. My stubborn resistance to uniformed corruption finally came to an end on the East African island of Madagascar, on a dark road, in a city under partial curfew, at the end of the barrel of a gun being pointed at my face by a stoned teenage soldier.

We'd been travelling across the island and were ending our two week trip back in the capital, Antananarivo, where we'd started out ten days earlier. With no cellphone coverage or access to TV news, we had no idea what was going on in the world, or for that matter, within Madagascar, but as our minibus began to negotiate the city's crumbling, steeply hilled streets, it was clear that something was going on. The town felt different. On edge, wary and dangerous. Heavily armed men, wearing an array of camouflaged uniforms were patrolling the streets in armoured vehicles. Sinister figures in full-face balaclavas stood on corners, twitchily training their machine guns on the slow moving traffic. Local police in ill-fitting uniforms skulked in rusting patrol cars, seemingly keeping a low profile.

All was revealed by Pascal, the cheerful owner of our guest house, as he met us at the gate.

"My friends, you missed all the fun. We had a coup while you were gone! The mayor of Antananarivo and some crazy army generals tried to take over the country."

"But we've only been gone ten days. No one mentioned it!"

Pascal responded with a gallic shrug and smiled. "Well it wasn't a good coup. It only lasted a few days. Nearly back to normal now....whatever that is!" He laughed and led us into the garden where we sat and drank vanilla tea, as he tried to explain the murky world of Madagascan politics to us.

"Too many factions, all plotting against each other. None of them trusts each other. You know Tana Plaza?" I nodded, it was a hotel in the centre of town.

"Someone threw a hand grenade through the window, whilst some big shot politician was having lunch. If you see a lot of suits in a restaurant, avoid it!"

I mentioned the armed presence on the streets and asked who they were. Pascal shook his head with a rueful smile.

"Who knows. National Police, local Gendarmerie, Army, someone's private mercenary militia, maybe even French special forces? It's hard to know who anyone is. There is meant to be a night time curfew too, but I ignore it. Take a taxi, you'll be okay."

That afternoon, we were walking close to Antananarivo's chaotic market, when we heard a loud report of gunfire from close by. The effect on the crowds in the narrow streets was electric, and brought to mind my experiences of football riots in the 1980's - that crackle of adrenaline ignited by the likelihood of imminent violence. Some faces betraying fear and panic as they pushed and jostled to escape. Others excited, eyes wide, bouncing on their toes, grinning manically and heading at speed towards the danger.

Kirsty and I were in the former group, and found ourselves carried along by the force of the crowd, surging between the market stalls, people glancing over their shoulders with panicked expressions, as children and the elderly stumbled beneath the feet of the charging throng. We eventually found a café with a first floor balcony, and grabbed a table to observe the confused scene, as rumour and counter rumour were discussed and dismissed by the café clientele. If the locals didn't understand what was happening, we had no chance.

That evening we took Pascal's advice and caught a taxi outside L'Hirondelle, a neighbourhood bar close to our guest house. It seemed the curfew was being taken more seriously by other visitors than by our host. We were the only foreigners present, and the resident hookers slouched listlessly at the bar, bemoaning a lack of dollar-paying punters.

We flagged down a passing taxi and jumped into the back seat of the old Renault, then wriggled around to avoid the protruding upholstery springs, as our driver chugged along the strangely deserted road. We were heading to a restaurant we'd read about in Lonely Planet, which Pascal had also endorsed. 'No Suits tonight, hopefully!'

As we passed an area of open ground with scrubby bushes and a makeshift camp of street dwellers, I became aware that the car was slowing, and my heart sank as I spotted a flashlight moving slowly up and down on the pavement. Our driver sighed and glanced at me in the rear-view mirror, muttering something I didn't quite catch, but seemed to convey a Malagasy version of 'Oh Bollocks.' We were being stopped by the police. Or the army. Or one of the other mysterious armed groups.

The taxi drew to a halt and I was blinded by a torch shone through the window into my eyes. A rifle barrel tapped on the glass and I was summoned out onto the pavement. Kirsty and the driver gave me a 'rather you than me' look as I clambered out, my departure hastened by a sharp seat spring in the buttock.

Initially, I was quite relieved to see that we'd been stopped by a single person rather than a group. At least that will avoid the playing-to-the-gallery, showboating tough guy act, I thought. However, when I observed my opponent in the orange glow of a single street lamp, I had cause to be worried again.

Late teens, with a pock-marked face and large, drooping lower lip, he cut a comical figure. However, his swaying stance, bloodshot eyes and retch inducing aroma of sweat and strong local rangani cannabis, told me this probably wouldn't be a particularly sophisticated negotiation. His tattered olive uniform was two sizes too large for his skinny frame, and smelt like it hadn't been washed since its previous owner had died while wearing it. Tellingly, it bore no identifying marks to denote which militia he belonged to. Slung carelessly under his arm was an aged wooden-barrelled carbine rifle, which looked like it had probably seen action in the Malagasy Uprising of the late 1940's. I decided to go on a charm offensive and smiled my friendliest smile as I extended my hand.

"Hi! Je suis Matthew, de Angleterre. Comment vous appelez?"

Looking down at my hand then back at my face seemed to unbalance the young stoner, and he swayed, then staggered back two steps.

"Frankie. I am Frankie," he slurred through his wobbly lip. Madagascan cannabis is renowned by users across the world as being a powerful sedative, and Frankie looked like he'd been on it all day.

"Mr. Matthew, I speaking small English." He accepted my hand. His felt like a small, wet fish.

"Je parle Francais un peu seulement, aussi." I smiled, establishing some common ground via our shared limited linguistic skills. Frankie smiled back and swayed. At this point, I became aware of a waist high presence on my left, and noticed a barefoot urchin of around ten who had decided to stop and watch the show.

"Mr Matthew. Vous avez un cadeau pour moi?" Frankie lurched forward towards me and I was hit by a breeze of fetid dope-smoke breath. I tried to play down the possibility of a 'gift' with a smile and a friendly pat on his skinny arm.

"No, pas de cadeaux Frankie, I'm sorry."

He wasn't about to be brushed off that easily though and gripped my upper arm with surprising force.

"Yes! Donne-moi un cadeau." The smile had been replaced by a scowl and he seemed to be struggling to keep his eyes open, as he swayed back and forth like a spruce tree in a strong breeze.

When travelling in African cities, it's sensible to keep a bundle of small value notes in a separate pocket to your main cash stash, and I decided it was now time to reach for my 'mugging-shrapnel.' After fishing around in the pocket of my jeans for a few seconds, I produced a bundle of soiled Ariary bank notes which I passed to Frankie.

"Votre cadeau, Monsieur."

Frankie turned towards the street light and screwed up his nose and eyes, as he tried to determine the value of his gift. The little street kid craned his neck to watch Frankie slowly shuffling the cash, as he struggled with the addition of multiple small denomination notes. After several tense seconds of assessment, it was the little barefoot observer who turned to me, shaking his head to deliver the unwanted, but not unexpected verdict.

"It's not enough," he whispered sadly in English. (If you ever need an interpreter in the developing world, grab a street urchin. They're usually multi-lingual!)

Frankie obviously agreed and thrust the unwanted notes towards the grateful boy. Turning to me, his voice lowered and took on a menacing tone.

"Mr Matthew, we have BIG problem."

I began to explain in my schoolboy French that we hadn't had time to go to the bank, and were actually on our way into town to try and locate Antananarivo's only ATM when he'd stopped us, but Frankie wasn't in the mood for discussion. With his half closed, bright red eyes boring into mine and his lower lip drooping ever lower, I could sense that Frankie felt insulted by my meagre donation. This was confirmed as he raised his rifle, and prodded the barrel into my chest while fingering the rusted trigger.

"More money!" he growled.

"Oh, this is danger!" Our little barefoot commentator summed things up quite well.

I raised my hands and maintained eye contact with Frankie. Looking at his boyish, acne scarred face, I very much doubted he had any intention of blowing a European tourist away for a few dollars. However, he was stoned, probably drunk, and looked like he hadn't slept for a week. His weapon was about three times as old as he was, and potentially either wouldn't fire at all, or could inadvertently blast a large hole in my chest, as a result of one of Frankie's frequent drug induced stumbles.

I glanced towards the taxi and saw Kirsty and the driver's expressions of horrified fascination, as they watched the drama unfold.

"Give him money mister. He is crazy." My little security advisor had wisely taken up a position several feet to my left, to avoid becoming collateral damage.

"Go to the legs." Frankie gestured to the pavement and I suspected he wanted me on my knees, which all felt a bit too much like a bad movie cliché, so I pretended not to understand, but this only caused him to raise the rifle towards my face, so I was now literally staring down the barrel.

"Money!" He shouted excitedly and jerked the gun towards my nose, which caused my heart to leap into my mouth and my bowels to momentarily liquidise. My hand was shaking so much I could barely get it into my pocket to retrieve my main wad of cash, which totalled the equivalent of about forty dollars, and probably represented about three months wages to Frankie. Consequently, the huge grin which spread over his simple face as he totted up his prize, was unsurprising.

"Mr Matthew, my friend! Angleterre!" He laughed and raised his rifle above his head like a Cheyenne brave, as I scuttled back to the taxi. The street urchin nodded sagely as I passed, in a gesture which I took to mean 'some you win, some you lose.' He was happy enough – he'd inherited my pocket full of mugging shrapnel.

Luckily, Kirsty was also carrying some hidden cash, so we carried on to the restaurant, where I needed several beers before I could contemplate the menu. Half way through the meal, four large cars drew up outside, and a phalanx of heavily armed men in suits piled through the door, and wandered around the room, assessing each table of now silent diners. Satisfied that we presented no threat, they signalled to colleagues at the door, and two small, elderly men, who looked like middle ranking accountants on a disappointing works night out, were ushered in and seated at a table in the corner.

The waiter turned off the background music and a hushed, tense atmosphere settled upon the previously lively dining room. The shuttered windows were open to the warm night air and I sensed worried glances cast towards them from all tables, until, within half an hour, Kirsty and I were the only remaining customers. Clearly the risk of a flying grenade hors d'oeuvres had to be considered when booking a table for dinner in Antananarivo.

The evening ended with Kirsty and I huddled under a blanket on the floor of a taxi as we headed back to the guest house. Our driver saw our white faces as too big a security risk in a lawless city after dark, and gave us the choice of backseat floor and blanket, or in the boot, which we thought was a little too secure.

Pascal was stood at the gate of the guest house smoking his customary Gauloises and swigging from a glass of brandy as the apparently empty taxi pulled up. He looked on quizzically as the driver opened the rear door of the cab and revealed his concealed cargo.

We emerged from under the blanket and crawled out, as Pascal laughed and saluted us with a glass of Remy Martin, "Welcome to Madagascar, land of law and order!"

A week later I was sat in a council office in Bradford,

undertaking my second speed awareness course, in order to avoid three penalty points and a fine.

The woman next to me, a high-powered legal P.A, was bemoaning the wasted time our full afternoon course represented.

"It's ridiculous. We should just be able to pay the fine to the police at the roadside. That's how they do it in a lot of countries, and it works just fine."

I gave her a sideways glance and could easily imagine her haranguing an incompetent, bribe seeking West African officer, but how she'd fare facing Frankie's twitchy trigger finger on the M606 roundabout, was a different matter!

15 ONCE IN A LIFETIME

Why do we travel? What is it that compels us to utilise scarce financial resources and precious work holidays, in order to file along in slow moving lines, through soulless, overpriced airports, then be crammed aboard a metal tube and propelled skyward at breakneck speed? Why do we leave our comfortable, safe, home environments to potentially experience discomfort, illness and challenging situations? A visitor from another planet would probably view the human desire to travel as a strange calling.

For many people, the sole reason for their annual holiday is a chance to recharge their batteries after a year of work and to spend time with the family near a beach, with some guaranteed sunshine thrown into the mix. For the younger generation, magazine and newspaper articles inform us that 'for millennials, life is all about experiences.' Twenty and thirty-somethings spend more on travel than any previous generation, but rather than a fortnight of cheap booze in the Balearics, it's now all about 'curating bespoke experiences.' Forget sizzling on an all-inclusive resort sun lounger. Today's young traveller wants cultural immersion, a journey of self-discovery, and a feeling of having contributed and left their mark on the world - something more than a vomit stain on a Tenerife flop-house balcony.

Crucially, their trip needs to be highly visible on social media, and a discerning young adventurer will always have an eye on the Instagram and Facebook opportunity when planning where to go and what to see. Consequently, organised trips and excursions feature highly on their agendas, as do the 'must-sees and must-dos' listed in each country's Lonely Planet guide. Alongside the bars, cafes and laundries in the streets of every traveller hub around the world, are a profusion of tour companies, guides and fixers, all trying to push their products to young tourists - sunrise mountain hikes; snorkelling with whales, sharks or manatees;

302

authentic village homestays, or maybe the chance to be shoved from a bridge over a deep gorge, while attached to a long piece of elastic.

It's a different world from when I was in my twenties and thirties, and sharing your travel experiences with family and friends meant a packet of low quality Supa-Snaps photos spread across the bar of your local pub or your Mum's kitchen table. I started travelling in a world with less 'must-sees and must-dos' and consequently have a different view of what makes a great travel memory.

I tend to find that the real, once-in-a-lifetime, never to be forgotten, travel experiences are those unexpected 'right place at the right time' moments, where you witness something unique and totally unexpected. Or the sense of achievement you get from a challenging journey where you have to overcome significant obstacles to reach your destination. Also of course, there are the unforgettable brushes with nature at its most spectacular - sights that no Hi-Res photo or You Tube video can do justice to. Then there are the cases of extreme culture shock, which change your whole view of the world and your place in it.

That's not to say I haven't indulged in 'must-do' activities myself in the past. Kirsty and I have ridden elephants and camels. Snorkelled with sharks and stingrays. Hiked up mountains and volcanoes. Ridden quad bikes in the Namib desert, and in the same location, slid down a two mile sand dune on a sheet of waxed plywood at 45mph. We never strayed into the 'must-do' category of extreme sports though. The closest I got to that level of excitement was zip-lining. And that ended badly.

We were in the Central American nation of Costa Rica, staying close to the El Arenal volcano, which, though still active, remained stubbornly hidden behind a thick cloud blanket during our visit. At the time, zip lining was a fairly new phenomenon and Kirsty and I signed up for the activity without really appreciating what was involved. I'd anticipated a gentle descent through the cloud-forest canopy, with the opportunity to observe exotic birds, butterflies and primates as I swung sedately through the foliage. The reality was an uphill hike to a wooden shelf, suspended several hundred feet above the forest, followed by a high-speed descent via a series of treetop platforms. Basically, once you'd set off, there was no way back other than via the zipline.

We were given some basic instruction – the left hand was to remain on the harness in front of you. The right hand, clad in a thick mitten, was to loosely grip the overhead cable to which you were attached. Your legs should remain extended straight in front of you, with the right hand used as a type of rudder, to ensure you stayed pointing ahead. The first line was a couple of hundred feet in length, and the 'ride' lasted about twenty terrifying seconds, by which time I was already wondering why I'd signed up for it. Kirsty came flying in to land a minute after me, at such velocity that she nearly took out the two diminutive locals employed as 'catchers' on the platform.

The next zipline was longer, initially through dense foliage, but then emerging to soar high above the treetops for around a minute. Disconcertingly, as I flew at around 40mph through wispy clouds of mist rising from the forest, my legs began to swing to the right and by the time I was fast approaching the landing platform, I was travelling sideways. From the corner of my eye I saw the catchers attempt to reposition themselves to avoid the inevitable impact, but I still managed to deliver a high-speed knee to the stomach of one unfortunate, slow moving employee, as I came crashing in to land. Clearly concerned for my own, and their colleagues' welfare, I was subjected to some additional instruction on how to keep my legs facing forward.

"Use the right hand to steer. Remember, the right hand," implored an older instructor in a red helmet, as his young co-worker crouched alongside us, holding his guts and moaning.

I managed to negotiate the next line without incident but once all the group were safely assembled on the platform, we were informed that the next stage was 'challenging.' The wire extended over a mile across a deep river gorge, and a fine mist of drizzle had begun to drift across the forest, obscuring the mountains ahead. The guides on this platform had clearly been informed they had a problem client to contend with, and as three American college boys eagerly took their turns at swinging into the jungle void, they repeated the mantra 'Right hand to steer,' at me.

Strapped into my harness, I perched on the edge of the platform. An instructor tapped my helmet twice.

"Ready?" I nodded.

"Okay. Legs up."

I raised my legs and accelerated rapidly away from the ledge. This time I was determined to keep my legs extended rigidly ahead of me. It was therefore no surprise that as I quickly gathered speed and flew above the jungle canopy, the very thing I was trying to avoid, happened. I watched in horror as my legs began to swing to the right. The more I tried to reposition them to a forward facing angle, the more they swang outwards, until eventually I had rotated a full 180 degrees, and was facing the now distant platform I'd just leapt from, hurtling backwards high above the treetops.

At this point I recalled the instructions I'd been given and squeezed the cable above me with my right hand. I wasn't entirely sure how this was supposed to redirect me, and indeed it seemed to have little impact other than to slow my descent. I therefore applied a bit more pressure, and experienced a welcome reduction in my speed. So I squeezed the cable even harder, and came to a juddering halt.

I was now stationary, revolving slowly through 360 degrees as I was buffeted by a strong breeze blowing down the valley. I could hear distant shouting, and looked up to see two instructors, plus the three American college boys, waving and gesticulating towards me from the platform I had failed to land on. Instead, I was suspended some way below them, my reduced speed having failed to negotiate the final slight incline of the zipline. Back on the previous platform, waiting for the all-clear which meant the next participant could leap into the abyss, Kirsty heard the radio crackle into life.

"Tenemos un problema. El ingles esta atrapado." The two instructors alongside Kirsty exchanged knowing glances and smirked at her.

Hanging from the wire, I revolved pitifully, whimpering and clinging onto the cable in front of me with shaking, sweat soaked, gloved hands. Each slow revolution brought the instructors temporarily into my line of sight and they waved their arms and shouted directions. Eventually I realised what they were asking me to do – grip the cable above me with both hands and haul myself up to the platform. Foolishly, I looked down towards a series of raging white rapids around two hundred feet below me, and felt my testicles ascend into my stomach, as a cold, clammy terror-induced sweat made me shiver. My hands gripped the cable in front of me like claws, and I closed my eyes, fearing I was about to vomit, or worse.

I seemed to be trapped for hours, though in reality it was probably less than ten minutes. I was literally frozen with fear, and the instructors obviously realised there was no way I could haul myself out of this predicament. There was only one thing for it – a rescue mission.

Strapping on an additional safety harness, one of the instructors was forced to abseil along the cable towards me. He was a small, muscular, dark skinned local of the Cabecar tribe, and he regarded me with ill-disguised disgust as he drew alongside and wrapped his legs around me. Never have I felt so inadequate, as this little man, who was six inches shorter and about four stones lighter than me, gripped my torso with his powerful thighs, and began to haul us both manually along the cable. Our faces were less than a foot apart and his dark eyes bore into mine as he strained to tug us up the slight incline of the cable, with not a word spoken between us, but with his mouth curled into an unmistakable sneer of contempt.

On Kirsty's platform, the radio crackled into life again, and she heard the words 'El Ingles es rescatado,' above the sound of laughing and ironic cheering from the college boys, which signalled the end of my only foray into the world of adventure sport travel experiences.

Although I can recall all my 'must-do' experiences, often for the wrong reasons, I find it's usually those seemingly insignificant, unexpected occurrences which provide the best memories. When Kirsty and I travelled to Cambodia in 2003, Lonely Planet released a new edition of their guide to the country just before we departed on the trip. The cover depicted a scene from Ta Prohm, the temple within the Angkor complex, made famous by countless images of the surrounding forest seemingly devouring the 12th century architecture. Mostly unrestored, the temple's stone pillars and ornate carvings are entwined with giant branches and tree roots, which have slowly reclaimed the site over hundreds of years. The striking image on the Lonely Planet cover, was of a carved stone doorway framed by thick, sinewy roots. In front of the doorway was an ancient man in a dusty blue smock. Shaven headed and hunched, he clutched a broom - a tiny troglodyte caretaker sweeping up stray leaves in his wild jungle garden.

Kirsty and I had ignored advice on travel forums which said that renting your own scooter to tour the Angkor temples was impossible, and we quickly located a rental shop in Siem Reap. We were therefore able to make up our own schedule to explore the huge site, which extends over two hundred and fifty square miles, and includes important Khmer archaeological sites such as Angkor Wat, the Bayon, Preah Khan and Ta Prohm. Crucially, having our own transport meant we could follow a different circuit to the tour groups, and therefore had many of the sites to ourselves.

This was the case at Ta Prohm, and we wandered alone through the alien, jungle enveloped complex, made famous by Angeline Jolie's Tomb Raider movie. I sat on an ancient carved stone trough and gazed up into the canopy of fig and banyan trees which shaded the site, until I became aware of a rustling, scuffling sound behind me. I turned and came face to face with the elderly man on the cover of the guide book I held in my hand. He didn't acknowledge me, and continued to work with his home-made broom, carefully sweeping fallen leaves and twigs into a pile.

I called Kirsty over and pointed to the old man, then to the Lonely Planet. It was definitely him. He was wearing the same blue smock and wielding an identical broom. It was almost as if he'd stepped straight from the book's cover and come to life before our eyes. He looked up and smiled as I approached, not surprisingly looking confused at this European who was grinning, and pointing at a strange book held in his hand.

At first, he seemed to stare straight through the book I brandished in front of him, and for a moment I wondered if he was blind. At close quarters I could now appreciate his age - over eighty, with a totally bald head and thin, unlined skin stretched taut across a small round skull, looking misbalanced by a pair of unfeasibly huge ears. Barefoot and bow legged, with a pronounced stoop, his appearance was that of a kindly elf or forest dwelling sprite.

The old man's eyes eventually began to focus on the photo on the front of the book, and he looked quizzically from the picture to me and back again, obviously wondering what I was trying to tell him. He shook his head and looked away, back to the leaves he was sweeping. Then a slow flicker of recognition caused him to glance back at the book. Some distant memory rekindled, maybe from a time in the past when he owned a mirror, perhaps lived in a house and had a family, before he adopted this ascetic existence in a cave in the jungle.

Slowly, he bent forward and stared at the image, reaching out with gnarled hands to gingerly take hold of the book, which he raised to the tip of his nose in order to see better.

"It's you!" I pointed at the book, then at the old man. He finally understood, and a huge toothless smile lit up his ancient face. He shook his head and chuckled, struggling to comprehend how his photo had ended up on the glossy cover of a book purchased in a busy city at the other side of the planet.

I've no doubt hundreds of other travellers subsequently recognised the old man, and showed him that Lonely Planet cover, but the moment he first saw it, and the expression of wonderment on his face, is something I'll never forget. An unexpected, but truly memorable travel moment. Needless to say, our copy of the Cambodia Lonely Planet, 2003 edition is missing its front cover. Torn from the book and handed over to a smiling old man in a jungle clearing, I'd like to think it still has pride of place in his cave to this day.

The encroaching jungle at Ta Prohm is a perfect example of the natural world being conquered by civilisation, only for the tide to turn over the course of time, as man's influence recedes and nature regains control. I have been lucky enough to see some of the planet's great natural attractions, including five of the 'official' seven natural wonders of the world, missing only Mexico's Paricutin Volcano, and the Aurora Borealis, which remained hidden behind thick Icelandic cloud for the whole weekend which Kirsty and I spent searching for those elusive lights in the sky!

However, having snorkelled at the Great Barrier Reef, clambered along the rim of Victoria Falls and scrambled up Uluru, I have to say my favourite travel memory of the natural world is far simpler. Scandinavia is the perfect location for a campervan excursion, with its 'Everyman's Law,' which permits 'wild' camping, enshrined in local custom. For Kirsty and I, visiting the region at the height of Summer, meant twenty four hour daylight, and the chance to witness the phenomenon known as the midnight sun. We'd fly into a town in Norway, Sweden or Finland within the Arctic Circle, at a latitude greater than seventy degrees north, then rent a campervan to set off to explore the mountains, lakes and forests.

The tenets of Everyman's Law are the rights to hunt, fish and light fires on common land, and whilst the former two held no appeal, my pyromaniac tendencies, forged in childhood in the woodlands of North Leeds, served me well in Scandinavia. Finding a secluded spot for the night, usually by a river, lake or Fjord, we'd crack open a couple of beers and Kirsty would start to prepare a meal, while I'd forage for firewood. Unlike in the wilds of Africa, where our fire was required to keep us safe from deadly predators, in the far north the smoke was protecting us only from the voracious midges, and the fire was more a social focal point than a necessity.

The midnight sun is usually visible as a milky glow, and continues its slow descent towards the horizon until around 1am, when it pauses, then slowly begins to rise again. For that brief moment in which the sun hangs there, seemingly hovering in a moment of indecision, before beginning its ascent, there is a sudden sense of silent, absolute calm. The breeze drops, the Fjord becomes as smooth as glass, and smoke from the campfire drifts slowly across its surface. Strangely, birdsong falls totally silent.

It lasts only seconds, and soon the sun begins its steady climb, to herald the start of a new day. Then the dawn chorus begins, only minutes after the roosting tweets of the previous day have ended.

This should be an obvious time to turn in for the night, but as the rising sun begins to regain its power, it's all too tempting to crack open another beer and throw another log on the fire.

You can't take a bus tour to it, or take a photo of it for Instagram. You can't check yourself into it on Facebook. Maybe that's what makes that moment, between an imperceptible sunset and sunrise, in the wild and away from the sounds of traffic and people, my favourite memory of the natural world.

Whether it's negotiating rainy season roads, crossing infamously corrupt borders or banking on an erratic ferry turning up, the achievement of overcoming travel challenges can provide great memories to look back on. Inspiration for those potentially tricky journeys can come from a variety of sources - books, magazine articles and on one occasion, for me, after seeing a TV programme. The show was Extreme Frontiers, featuring Ewan

McGregor's posh-boy pal, Charlie Boorman, and telling of his adventures driving some of Southern Africa's scariest roads.

The particular episode which piqued my interest, featured a hair-raising ascent of the legendary Sani Pass, the 3000 metre high dirt track which runs between South Africa and the mysterious mountain kingdom of Lesotho. I'd been considering a visit to South Africa's Kwa-Zulu Natal province, with its opportunities for a self-drive safari and visiting historic sites such as the Boer War battlegrounds of Isandlwana and Rourke's Drift. The fact that Sani Pass was situated nearby, and that the Chinese were suggesting tarmacing the pass at some point in the future, to provide easier access to Lesotho's mineral wealth, convinced me that the time was right to attempt the challenging drive.

Boorman undertook his ill-fated attempt at crossing the pass in winter, when a layer of ice covering the gravel road made the already treacherous ascent almost suicidal. I watched open mouthed as his Land Rover, driven by a local guide, slid with wheels locked towards the edge of a sheer drop, his producer having already leapt, terrified, from the vehicle. Boorman survived but had to undertake the final section to the Lesotho border and the 'Highest Pub in Africa' on foot.

I was determined that wouldn't happen to me, as Kirsty and I nursed a couple of beers in a local bar in the small town of Underberg, the night before we were due to drive the pass. As is always the case in South Africa, the locals were happy to talk, and we engaged in friendly sport-based banter, occasionally drifting into the ubiquitous S.A. subjects of crime and politics. As we attempted to leave, citing an early start as a good reason for our premature departure, we were encouraged to have another Castle lager or two.

'Where are you headed tomorrow anyway?' asked one of our new drinking buddies at the bar.

'Up the Pass to Lesotho.' I responded, trying to sound nonchalant but feeling distinctly apprehensive.

'Who are you going with?' A couple of tour companies based in Underberg offered guided trips up the pass, and I sensed an increased interest from drinkers at neighbouring tables, as I announced our intended destination.

The mood changed noticeably at my response. 'On our own. I'm driving it myself...'

There was a pause from the drinkers as eyebrows were raised and teeth were sucked. Now everyone in the bar was interested and had an opinion, and a deluge of questions and advice began, ranging from the type of 4X4 I'd be driving, to detailed descriptions of how to handle specific sections of the drive.

I decide to order another drink but the man next to me, a typically brash and confident thirty-something with a hideous flashed mullet hairstyle, had changed his views on my alcohol consumption.

"No more. You need to go home if you're driving the mountain tomorrow. You have to treat it with respect." He placed his palm over my glass to emphasise the point.

I smiled, assuming he was joking. He wasn't, and we left the pub feeling even more nervous than before.

The previous day had seen the Drakensberg mountains shrouded in a pea-soup of damp cloud, but as we woke in our B+B at 7am, the sun was already finding its way through the gaps in the curtains. I pulled them back to reveal a perfect morning with not a cloud in the sky, and the mountain gateway to Lesotho visible in the distance. With a few final Pass driving tips from Stuart, the owner of the B+B, we pulled the Nissan Bakkie onto the road and set off to Sani Pass, and hopefully, Lesotho.

I'd read a lot about the pass, watched YouTube videos from previous travellers, and posted numerous questions on travel forums to try and get a feel for what I should expect. The Wikipedia entry for Sani Pass provided a good summary-

Sani Pass is located at the western end of KwaZulu-Natal province on the road between Underberg, South Africa and Mokhotlong, Lesotho. It is a notoriously dangerous road, which requires the use of a 4x4 vehicle. The pass lies between the border controls of both countries and is approximately 9 km in length and requires experienced driving skills. It has the occasional remains of vehicles that did not succeed in navigating its steep gradients and poor traction surfaces, and boasts a catalogue of frightening stories of failed attempts at ascending the track over the Southern Drakensberg mountains.

The South African border guard checked our vehicle, wished us luck and waved us off on our adventure. The road was rough gravel initially, and we soon passed a sign forbidding further progress by non 4X4's. There was one other vehicle making the drive and as we rounded the increasingly steep bends, I could see it as a tiny white speck, winding along the narrow road a couple of miles ahead of us. There was no one following us, and I tried not to imagine how long we may have to wait for rescue if we were unable to complete the ascent for some reason. I soon dismissed that thought. The sun was shining, the views were amazing, and we found ourselves stopping for photos whenever the road levelled off enough to give us confidence that we'd actually manage to set off again.

We eventually reached the infamous section of hairpin bends with names such as Haemorrhoid Hill, Suicide Bend, Ice Corner, Reverse Corner and Big Wind Corner, at altitudes approaching 3000 metres and all affording spectacular, but stomach turning views. There was no chance of stopping here. With 4-wheel-drive engaged, I remained in second gear and tried to maintain a steady speed as we bumped and bounced our way around the vicious curves. Our friends in the bar had told us that ten years ago, it was necessary to execute three, five or even seven point turns to navigate these corners, but the road had now been widened enough to just about get around with full lock on the steering wheel.

Eventually, after an exhilarating ninety minute journey, we

lurched onto the plateau of Sani Top with the Sani Lodge hotel perched on the lip of the cliff, enjoying fantastic views over South Africa. Billed as the world's highest pub, at 2874 metres, Sani Lodge was a strangely low-key affair. With faded sepia photos, a dusty dining room with no obvious signs of any cooking taking place and a musty moth-eaten bar, it seemed deserted. We took the obligatory photo with the 'World's Highest Bar' sign, and drove on to the Lesotho border post, around one hundred feet further along the dirt road.

If we'd viewed the lodge as eccentric, Lesotho's passport control was truly bizarre. A paint splashed breeze-block building with no windows, proclaiming itself as 'Lesotho Bordar' in mismatched, hand painted letters, and a three-legged plastic classroom chair, propped alongside a kitchen table on a rickety balcony, was our welcome to the mountain kingdom. Unsurprisingly, we had to rap on the door to rouse a slumbering official from his mid-morning nap, and he painstakingly stamped and signed our passports while peeking from beneath a colourful blanket like a sleepy toddler.

We had no real expectations of Lesotho, as it's one of the least travelled locations in Africa, and indeed, the world, but we were soon transfixed by the scenery. Rough, mountainous dirt roads led through dramatic valleys with a profusion of unlikely colours. Tan, burgundy, violet and a vivid range of greens had me reaching for my camera at every turn. Villages of traditional rondavel huts were populated by smiling, mule-riding Basotho people, clad in blankets, wellington boots and wearing wide brimmed hats. There was no traffic, save for the occasional pack horse train, or a flock of sheep being herded by shepherds in full face balaclava helmets.

It felt like climbing the mountain pass had transported us back in time by a couple of hundred years, and we'd discovered a secret kingdom, long forgotten by modern civilisation. Then we'd see scrubby fields, with local people ox-ploughing and hand hoeing, as they have for centuries, alongside an ugly diamond mine or engineering development. Here, Chinese overseers were managing local labour, and it reminded us that the modern world is well aware of Lesotho's natural wealth, and the traditional scenes we were witnessing may be gone in less than a decade.

After seven hours of driving at high altitude on challenging gravel roads, we encountered a freak storm at 3000 metres, with golfball sized hail stones, which had me fretting about my rental insurance cover as they rebounded off our roof in a deafening crescendo. Eventually we arrived at Africa's one and only ski resort to find the electricity had been knocked out by the storm. We were the only guests, and the owners lit candles and served us a welcome Maluti beer, smiling as we described our journey, and congratulating us on completing a drive that had defeated Mr Boorman! A memorable day, travelling in an unusual, remote country was made even better by the feeling of achievement in conquering one of the world's most challenging drives before it's sanitised into mundane normality beneath a layer of Chinese tarmac.

For many people, two weeks of guaranteed sunshine, away from the daily grind of work, is all that's required for a great two week holiday. But for others, myself included, travel needs to be something more than relaxing on a beach for a fortnight. Experiencing different cultures and beliefs, and witnessing the daily struggle to survive, can help us appreciate our own privileged existence. Facing challenging situations, making split second decisions and being able to recognise imminent danger, are life skills which are useful for anyone. For me though, one of the greatest rewards of travel is its ability to make us question our own beliefs and understanding of the world. To recognise that our high-tech, scientifically informed civilisation may not have all the right answers. To return home from a trip with a changed mindset and an altered perception is, for me, one of the greatest gifts travel can give.

I read a lot of travel books. The best travel writing leaves you wanting more, in terms of a greater understanding of the region you've read about, or maybe even a desire to visit that country.

Rarely, a book leaves you scratching your head in puzzlement. Confused by what you've read, you feel compelled to learn more on the subject. One such book was Toby Green's 2001 book 'Meeting the Invisible Man,' in which the author travels to Senegal and Guinea-Conakry, to explore the secretive world of West African spiritualism and magic. Initially sceptical, Green spends time with sorcerers, witch doctors and Islamic mystics known as Marabouts, and witnesses a number of unexplained phenomena, including an instance where he appears to be rendered invisible. He describes complex rituals and the acquisition of 'gris-gris' amulets, which bestow upon him a strange force which supposedly delivers superhuman qualities of invulnerability. Much to his own surprise, Green allows himself to be repeatedly stabbed with a large knife and sustains nothing more than superficial bruising.

The book's strange ending, and the author's shift in attitude following his experiences, prompted me to read more about African magic, and the mysterious practices surrounding the belief system we know in the west as Voodoo. Still puzzled, and seeking answers, I began to research the possibility of a trip to Benin, the thin sliver of a country sandwiched between Nigeria and Togo, where 60% of the population cite Voodoo, locally known as Vodun, as their main religion.

We travelled from Ghana by taxi-brousse, and stayed for a couple of days in the scruffy Togolese capital, Lome, where we visited the most disturbing market I've ever experienced – Le Marche des Feticheurs, the fetish market of Akodessawa. This fly infested courtyard is basically a wholesale market for West Africa's witch doctors and fetish priests, and is piled high with body parts from every imaginable living beast, plus some almost unimaginable ones. These are used as the aforementioned 'Gris-Gris,' also referred to as 'Ju-Ju' in some regions – amulets and charms to ward off evil spirits, or mysterious powders or potions concocted from body parts, boiled, ground or roasted.

We smelt the market long before we found it, and followed our noses until we arrived at a compound filled with trestle tables piled high with death. Predictable contents of a witch doctor's cauldron – monkey fists, the rictus-grin heads of baboons, dogs and cats, and a pile of desiccated hippo toes sat alongside more exotic ingredients. Two small boys wielding a live python, pointed out plastic sacks of pangolin scales; the dried, yet still pink, nose of a mandrill; and a glass bowl of pickled mules' tongues, resembling a bizarre corner shop 'pick and mix' sweet jar.

As we meandered between the stalls, holding our t-shirts over our faces to reduce the stench and keep the swarming flies out of our nostrils, an elderly man in a crumpled beige suit approached. Unshaven and tobacco stained beneath a dusty panama hat, he spoke with the clipped tones of an old Etonian.

"They say you can buy anything in this place. And I mean...anything." He looked at the young snake carriers and licked his lips. "Do you find this place upsetting?"

He seemed disappointed when I said that although the smell wasn't pleasant, I found it quite interesting.

"Many Europeans find it utterly sickening." There was a hint of a satisfied smirk, as he absent mindedly fingered the severed head of a young chimp, it's prominent teeth bringing to mind Bingo, the shades-wearing simian from the Banana Splits.

"Are you here to visit a feticheur?" He used the French term to reference the Fetish priests who operated in the market, acting as a conduit between the world of the living, and the Voodoo Gods, the Loa, via rituals which utilised the body part offerings on sale.

"I don't think so. Are you?"

He evaded the question. "You don't choose to become a feticheur, you know. The Gods choose you. The power of spirit communication is passed along the blood line."

The chimp head had been replaced in his trembling hand by the skull of a dik-dik antelope, complete with tiny antlers. As he surveyed the macabre jumble sale of decaying bone and flesh, he said something which I recalled later in our trip.

"You must understand, these people know things which we forgot hundreds of years ago." He carefully placed the skull back on a pile of similar tiny craniums, waved without looking at us, and shuffled out of the market.

Glad to escape the stifling heat of Lome, we next headed to the town of Ouidah in Southern Benin, widely regarded as the spiritual home of Vodun. We stayed in a dusty compound, close to the Door of No Return, a memorial arch dedicated to the memory of the estimated one million Africans who were shipped to the Americas from the town's slave port in the 17th and 18th centuries.

We hadn't appreciated the distance between our auberge and the town, and the Lonely Planet guidebook warned of bandit attacks on the dusty, unlit road we'd be forced to travel on. I therefore asked around and managed to secure transport in the form of an ancient Chinese motorbike, loaned by Jean-Claude, the desk clerk. He told me his shift ended at six, and I assured him we'd be back by then, not wanting to travel the bandit road after dark. We set off with Kirsty initially tramping along behind me on foot, as I struggled to control the heavy bike, plus a pillion passenger, in the deep sand which covered the track.

Our first stop in Ouidah was the Python Temple, dedicated to the Serpent God, Danballa. We left the Chinese rust-bucket to be polished by a group of eager street urchins, and were greeted by a chubby temple attendant with tribal facial scarification, and a brightly coloured boubou smock. He showed us around, accompanied by a frail poodle, pirouetting on its hind legs, which had me wondering whether it was friend or food.

He explained that the temple housed around sixty snakes, which were very much of the 'free range' variety. They spent their days lounging within the temple compound, but at night were released to slither unhindered through Ouidah's streets, where they often found their way into local homes. Viewed as the returning souls of deceased relatives, each reptile was fed and pampered before being safely delivered back to the temple the following day, like a teenager skulking home on a Sunday morning, still clad in their nightclub clothes. The Beninese slither of shame.

The temple's main chamber was a shady, high ceilinged room with convenient ledges and shelves for its serpentine occupants to relax upon. It felt cool and peaceful, hidden away in the shady temple compound, away from the punishing rays of the West African sun. Kirsty and I sat in the semi-darkness, enjoying the unfamiliar chill, whilst a writhing knot of pythons slid and twisted around us. Sitting in a pit of snakes had never felt so relaxing!

Back in Ouidah's dusty backstreets, we witnessed the ubiquitous presence of Vodun in the lives of the Beninese people. The God Legba is viewed as the guardian spirit of homes and places of work, and shrines to this mischievous entity are as common as bus stops in England. Varying in design from an intricately carved statue with a rampant, erect phallus, to an ambiguous blob of concrete, these shrines were everywhere. Coated in a mixture of candle wax, the local palm spirit, Sodabi, and the feathers and blood of sacrificed livestock, they often resembled a meeting point for local catarrh sufferers, being coated in a thick layer of sticky, foul smelling goo.

At the sudden onset of the equatorial dusk, the streets began to clear and smoke drifted from the many open-air grills, selling goat brochettes and smoked fish. Now, in the fading light, you had to be alert to the presence of an unofficial local police force – followers of the cult of Zangbeto, who patrolled the streets, wielding whips and sticks, which they used to scatter crowds of terrified locals. The appearance of these 'guardians of the night' was made all the more terrifying by the fact that they were dressed as giant haystacks. Not the strangely named British wrestler of the 1970's, but a huge, straw covered presence, alternately spinning, jumping and crawling, whilst emitting an eerie humming noise. The terror inspired in the locals by the appearance of a Zangbeto adherent in a crowded street, can be explained by a fact that any Beninese will explain. The belief is that there is no man beneath the haystack outfit, only a spirit. Once the street has been cleansed of potential wrongdoers, the haystack will reduce to a pile of straw, from which the spirit will appear as a large frog, who, job done, will then hop away into the night.

We located our now well-polished bike back at the snake temple, and headed towards the bandit road, as the sun was setting over the distant Atlantic. A cloud of bats evacuated a church tower ahead of us; office workers in ill-fitting suits and brightly coloured kufi caps cycled home; and a knot of pythons slid silently into the sidestreets, in a uniquely Beninese rush hour.

Next morning, we were poring over our Lonely Planet map of Ouidah with Jean-Claude, as he tried to locate a Vodun temple on the outskirts of town. I'd asked him to keep his ear to the ground, and let me know about any authentic Voodoo gatherings, and he'd heard that there was to be a ceremony to initiate new adepts, or followers, to this temple. We were surprised to hear that the ceremony would be likely to include small children, and Jean-Claude explained that kids as young as five may become Vodun initiates, dedicated to the temple in response to a pressing need by their family for divine assistance – serious illness or financial dire straits requiring intervention from the Vodun Gods. These young initiates will enter the temple and devote their lives to the religion, unlikely to ever see their family again.

We identified the location on a map and set out in the early afternoon, again borrowing Jean-Claude's bike to make the journey to town, and again promising to be back before six. The temple was situated in a dusty walled compound with a large marula tree at its centre. We asked to see the temple guardian, and an old man with a distended belly, wearing a stained blue boubou emerged, rubbing his eyes. It was clear we'd disturbed his pre-ceremony nap, as he looked us up and down critically, and told us it was 'tres difficile' for 'etrangers' to witness a ceremony. Predictably, the West African franc notes which I thrust into his hand, seemed to make things less 'difficile', and we were told to return at four.

Two hours later, we pulled up to the compound gates and did a double take at the transformation which had taken place in our absence. The sun had dipped, and the sandy courtyard was now dappled in the shade of the central tree. Multiple rows of cycles and motorbikes parked outside the gates told us that we weren't the first arrivals. A guard of thickset gatekeepers watched us park our bike and waved us towards the rusty metal gates. We were clearly expected. As we were ushered through to the compound, five hundred pairs of eyes turned in our direction. It seemed that half the population of Ouidah was crammed into the dusty courtyard, and they craned their necks and stared and pointed, and chattered excitedly, as we were shoved through the crowd towards a row of four red plastic seats strategically placed in front of the jostling, swaying throng.

Two of the seats were already occupied, by a sweating, middle-aged European couple who seemed relieved at the arrival of two more white faces, but still looked terrified. As we sat down, they introduced themselves as Rolf and Anna from Dortmund, who had handed over an exorbitant amount of cash to a local fixer to witness 'genuine Voodoo.' It was clear that the four of us were the guests of honour, and we sat conspicuously on our plastic thrones, at the edge of the ceremonial circle, fending off vendors hawking goat kebabs, horse-tail fly swats and plastic bags of toxic looking coloured liquid. The old guardian patrolled the perimeter of the circle, wearing brightly coloured pyjama trousers and a white skull cap. Bare-chested, displaying his pot belly and small plump breasts, he was snapping at youngsters and flicking a small whip at anyone who dared to encroach slightly into the central arena.

After the usual lengthy and confusing delay which precedes any event in Africa, two rows of seats beneath the marula tree were slowly filled by colourfully dressed temple elders, and a troop of white-robed drummers. The sun was beginning to set as the first repetitive beats thudded from a row of hand drums, and a clanking bell heralded the arrival of the adepts - a line of a dozen dancers, hunched low, faces expressionless, staring at the ground, swinging their arms in a jerky, deliberate motion as they entered the central courtyard, swaying and bowing before the elders. All wore brightly coloured wraps around their legs and were bare chested, their upper bodies adorned with strings of beads and cowrie shells.

Amongst their number were three children, aged around six. With their heads shaved completely bald, it was impossible to gauge their sex.

The formality of the entrance of this initial line of dancers preceded a contrasting ragtag band of strolling women, wearing extravagant hats of the type worn by Ascot racegoers, and carrying plastic bottles filled with pebbles, to be used as makeshift maracas. Next to appear was a line of men in flowered women's dresses with red frill hems, carrying what appeared to be large, upturned garden umbrellas, garnished with red feathers. Each new group joined the dancers as they circled the courtyard to a soundtrack of drumming, bell ringing, chanting and ululation. Everywhere we looked, we saw another incomprehensible sight, so strange and foreign, that all the four of us could do was to sit in silent, baffled confusion.

As the light faded further, the drumming and bell ringing intensified, smoke and dust filled the courtyard and the non-stop procession of dancers passed in a continuous circle around the central tree, under which the impassively faced elders sat. Occasionally a quickened drum beat would propel the dancers into frenzied gyration, but mostly their circulation was a robotic, jerking stagger, with each step in time to the thudding percussion.

The constant drumming was hypnotic to witness, and it was no surprise when some of the dancers, sweat dripping beneath their Sunday-best headware, began to enter a trancelike state. One woman's eyes rolled in her head and she collapsed to the ground in front of us, jabbering incomprehensibly from foam-coated lips, her body convulsing as she was possessed by the spirits. Attendants dragged her aside as her limbs thrashed wildly, to allow the circle of dancers to proceed.

With darkness falling and an awareness dawning that the ceremony was likely to go on all night, I cast a nervous glance at my watch. Already 6.15. I imagined Jean-Claude pacing in reception at the end of his shift, and the bandits taking up position on the dark road we still had to ride. It was clear we needed to leave, but how? We had the best seats in the house, prominently sited on the front row. Behind us were massed ranks of worshippers and observers, and ahead of us was a shifting procession of dancers, many who were now in advanced states of quivering delirium. There seemed no way out, and I was vainly hoping that there would be an interval for drinks and ice creams, when the mood in the compound suddenly changed.

An electricity of tension filled the air - that anticipation of imminent danger or violence. From my seated position it was hard to see what was happening. Women and children screamed, men shoved and postured, fists clenched, eyes wide. Through the parade of dancers, who continued their endless frenzied march, I caught site of a silhouetted, hooded figure which had appeared on one of the perimeter walls of the compound. Its face and body were concealed beneath a thick cowl, and the appearance of this monk-like presence had set off a panic in the crowd. People were shouting angrily, arms waving, and I saw one man pick up a bamboo pole and thrust it towards the menacing figure seated high on the wall.

Anna from Dortmund looked close to tears as the drum beat quickened, children squealed, men shook their fists and one of the dancers bared her breasts, shook uncontrollably and screamed like a wounded animal. Amongst the chaos, I sensed our chance to escape and grabbed Kirsty by the hand. My plan to sneak around the perimeter of the circle was thwarted by a large man, who either had spectacular tribal scarification on his upper arms, or had been afflicted by a terrible plague of localised boils. He grabbed me by the shoulder and yelled something which I failed to understand amongst the cacophony of drumming, bell ringing and shrieking. I pointed at the exit and to my horror, he took hold of my arm and dragged me into the circle of dancers. Kirsty had no choice but to follow, and was perfectly placed to see the entire crowd yelling and pointing excitedly as the white man appeared, centre of ceremony, being dragged by a large temple minder, and the pot-bellied old guardian attempted to lash me with his home-made whip.

"Money!" yelled our 'rescuer,' predictably, at the gate, and I thrust a handful of notes at him, and dashed towards the motorbike. We slewed and fishtailed along the dark sandy road, but thankfully avoided bandits, and delivered Jean-Claude his bike, only an hour late.

The adepts' initiation certainly felt like a genuine Voodoo event, rather than something cooked-up for tourists, and although it was undoubtably a strange and unsettling experience, I'd seen nothing to suggest that practitioners of Vodun had any special knowledge or powers. I decided that the best place to experience the sort of magic which Toby Green had apparently witnessed was the countryside, so we headed to the small coastal town of Grand Popo.

Checking in to an auberge next to the beach, I put out some feelers amongst the staff and was told that I needed to speak to 'Voodoo people.' I asked how I could find such people, and was told mysteriously, 'Don't worry monsieur, they will find you.'

It was of little surprise therefore that the following day, while we were munching on our breakfast baguettes outside a café in town, a bow-legged man in a pink polo shirt pulled up a chair to the next table, lit a cigarette and spoke in English.

"So, I hear you want to see Voodoo in Benin?" His eyes stared outwards from the side of his face, like an iguana, so neither one looked at you directly.

"Are you a Voodoo person?" He certainly didn't look like the adherents in the Ouidah temple, with his stylish western clothes.

"Not me, but I know people who are. I can take you."

"Real Voodoo, not for tourists?"

"C'est vrai, it's real. We don't see many tourists here anyway." He smiled, we agreed a price, and he introduced himself as Romeo, an unlikely name, given his unfortunate eye alignment.

The next morning, at eleven, Kirsty and I set off out from

Grand Popo, to search for Voodoo. I was riding pillion on Romeo's Honda Dream and Kirsty bumped along behind his taciturn friend, Yannick, who Romeo assured us knew 'many Voodoo people.'

After visiting a couple of villages where we observed the ubiquitous, gunk covered Legba icon and some dusty, deserted Voodoo temple compounds, I was beginning to suspect that Romeo and Yannick may not be as well connected with the literal movers and shakers of the Voodoo world as they had led us to believe. Next, we arrived at a scruffy cluster of shacks, and were led to a concrete hut by a shirtless man whose back was a pustulating mass of fresh insect bites. It looked like he'd fallen asleep on a nest of fire ants, and it was clear that whatever protection his Loa offered him, it clearly didn't cover biting parasites.

"He is now going to conduct the ceremony," Romeo whispered excitedly as we were ushered into the hut and told to squat on the dirt floor. On a shelf in front of us were an array of crude clay shapes, which Romeo told us were 'idols,' and the usual paraphernalia employed by Voodoo adherents to communicate with the spirits – shells, beads, tobacco, plastic children's toys and assorted body parts hacked from dead animals and birds.

The ceremony began with the welt-covered man lighting three cigarettes at the same time. Two were then positioned, alight, on the makeshift altar, and the third remained dangling precariously from his lips. Next, he reached for a bottle of cane spirit and took a couple of healthy swigs, between drags on his cigarette. I wondered if this part of the ceremony provided a clue as to why he'd spent the previous night sleeping on an ant hill. After his third glug from the neck of the bottle, he expelled the liquid with a dramatic hiss, spraying it across the icons on the altar. He repeated this three times, with each spray of liquid followed by a puff on his cigarette, and an exhalation of smoke towards the alcohol soaked clay blobs. Then he seemed to fall asleep.

After a few minutes of uncomfortable silence, he suddenly

lurched back to life. Kirsty and I jumped in the gloom, as he began to chatter in an animated fashion, seemingly to the clay figures in front of him, while waving his arms, as if engaged in a complex debate.

"He is speaking with the Gods now," whispered Noah reverently.

A visitor with a mind completely open to the possibilities of communicating with the pantheon of Voodoo deities, via three Lambert and Butler and a bottle of supermarket booze, may have been thrilled to witness the spectacle. To me, this seemed no more than an old drunk, muttering nonsense at some blobs of mud in a garden shed. He did seem committed to the act though, and after twenty minutes was still engaged in a heated discussion with some unseen force. He didn't even seem to notice when we got up to leave, my frown conveying a 'must do better' message to Romeo.

Unfortunately, our next visit was similarly underwhelming. After a whispered conference with Yannick, Romeo informed us with a flourish that he'd secured us an audience with local royalty – a high priestess known as the Queen of Voodoo in the area.

Half an hour later, Kirsty and I were sitting cross legged on the floor of a breeze block bungalow, being observed by an obese pensioner in an extravagant, white layered frock. Her huge hippo-like face stared from beneath a towering red turban, and the gold covering her fat fingers made it clear that she'd obviously done well financially from her close relationship with the Loa.

Romeo sat to our right, fidgeting nervously, and it soon became clear that she had no idea what these perspiring, fly-swotting Europeans sat on her floor wanted from her. Nor did we. Did we expect a magic act? An animal sacrifice? More jabbering at statues? We didn't have a clue. So we sat there, nodding and smiling embarrassed smiles, as she gazed back with her little hippo eyes, also smiling with bemusement. Eventually, Romeo thankfully brought the awkward visit to an end, and said we must leave. The queen muttered something, and he looked sheepish.

"Erm, it is customary to bring a gift for the queen."

No surprise there, I thought, and fished in my rucksack to retrieve the ideal offering. Holding out the shiny coin, I explained that this was my own queen, in England, and that I'd brought the gift as a tribute to the renowned Queen of Voodoo. She held the coin up to the light and examined it critically, mumbling something to Romeo.

"She wants to know if it's gold," he translated.

"Of course." I smiled. "One pound coins are solid gold and are very rare. My queen wanted her to have it."

If the Voodoo queen was satisfied with her gold coin, I was less impressed with Romeo and Yannick's supposed inside knowledge of Grand Popo's mysterious Voodoo people. We spent the early afternoon visiting more shrines, sites of sacrifice and supposed sacred baobob trees, and I reflected that it had taken Toby Green months to gain access to the real secrets of West African magic. Maybe I'd been naïve to think I could experience genuine Voodoo on a two-week trip.

At around 3pm we were bumping down a rutted, dusty track, when Yannick spotted a motorcycle approaching from a side road and drew to a halt. A brief exchange turned into a more detailed discussion. Romeo was summoned and I could tell from his expression that something had piqued his interest. The three men were now engaged in an animated debate, with occasional glances over to where Kirsty and I were slumped disconsolately by the roadside.

Though seemingly reluctant, the stranger was persuaded to make a phone call, and his battered Nokia was soon being passed to Romeo, who appeared to be entering into some form of negotiation. Once concluded he bounded over to us, his protruding eyes bulging with excitement.

"Yannick's friend is a moto-taxi driver. He has just taken a boy to a village close to here." He paused to catch his breath.

"He has a dispute over a debt with a man from another village. That man has threatened to kill him." We waited for the punchline, and it didn't disappoint when Romeo finally delivered it with a grin.

"The boy has gone to the village to see a famous houngan. He has gone to take the power."

I played dumb. "I don't understand. Why has he gone to the village? What is the power?"

"The houngan is a very powerful Voodoo witch doctor. He will perform a ritual to give the boy the protection of the Gods. Once he has the power, no man can harm him!" Yannick was revving his bike impatiently and Kirsty jumped on behind him. Romeo was already accelerating away in a cloud of dust before I was even properly seated on his machine.

It soon became obvious that we were travelling in an area which was unfamiliar to our fixers, and it took a number of stops to ask directions before we finally skidded along a narrow track between wood and clay shacks, scattering piglets and chickens to announce our arrival.

If material wealth such as that displayed by the 'queen' demonstrated impressive Voodoo credentials, this place promised to be another disappointment. Even by rural Beninese standards, it was impoverished. Barefoot children are the norm in the African countryside, but this village didn't seem able to boast a pair of shoes between any of its inhabitants. Cooking pots smoked over an open fire in the centre of a scrubby sand compound containing a large, charred tree stump. It seemed the villagers had succumbed to short-sighted temptation at some point in the past, and chopped down their only source of shade, for firewood or building materials. Consequently, the late afternoon sun beat down unrelentingly and bleached the village in its glare. A handful of slumbering men raised their heads, and toddlers squealed in terror and ran for cover as the rasp of our engines signalled the arrival of strangers.

I sensed Romeo shrink into the background and he allowed Yannick to do the talking to a tall, bare chested man who loomed, scowling from the gloom of one of the shacks. It was difficult to know what was going on, but I sensed negotiations hadn't been fully concluded in the phone call, and voices were raised as more men and youths appeared, to join what was fast becoming a heated discussion.

"Wait here. These people are....wait here." Romeo dismounted and adopted a submissive stance, with head dipped and arms outstretched as he nervously hurried across to enter the debate. Again, glances were cast in our direction, arms were waved, heads shaken and at one point, Yannick was shoved forcefully in the chest.

"This isn't looking good." I whispered to Kirsty, stating the obvious. We were miles from town, in a wild and potentially lawless area, searching for adherents of a sacrificial cult, with two fixers who were clearly well out of their depth. Romeo looked in my direction, though as usual his eyes were focused elsewhere, and gave me a furtive raised hand signal which I took to mean 'Don't worry, it's under control.' It looked anything but.

After ten minutes of discussion, and various comings and goings from the tall man who seemed to be acting as a go-between, Romeo waved us over.

"It's okay. Don't worry." His voice was shaking, and his lizard eyes darted around nervously.

The tall man was standing in the doorway of a tin roofed clay hut, and beckoned us to enter. Inside it was too dark to see, but it smelt of damp and dirt and smoke. Someone grabbed my arm tightly, but I couldn't see who. I reached out for Kirsty's hand and we were led towards hushed voices in the gloom. We rounded a corner and entered a room, lit by a small fire, around which five men were crouched. All barefoot, they wore an incongruous mix of patterned boubou smocks, beach shorts and long sleeved patterned shirts. None of them looked up, as unseen hands pushed us down to the cool of the dirt floor. They remained focused on the task at hand of assembling the tools of their trade – a metal bowl containing a mixture of syrupy liquid and ground plant matter; cowrie shells and coloured beads; figures carved from wood and fashioned from clay; cigarettes and alcohol. A stifled clucking in the shadows signalled the end of a chicken and the introduction of its bleeding heart to the bowl.

"Don't be scared, it will be okay." I smelt the tobacco on Romeo's breath as he whispered in my ear.

"I'm not scared. Are you?" He didn't answer immediately.

"No. Maybe, a little. But these people..." His voice tailed off and I knew he was terrified.

There's a particular smell we associate with death. A subtle aroma of decay which surrounds the soon to pass, and the recently departed. And these boys had more than a hint of it about them in that dark, damp, smoky hut. Their eyes, caught in the flicker of the cigarette lighter being used to ignite tinder in the metal bowl, suggested they had seen, and maybe done things that precluded them from sound sleep of an evening. They spoke with hushed tones until the preparations were complete. Then the patterned shirts and tattered silk shorts shrank back into the shadows to let the houngan begin his work. Though squatting on his haunches, it was clear he was a tall man. Dressed in a shapeless grey t-shirt and grubby brown cargo shorts, his appearance was the antithesis of the Voodoo Queen's theatrical outfit. His face remained impassive, as he began a quiet incantation, accompanied by the repeated tossing of a handful of cowries. Only when the formation of the scattered shells was correctly aligned, were the final ingredients added to the bowl containing the chicken's bloodied organ. Then, in a repeat of the ritual we'd seen earlier in the insect-bite victim's shed, cane spirit was spat across the mix, followed by blown smoke from three cigarettes which the houngan puffed on simultaneously.

At this point, I was unsure which of the men was to be the

recipient of the spell which would deliver to him 'the power,' and proceedings became even more confusing as the houngan and his attendants slowly rose, and shuffled away into the blackness of the shack. Kirsty and I were unsure of what was happening, and remained crouched in the dark, with the only light provided by the embers of the dying fire. I established that Romeo and Yannick were still present from their hushed whispers, which I assumed were speculating what was going on.

Suddenly, the croaking voice of an unseen old man, wheezed something undecipherable from close-by in the darkness, and Romeo nudged us to get up and follow him outside. We blinked at the harsh light in the courtyard, and Romeo explained that we had witnessed the preparation of the spell. The actual administration of the 'power' to its recipient, was now taking place in private.

"We don't want to see that. Too secret." Romeo cut me off before I'd even asked the question.

We sat in the shade of one of the huts and watched a toddler dance to some Afrobeat music being played on a battery radio. Village women laughed and encouraged the little girl to wiggle on wobbly legs, as they washed clothes in a wooden bowl and tended the fire. An old man was admiring Romeo's motorbike and two puppies fought in the dust. If this sense of mundane normality felt strange after witnessing the ritual in the hut, it was going to get a lot stranger.

After around half an hour, the houngan led his entourage back into the compound. They were accompanied by a young man of about twenty, bare chested, wearing jeans cut off at the knees, and fake Adidas trainers. His hair was shaved at the sides and shaped into a short flat top, and he bore a badly etched homemade tattoo on his left shoulder. I was absent mindedly tapping out an accompanying drumbeat to the toddler's dance tunes, using a three-quarter-litre cane spirit bottle I'd picked up from a pile lying outside the shack. I was surprised as the houngan strode towards me, took the bottle and handed it to the young man.

Without hesitation, he turned to look at me, then smashed the bottle hard into his own face, shattering the glass on his forehead with a sickening crack. He nonchalantly brushed some glass fragments from his shoulder, then raised the broken bottle to his mouth and bit hard on the jagged edge. Kirsty and I, plus Romeo and Yannick cringed as we heard his teeth crunching glass, and he spat a number of large shards onto the sand. As a finale, he opened his mouth and stuck out his tongue to reveal no obvious damage. Apart from a small dark mark on his forehead, his face was similarly unmarked. He gave us a big smile – he now had 'the power.'

He handed the broken bottle back to the houngan, who, in turn passed it back to me. Dumfounded, I gingerly ran my finger along the jagged broken edge and felt its sharpness. The houngan stood above me, retaining his impassive expression. He then took the remains of the bottle, placed it on the ground in front of me and smashed it with his bare foot, taking care to slowly ground the glass fragments into the sand. Then he walked away, leaving us to ponder what we'd just witnessed, as the words of the old Englishman in Lome's fetish market returned to me. 'These people know things we forgot hundreds of years ago.'

Less than a week later I was back at work, attending a team meeting in London. Well aware of my recent trip, and probably anticipating an interesting meeting 'ice breaker,' our boss teed me up for a tale.

"Do anything interesting then?" Twenty expectant faces looked down the table towards me.

A jumble sale of animal parts. Free range snakes. A Voodoo queen and an old man jabbering at clay effigies in his garden shed. Hooded figures and whip-wielding men dressed as haystacks. The Power. Things we forgot that they still know, and that I now believe too.

"Just the usual holiday stuff," I smiled. Sometimes the tales of a Two Week Traveller are best left untold. I opened my laptop and tried to focus on the forthcoming months of work, and of course, and more importantly, planning my next trip.

16 EPILOGUE

Montanita, Ecuador, May 2019

The beginning of 2019 marked the end for me of more than thirty years as a two-week traveller. Kirsty was between jobs, having left our company in 2018, and the time seemed right for us to take some of the trips we'd dreamt of over the years, but felt couldn't be properly undertaken in two weeks. I therefore applied for a sabbatical and was granted eight months of unpaid leave. This was to be a different way of travelling for us. Time was no longer the limiting factor we were used to, and with no income for either of us, money became a key consideration!

We set off for New Zealand at the start of January 2019, and rented an ancient campervan to tour both islands, wild camping for the vast majority of the journey. We washed in lakes and rivers, overdosed on barbecues, and drank supermarket wine and beer beside crackling campfires in spectacular locations of an evening. For once, we had no plans. No time limit. No schedule. We decided where to go each day whilst eating our breakfast. It was something of a shock for someone used to the meticulous planning of trips to fit into a tight two week timeframe.

Next we explored Fiji, then chilled out in Thailand for a few weeks. Then on to South America, where again, we set our agenda on a daily basis, travelling overland through Paraguay, Bolivia, Peru and now, Ecuador, where I'm writing this final chapter while watching sunset surfers catch the last Pacific waves of the day, with a cold bottle of Club beer in hand, (that's me, not the surfers!) For our South American overland journey our usual rental car has been replaced by my old nemesis, the long-distance overnight bus, though I'm pleased to report that Latin American buses are a major improvement on their Moldovan counterparts!

With an accommodation budget of $15 per night, we've stayed

in cheap hostels, where we're usually the oldest guests by a margin of around twenty years. We've also made good use of the Air B&B app, and stayed in an eclectic mix of low-cost apartments, some great, some less-so, but all invariably hosted by interesting and interested locals.

Kirsty and I have both worked to improve our sketchy Spanish using the Duolingo app, which has proved invaluable in South America; I've attempted to improve my photography skills with an online course, and I've also squeezed in time to write this book! All are things that I've thoroughly enjoyed doing, and to me, have felt so much more worthwhile than working long hours for a huge multinational company.

Our plan is to head back to Europe for the Summer and take our beloved campervan on an extended tour of the continent. Again, something we could never fit into a two week schedule.

What will the next chapter hold? Who knows. But the recent months have shown that the transition from our previous well planned, time limited schedules to unplanned, longer and lower cost trips is one we can easily make. Hopefully at some point in the near future the Two Week Traveller will have the opportunity to become an All-Year Adventurer!

In the meantime, I'll return to work and on my first day back, tackle THE most important task - calculating how much holiday allowance I'm due for the remainder of 2019. After all, I'm sure there'll be time to squeeze in a two-week trip before the end of the year!

Printed by Amazon Italia Logistica S.r.l.
Torrazza Piemonte (TO), Italy

10464317R00198